AU[

D0384336

FINDING MY
BADASS SELF

~~~• A YEAR OF •~~~
TRUTHS AND DARES

SHERRY STANFA–STANLEY

SHE WRITES PRESS

Published 2017
Printed in the United States of America
Print ISBN: 978-1-63152-290-1
E-ISBN: 978-1-63152-291-8
Library of Congress Control Number: 2017937953

For information, address:
She Writes Press
1563 Solano Ave #546
Berkeley, CA 94707

Cover design by Mimi Bark
Interior design by Tabitha Lahr

She Writes Press is a division of SparkPoint Studio, LLC.

Names and identifying characteristics have been changed to protect the privacy of certain individuals.

CONTENTS

FALL

WINTER

To Jorden (Son #1) and Kyle (Son #2): Being your mother has been more rewarding than any experience in this book. There. Does that make up for the embarrassment I've caused you?

And to my parents, Denny and Gloria Stanfa: Thanks for teaching me the family motto, "When it's too rough for everyone else, it's just about right for us."

"I have already lost touch with a couple of people I used to be."

—JOAN DIDION

"Promise me you'll always remember: You're braver than you believe, and stronger than you seem, and smarter than you think."

—CHRISTOPHER ROBIN TO POOH

"Shoulda, woulda, coulda is way more terrifying than ready, set, go."

—LEIGHANN LORD

Prologue:

THE BEGINNING

Often, life serves us vanilla ice cream, and we're fine with that. Vanilla is sweet. It's generally satisfying. From time to time, that vanilla is exactly what we want.

Until one day, we crave something different. Perhaps a new flavor. Or maybe, a sprinkle of nuts: a crazy new experience, say, exfoliating a rhinoceros or going on a raid with a SWAT team.

But I digress. Let us back up.

My life had taken the prescribed and expected route in many ways: I graduated from college, married, made a couple babies, and embarked on a long and arguably successful communications career near my hometown of Toledo, Ohio.

Then, stumbling into my fifties as a divorced empty-nester, I found myself simultaneously unsettled and *too* settled. I'd lived in the same house and held down the same job for twenty years. I realized I'd spent most of the last three decades doing the same ordinary things.

I wouldn't call it a rut—more of a crater.

I knew many people in a similar situation, particularly midlifers or else young mothers who spent more than their share of evenings folding clothes in front of the TV, daydreaming about the world out there while they contemplated having that second bowl of ice cream.

So, I sold my home of twenty-one years, bought a condo, and dropped thirty pounds. (Disclaimer: I later regained those thirty and lost them again. Rinse and repeat. Ahem.) Then, I pondered how else I might shake up my life. I needed something more radical.

Why this epiphany at this time in my life? Was the anticipation of turning fifty-two some significant or magical moment? Maybe I was simply bored. Perhaps it was midlife hormonal psychosis. Or maybe I was subconsciously driven by the fact that my father died a week after he turned fifty-three.

Regardless of our motivations, at some point we decide to either continue sighing at the status quo of our lives or else we open our minds and our arms to embrace change. I chose change, albeit with trembling hands and a wavering mindset. If we want to change our lives, we have to get past what is holding us back. Generally, that's our own fear.

Thus was born The 52/52 Project: my year of fifty-two new enlightening, exciting, and frequently just-kill-me-now experiences.

A bucket list this was not. It was more an *unbucket* list. The weekly ventures I planned were intended to push my boundaries, discover my capabilities, and change my life. I fought inertia and stared down fear through a year of experiences I'd never before faced, all outside my comfort zone. They ranged from visiting a nude beach (naturally, I had my seventy-five-year-old mother in tow), to babysitting quadruplets, to auditioning for *Survivor*.

Aside from choosing experiences that frightened me, I included a number of outrageous items primarily designed to make me laugh—at least in retrospect. As adults, most of us have forgotten how to be silly. The first rule of going outside our comfort zone is learning to laugh at ourselves.

Just a couple weeks into the project, I began blogging and started a Facebook page about The 52/52 Project. I had no idea if people would care enough to read along, and the idea of publicly sharing snippets of my stories scared me nearly as much as some of the escapades themselves. But thousands of people, most of them strangers, jumped on board.

My online readers not only provided the reward of an early and continuing audience, they also held me accountable for seeing this project through to the end—often a challenge in itself. This group of good-natured sadists appeared charged and excited. We motivated each other every day. Together, we jumped the curb, taking a detour from the safe and secure cul-de-sac of our lives, to visit personally unexplored territories.

At the start, I wasn't certain whether I'd be opening the door to an exciting new life or opening Pandora's Box.

Turns out, the two are not mutually exclusive.

SUMMER

Chapter 1:

BELLYING UP TO THE DANCE BAR

ere's the thing about belly dancing: You seldom look as sexy as you hoped.

Given my middle-aged figure and history of uncoordination, looking sexy was a long shot. The most I probably could hope to pull off was getting a bit of exercise, enduring minimal humiliation, and walking away without any body parts permanently out of whack.

I knew belly dancing classes, as the first of my new experiences, would challenge both my physical ability and my pride. I did seem to have at least a couple of the physical prerequisites. A well-meaning older girl informed me, when I was thirteen, that my big hips would come in handy for birthing babies, as if this were something every teenage girl dreams of hearing. (The joke was on both of us years later, when I ended up with two C-sections.)

And, at this midpoint in my life, Lord knew I had the necessary belly.

But the word "belly" proved to be far less important than the word "dancing." "Dancing" should have raised a three-mile-high red flag. The last structured dancing lesson I'd taken was a ballet class in the second grade. The song that my seven-year-old self practiced for weeks for our final recital was "I Can Learn to Do Ballet."

The problem was, I could not.

After my recital, my parents never once mentioned re-enrolling me. I assumed the classes were too expensive.

Forty-five years later and forty-five minutes into my first belly dancing lesson, my foremost thought was, "Holy Mother of God, please don't let this end in a public recital."

The instructor was a full-sized woman my age or a few years older, but far more agile and confident. She seemed to sense my trepidation. She tossed out a trickle of encouraging remarks: "Age, shape, and size don't matter here. Belly dancing is for women who want to celebrate life." She also was fond of telling us, "Belly dancing is different from that *other* form of dancing entertainment not taught here. We are ladies, not hussies." And my favorite, that first night: "I've only had you for an hour. I don't want to hear anyone say, 'I can't do this.' You can only say, 'I can't do this *yet*.'" During the first lesson, I muttered, "I can't do this *yet*," approximately five times. Or maybe fifty-two.

I mastered the hip thrust in minutes. It was a surprising feat, considering my romantic life had provided no opportunity for that particular move in a long while.

But the stepping and the swiveling and the pivoting? And accomplishing them all in a prescribed order? This appeared to require not just coordination but also some sort of geometric or algebraic equation. Math was not my forte.

"Step, touch—one, two, three, four, five, six, seven, eight. And back—one, two, three, four, five, six, seven, eight." Blah-blah-blah. If I couldn't remember the instructions three seconds after hearing them, you can be damn sure I can't recall them now.

The swiveling was particularly perplexing, much like hula-hooping in my school playground days. Even now, my ample hips were useless tools when it came to swiveling. Trying to memorize the additional stepping and pivoting sequences gave me the closest thing to a combined migraine and anxiety attack I'd ever experienced.

I wanted to believe I was faking my way through, or at least keeping up with the rest of the first-timers. My friend, Mary, while finishing off a bottle of wine the previous weekend, had agreed to join me in this escapade. I glanced over and noticed that as she was pivoting left, I was swiveling right.

I elbowed her. "This is impossible. Are you having a hard time keeping up, too?"

Mary shushed me, shook her head, and glided across the floor through the rest of the sequence.

I secretly vowed to never invite her along again.

Moments later, the instructor asked a finely tuned returning student to move down the dance line, so "others" could watch her and try to follow along. She was placed directly in front of me. I shrugged off her placement as a coincidence.

As we continued to swivel and step, I frowned. Each of us had chosen a brightly colored scarf, adorned with gold-colored coins, to wear around our hips. As my classmates danced, the dangling coins from their hips jingled. My own hip scarf remained noticeably silent. A terrible thought struck me: Perhaps the scarf was stretched so tightly around my ample hips that it had absolutely no room to sway and clink. Although it was also *possible* I was simply the victim of defective coins. I went with that.

I wasn't nearly as rattled about my non-clinking coins as I was about all the falling ones. Several coins from our scarves had dropped off and were now scattered across the dance floor. Mary mentioned this to our instructor, who reassured us not to worry about it.

Not to worry? After all the other dancers chose to disregard these rogue coins, I could think about nothing else but the collateral damage. I kept eying the floor. Each time we enjoyed a momentary break before segueing into a new sequence, I frantically scooped up every stray coin. Was no one else consumed with the fear of slipping on one of these menacing baubles? How would I manage a hip thrust with a broken hip?

My paranoia was not without justification. Through just a meager handful of physical and athletic pursuits, I had endured a lifetime of accidents.

During a workplace softball league in 1982, my future and now former husband assigned me the position of catcher. Our romance was still young, so I was eager to please. I crouched down and pounded my mitt with my right hand, as I'd seen professional players do. I was so preoccupied with this vital maneuver that I forgot to keep my eye on the pitcher—which is why the ball slammed straight into my face.

I'd like to say I crashed to the ground with the ball securely in hand. In reality, it knocked me flat and smashed my glasses. I rose to my feet, empty-handed, sore, and sightless. But I was tough. Besides, my boyfriend/coach pointed out that we didn't have any spare players. So, I continued playing the remainder of the game, squinting in right field, where my near-blindness had little opportunity to prove me any worse a player than I was.

As the years passed, my coordination and athletic prowess never did kick in. A rollerblading incident in 1999 ended with a CT scan in the ER, and in my second—and final—attempt at snow skiing, I fell off the chairlift.

Somehow, I managed to make it, free of any physical

crisis, through my first belly dancing class. And through a second one, too.

When time for the third class rolled around, I reasoned it wasn't worth investing more of my time or money. Why stick with something I'd given a shot if I didn't enjoy it and showed little promise? I had other seeds to sow. Other crosses to bear. Other clichés to write.

Although I became a belly dancing dropout after two lessons, the gig was not without its positives. Except for my nightly hot flashes, I hadn't sweated so much in years. I lost a pound in water weight over those two weeks.

That hip thrust could come in handy, too, if I ever got lucky again.

The point was, I'd tried something new. I'd gone outside my comfort zone, which was the idea behind this whole project. I'd also learned I was indeed a lady and not a hussy, no matter what *anyone* said.

I felt no shame in moving on.

Chapter 2:

STRANGER OF THE BRIDE

A little hint about remaining inconspicuous when crash-ing a wedding reception: It's probably best not to catch the bridal bouquet.

The bouquet toss was the furthest thing from my mind when I cruised party hall parking lots on a Friday night. Seek-ing another experience for my year of new adventures, I sim-ply anticipated a nice meal, a few drinks, and the opportunity to celebrate the wedded bliss of a wonderful couple. Sure, I wasn't invited, and I'd never met either of them. Minor details.

Crashing a wedding reception might have been more fath-omable and potentially fun if I were twenty-one, accompanied by a group of college friends, and half-plastered. At fifty-two, alone, and sober? Not so much. Considering most items still ahead on my unbucket list, however, this was one I thought *could* be enjoyable—in between the panic and paranoia.

After a half hour of circling the city, I scored with a full parking lot at the third place I passed, one of the most upscale reception halls in town. Surely, I'd struck gold with a three-star wedding. Yet when I stepped into the lobby, the first thing I spotted was a poster with a huge photograph and the words "Rest in Peace."

Since when did a party hall host a *wake* on a Friday night? I stepped back, contemplating my escape. As I reached the doorway, I paused. Crashing a funeral wasn't exactly what I had in mind, but it would indeed be a whole new experience.

And then, I spied a bigger banner, reading "Congratulations," along with a photo of a happy young couple. Apparently, the first poster was only their memoriam for a recently deceased loved one.

My shoulders drooped at this tearjerker tribute. My sentiments, however, quickly changed gears. Sure, this beloved friend or family member was unable to attend. But I was alive and on hand to take part in the celebration.

It seemed so wrong, yet so right.

I ignored my weak legs and wandered in. I'd morphed into a ten-year-old schoolgirl, wondering just how much I could get away with.

Next to a pile of scrapbooks on a table, I spotted a basket of tickets for dinner selections. I grabbed the last slip for chicken. "Boneless chicken breast with bread stuffing, topped with a garlic pan sauce." It sounded scrumptious! I was hungry. And thirsty, too!

I made a beeline to the bar—a rational move.

First appearances mean so much. My beer was served in a *real* glass. No plastic cups for my fabulous, newly wedded BFFs. This was a classy kind of gig. I was pretty certain I would fit right in—if I hadn't been some freeloading stranger walking in off the street.

I wasn't a true freeloader though. I *had* brought a congratulatory card with a gift certificate enclosed. I dropped it ceremoniously on the gift table and slowly swiveled my head around, hoping people might note this validation of my attendance.

As I saw the line forming for the dessert table, I realized I missed dinner. If only I actually had been invited, I might have known when the event started. What if dinner had been a planned seating arrangement though? I'd have been SOL, for sure. Maybe my timing was impeccable. I could make do with the dessert bar. Moreover, I wasn't too late for libations—and a chance to mingle with a hundred or so total strangers.

I joined a group around a fire pit on the outdoor patio and found myself fitting in more easily than expected. No one questioned me or my relationship to the bride and groom. While this eased the execution of my plan, I was a tad disappointed I didn't need to conjure up any of the pre-fabricated stories I'd prepared on the drive there. (My name: Shelly. My relationship to the new couple: Girlfriend of Jim Miller, who used to work with the groom. Where: Hmm. I can't remember—it was years ago. I'd have to ask him. Wow, the bride's gown is gorgeous, don't you think?)

I struck up a conversation with a trio of young men who advised me on the best way to illegally stream movies. Nice guys, if not a bit shady. I asked them to snap a picture of me with my new iPhone camera, which I didn't yet know how to use. I hoisted my glass of beer and smiled at the camera, not realizing it wouldn't be the last photo taken of me that night.

When I returned to the fire pit, another man smiled at me. "Having a good time?" he asked.

I nodded. "Great reception! I've never seen the bride and groom look so happy." True statement.

He nodded back. "I'm still looking for a sign about it all," he said. "I haven't been given one yet, but I've been look-ing as closely as I can, to the atmosphere, to the stars, and to the birds." As he continued to profess these powers in the universe and provided a litany of strange personal encoun-ters with stars and birds, I grew confused and concerned. Was he extremely spiritual or just extremely crazy? My instincts leaned toward "crazy."

"Uh-huh. Hey, excuse me," I finally said. "I see someone I need to talk to." Which would have been anyone but him.

Minutes later, while enjoying a conversation with a handsome, younger, and seemingly more stable guy, I turned to see the bride approaching us, looking eager to join the discussion. I backed away, avoiding her glance, and headed back inside.

As I watched people swinging it on the dance floor, I deliberated asking someone to dance. The thought terrified me, which made it all the more an obligatory move. I narrowed down my most obvious choices to the nice-looking younger guy by the fire pit or the dude searching for signs from the stars and birds.

I hadn't danced with a stranger in how long? A decade? As my stomach rolled, the DJ made the last call for all single women to join in the bouquet toss. I realized this wasn't only an easy out from dancing but also that a shot of the backs of a group of unidentifiable women, lunging for the spray of flowers, would be a terrific photo op. I hurried over, stationing myself a good twenty yards behind the line of waiting women. I pulled out my iPhone just as I heard the DJ begin his countdown.

Before I could manage to find my new phone's camera setting, I heard a collective rush of shouts, and then—silence. I looked up to see the crowd of zealous single women, as well as nearly every wedding guest in the room, staring at me.

I followed the direction of their glances. I looked down. Apparently, the bride was a former softball pitcher with a hell of an arm. Her throw landed the bouquet far past its intended aim. It was lying two inches from my right foot.

My eyes darted around the room, which had fallen so quiet you could hear my chin drop. All eyes were focused on me. I had no choice, really. I bent down, picked up the bou-quet, and clutched it. I smiled stupidly.

As cameras flashed, my heart rate quickened. I franti-cally contemplated what to do next. If all went according to normal wedding reception protocol, I knew I'd soon find myself posing for more photos: with a garter-snatching stranger feeling his way up my thigh. It was a halfway appeal-ing notion, but I was pretty sure I'd rather salvage the bit of anonymity I had left.

A little girl came to my rescue. She tugged at my blouse, pointed at the bouquet, and said, "Can I have that?"

I smiled down at my small savior and said, "Honey, it's all yours." I thrust the flowers in her hands and walked straight to the exit, pausing only to deposit my half-finished beer at the bar.

"I just accidentally caught the bouquet," I told the bar-tender. "Probably a good time for me to leave."

As I headed to the parking lot, I envisioned the bride and groom at their gift-opening party the next day, watching a replay of their wedding video. When they got to the bouquet toss, they would look at each other in squinted confusion. "Who *is* that woman? Wait, you mean you don't know her either?"

Although I didn't remain inconspicuous, I figured I did stay anonymous, at least until a discovery the next day when I posted my story and a photo online. Here's another little hint about wedding-crashing: It's best to not inadvertently be Facebook friends with the owner of the reception hall.

My anonymity was completely blown after I agreed, months later, to be interviewed about my experience on the TV news show *20/20*. When the episode aired, I bit off half my fingernails as I found myself included with a group of criminals and miscreants in a segment titled *The Moochers*. Rather than proving to be a cautionary tale (which wouldn't have been my first time), I was relieved that, mostly due to my wedding gift, I appeared to be the moral of this story.

"If you must crash a wedding," the voiceover advised, "crash with *class*."

Feeling redeemed, I managed to connect with the bride and groom, Mike and Helen (who was indeed a former softball player). They proved to be a good-natured couple, who remembered my unsigned card and gift. I'd chosen that card very thoughtfully. The pre-printed text read: "A toast to good friends: To a great couple, to your love, your future, and your happiness... and to the friendship that will keep us close always."

Below, I scrawled: "Thanks for an evening none of us will ever forget."

Wasn't that the truth.

Chapter 3:

THE PRINCESS AND THE PEE

I never set foot inside a tent until I was in college. And those trips entailed a more eager and experienced companion doing all the work while I sat and forged my enthusiasm by working my way through a cooler of beer. On one of these outings, we actually "borrowed" a cardboard beer display, shaped like a throne, from a carryout. I sat on it all weekend around the campfire and earned the ironic nickname "Sherry, Queen of Campers."

Yet camping was never my thing. I spent the next decade acquainting myself with hotel bars, air-conditioning, and room service. They were the best of times.

Meanwhile, I married and procreated. And when Son #2 was a mere rugrat, he expressed a burning desire to go tent-camping. His father and I cringed but finally caved. We were indulgent, albeit temporarily insane, parents.

That single night reinforced the most awful aspects of camping memories I had suppressed, or at least never experienced sober. I encouraged Son #2 to join the Boy Scouts.

He went on to become an Eagle Scout, finding his own happy arena for overnight nature excursions and leaving me off the obligatory camping hook.

Camping never again crossed my mind until The 52/52 Project clouded my judgment. I reluctantly decided to traipse out one night, alone, with a borrowed tent, a new sleeping bag, a can of mosquito repellent, and an assortment of campfire food. S'mores and Jiffy Pop, I prayed, would be the night's saving grace.

Important note: I agonized over the idea of bringing a six-pack of beer. While this had been my college routine and might have made for a more entertaining evening, it would also necessitate several nighttime expeditions to the bathroom. A campsite "bathroom" was obviously a misnomer. A porta potty was in no way an actual room and did not allow for any type of bath—except for the occasional backsplash from a full pit toilet.

My camping-savvy friend, Kim, suggested I try out Mary Jane Thurston State Park. She noted it had a beautiful riverside campground and, being just fifteen minutes away, it wouldn't necessitate much planning or travel. The added bonus: If necessary, I could make a quick escape back home.

I climbed out of my car, dragged my equipment down the trail, and surveyed the campground. The only other campers I spied were located directly next to my assigned site. Three adult men, all of them big bare-chested beasts, roamed about a makeshift compound of tents and tarps.

I watched them watching me. Just one thought came to mind: the movie *Deliverance*. Bringing along a baseball bat to keep at my side while I slept, as Son #1 suggested, might have been a wise move after all. Sadly, my only weapons of defense were a Bic grill lighter and a marshmallow fork.

I practiced my jabbing moves with the fork and tried to not make eye contact.

Finally, I spotted a woman and three children in the group. I blew out a relieved whisper of a sigh. There weren't any psychotic women in *Deliverance*, were there?

Pushing aside my paranoia, I focused on putting up my tent. This proved to be the easiest portion of the trip, thanks to Kim, who had walked me through a trial run that morning. Other than finding myself left with four seemingly superfluous stakes and a rain-fly I had no idea how to attach, I managed to build a shelter of sorts. I prayed the meteorologists were mistaken with their prediction of a storm.

The next step, as I watched the sun disappear below the horizon, was making a fire. Kim had also offered me a load of firewood and a propane fire-starter. I declined, ensuring her with much (feigned) confidence that I planned to rough it. Anything else was cheating, right? I was camping in a wooded state park, for God's sake. Certainly I could collect enough timber to build a fire. My son, the Eagle Scout, had assured me a ten year old could manage that.

I should probably have recalled the previous night's torrential downpour, which resulted in more than four inches of rain. The only pieces of wood I spied that weren't water-logged lay several feet off any path. Twice, I stepped through the jungle to grab some, until I realized I was knee-deep in red-stemmed, three-leaved plants. I wasn't much of a camper, yet I did fancy myself a backyard gardener. I realized, too late, that I had stepped through a healthy crop of poison ivy.

Regardless of the enflamed and itchy nightmare I'd deal with later, I stayed focused on the task at hand. I scrounged an armful of somewhat dry twigs and driftwood from the riverbank. I piled them, pyramid-style, in the fire ring, and flicked my Bic lighter.

My fire-starting attempt lasted, oh, about forty-five minutes—with nary a spark.

I finally decided a hot dog, slightly singed over the flame of my lighter, would need to suffice as dinner.

With no campfire to keep away the mosquitos, I applied another layer of repellant to every inch of my being. Given the amount of deet my skin absorbed that night, I guessed I would likely die a horrific death within weeks.

Or maybe I would die much sooner: Since the creepiest guy of all from the site twenty yards over suddenly appeared at my side.

I stepped back and gripped my Bic.

"Hey," he said, sporting a semi-toothless smile. "Looks like you're having a tough time over here. Need any help?"

I didn't *need* any help. I was fully (in)capable all on my own. But how did one say no to a potential psycho-killer? It would be rude. And from what I recalled, rudeness didn't get the victims in *Deliverance* anywhere.

I stood, several yards away, as he huffed and he puffed. Given my pitiful quantity and quality of firewood, even the mightiest of mountain men was sure to struggle with this task. Meanwhile, with one of my hands grasping my fork and the other wielding my lighter, we carried on a lengthy conversation.

"Herbert" eventually got the fire started. And...he turned out to be the nicest guy ever.

Perhaps fire-building wasn't the biggest lesson I learned that night.

I feared, left to my own devices, the campfire would soon fizzle out. I hurriedly cooked and scarfed down a hot dog, a can of beans, a pan of Jiffy Pop (half-popped and half-burnt, as always), and two S'mores. All within fifteen minutes.

As I finished off the food and began to feel queasy, I was struck with a sudden thought: What next? After gorging oneself on junk food, and having no companions or alcohol to fuel the night, what else—besides reapplying mosquito repellant (which I sprayed on myself three more times)—did one do while camping?

Reciting (to no one but myself) the standard fare of campsite ghost stories was out of the picture. The very real prospect of wild storms, wild animals, and wild men was frightening enough. Sure, Herbert and the other campers in the commune next door might be friendly enough, but legend had it that Ted Bundy and a host of other serial killers passed off as charming, too.

So, I conjured up every camping song I could recall. Although my Girl Scout career ended abruptly when I was kicked out of my troop at the age of ten, before we ever *actually* camped, I still remembered a few of the songs we sang in a circle in our school basement. I ran, silently, through refrains of "Found a Peanut" and "The Other Day, I Met a Bear." I ended with the college camping favorite of "Ninety-Nine Bottles of Beer" until it made me thirsty and a bit weepy that I didn't have a Miller 64 close at hand.

Once I ran out of songs and the fire died, I crawled into my tent. And there I lay awake, tossing and turning, until nearly sunrise.

Sleep was out of the question for many reasons. The heat and humidity of summer tent-camping was akin to sleeping in a greenhouse. I was sweaty, dirty, and stinky. The threat of storms remained constant. I tried to ignore the occasional cymbal crashes of thunder, although even that was preferable to hearing the strums of a banjo.

I still harbored a *tiny* suspicion that one of my *Deliverance* neighbors might tie me up and make me squeal like a pig.

Plus, even with a sleeping bag and foam pad, I could still feel every single stone in the ground below me. Although once the Ironic Queen of Campers, I was not The Princess and the Pea—I was far too wimpy and whiny.

However, the Princess and the *Pee* might have been more

accurate. Because after I fought the need all night to run to the porta potty, my bladder remained a full water balloon waiting to burst.

As soon as the morning sun began streaming through the thin walls of my tent, I climbed out and began breaking camp. After all, I was a busy, professional-type person. I had places to go and things to do.

My first task would be the pursuit of indoor plumbing.

I figured the Queen of Campers deserved a Royal Flush.

Chapter 4:

OF BUNNIES AND BATTERIES

S ex Ed in the seventies proved to be an enlightening experience, especially for a young girl at a Catholic grade
school. I wandered away from that single lesson feeling fairly
clear about the basics, but confused about where exactly my
"pistil" was hidden and how a male "stamen" might get there
to fertilize it.

Thankfully, the nun teaching the class assured us girls
we wouldn't have to worry about sex until our wedding
night. Those nuns were mighty strict, but they had a hell of
a sense of humor.

Most people I knew received their real sex education in
hushed circles on the school playground and later through
more hands-on experience in parked cars. There, on darkened streets, many lingering questions were finally answered.
These exploits were often accompanied by *new* questions,
such as, "Oh, shit, did that condom just break?"

Catholic sex education aside, I learned enough over the
years to enjoy a "romantic" life. Somehow, though, I made it
to my fifties before ever stepping foot in an adult bookstore.

One goal of The 52/52 Project was learning about the world around me. This particular objective was not only to visit an adult bookstore—or sex shop, to be more accurate, since books composed a tiny part of the inventory—but also to engage fully in the shopping experience. And, like many of my challenges, this one mandated that I could bring no one along for (im)moral support.

As the saying goes, "You're never too old to learn something new." Aside from the embarrassment I envisioned, my biggest fear was that this new information was coming too late in the game for me to put to good use.

What I later learned was that there were your garden variety "Adultmarts," and then there were trucker-style sex shops. Apparently, the one I chose for convenience, located just off the turnpike exit near the airport, was the latter.

I wandered the store for about ten minutes, soaking up the sights. The full-color photos on the packaging required little imagination. Many of them featured wide open legs, wide open mouths, and freakishly big male appendages.

The only thing bigger and wider might have been my eyes. I may have been fifty-two, but I giggled as awkwardly as a twelve year old.

I stifled my snickers. I had a serious research project to undertake. I needed to know more.

The twenty-something androgynous store clerk proved chatty and eager to pass along his knowledge. He seemed well versed, either by his training or by his own hard-wired interests, in personal entertainment for *both* genders. I found myself engaged in the longest, most graphic conversation I have ever had with a complete stranger. Or with anyone. In my entire life.

I shook off my awkwardness, blinked, and cleared my throat. "So, um, what are your best-selling items for women?"

He promptly led me to the battery-operated device aisle, where he pointed out an impressive variety of shapes and sizes. He noted the advantages of each: bigger, faster, and more lifelike. After providing thorough explanations of all the top sellers, he paused and watched me in anticipation, apparently awaiting my choice.

I hesitated, and finally pointed, randomly, at one. "Well, *this* one looks nice."

"Good choice. I think you'll like this."

He handed it to me. I shoved it under my arm without noting its cost or any of its special features. We moved on to an aisle of men's toys.

Ladies: If the dating pool seems shallower these days, it's likely because we've been rendered obsolete.

I'd anticipated seeing a number of devices used for simulating the most traditional sexual activity, which many women my age probably first discovered through the missionary position. What I didn't imagine were the *other* choices. My new clerk friend explained the most popular item. It resembled a flashlight, but with a tip resembling pursed lips. The package advertised that the "Fleshlight" accommodated any size, provided realistic physical sensations, and was a real pleaser.

I didn't have to rely on the manufacturer's marketing blurbs. While I tried to avoid eye contact with the store clerk as I scrutinized the Fleshlight, a customer behind us chimed in.

"Yeah, those are great! I have two of those!"

Well, then. It appeared variety truly was the spice of life, even when it came to artificial body parts.

With my shopping finished, I decided my visit wouldn't be complete without viewing a peep show. I'd seen porn flicks before; no biggie. (Pun intended.) They have their time and place. The ideal place for me, however, would probably *not* be a small back room in this sketchy turnpike-exit sex shop.

I soon determined it was unlikely that I'd ever manage to "get in the mood" here. Especially once I spied the cut-out holes in the adjoining walls of my tiny booth.

So horrified yet so transfixed by these "glory holes," I watched only snippets of the movie. For all I know, the particular peep show I chose through a random punch of a button might have been an Academy Award winner in the oft-neglected porn category, but I can't say it provided a climactic ending to my visit.

I left that day with a wealth of information and experience. In fact, my only remaining question when I headed home was, would my receipts for a peep show, a candy bra, and a pretty pink "Wonder Bullet" be sufficient for me to write this off as "writing-related research"?

Regardless, now that I was a semi-professional sex store shopper, I was equipped to share what I learned in my crash course.

I learned that rabbits, butterflies, elephants, dolphins, beavers, and hummingbirds apparently were *not* just characters in a Disney cartoon.

I discovered the top-of-the-line female sex toys came with rechargeable batteries and a remote control and were guaranteed to last ten years. One of them even did all the work for you. The clerk called it a "nice, lazy little toy." Apparently you just sat back and watched it do its thing, while it brought you great pleasure. Much like a Slinky, I guessed.

If you are particularly choosy, you should be sure to look for the items marked "Pleasantly Scented." And, if you are the patriotic sort, you'll be glad to know you can find one bearing the proud label, "Made in America!"

Just like McDonald's, where the drive-through cashier asks if you'd like fries with your burger, adult bookstore clerks are trained to be equally helpful. As you hand over your purchase, they will ask if you'd like batteries or some lube with it. I declined both.

Sadly, I learned you cannot return an item, even if you discover it to be the wrong size.

In addition, that outdoor sign boasting 25-cent videos? It likely has not been changed in decades. A peep show will now cost you a minimum of five dollars—or ten dollars if you are paying by credit card. I suggest you bring cash. Needing to leave the booth and cross the store floor, twice, to ask for assistance with your credit card might push your comfort zone even farther than you imagined. In addition, operating the video player or using the doorknob in the booth might be more sanitary if you wear gloves—or maybe a hazmat suit.

And be forewarned: If you get creeped out by the glory holes in the walls of your booth, suspect the ominous movement in an adjoining booth is growing inches closer, and decide to make a quick exit, you will not get your money refunded.

But rest assured you won't miss much if you do decide to leave the movie prematurely.

I have a hunch they all have a happy ending.

Chapter 5:

PIZZA PIE IN THE SKY

C oming off a thirty-pound weight loss, I knew only one reasonable way to follow it up—with a pizza-eating contest.

I excelled at eating, and the adventure of participating in such a thrilling—albeit intimidating—experience had landed this endeavor on my list early on. So when Caper's Restaurant and Bar advertised just such a challenge, I was in. Goodbye, low-carb diet! Hello, elastic-waist pants!

I pushed aside my dieting guilt and justified this as a necessary evil for my project. Besides, endless pieces of pizza.

Heading into this for the food and the fodder for a new experience didn't mean I wasn't serious about waddling away as a winner. So, like any true athlete, I went into training. I sat myself down and spent ten minutes Googling "pizza eating contest hints."

The various search results were conflicting: Arrive with an empty stomach or eat normally beforehand? Dunk the pizza crusts in water or avoid any form of liquid at all? Puke before you gorge or puke afterward?

I seized upon those ideas I deemed most promising. I would eat a protein-rich meal five hours beforehand. Once the contest started, I would fold each slice of pizza, gobbling the cheesy innards first and saving the crusts for last. I'd avoid any liquid except the occasionally necessary sip of water. And, I found this final suggestion particularly helpful: "When you begin to feel slightly full: stand up and wiggle your hips from side to side for five to ten seconds. This makes the food go down your esophagus faster and squashes it up in your stomach."

Given my two recent belly dancing lessons, I was practically a professional hip-wiggler. My win was nearly guaranteed.

I discouraged friends from coming out to watch. After all, dribbling tomato sauce down my chin might be best endured in front of total strangers. When my mom and her friend, Suzanne, showed up anyway, I was secretly pleased. A small fan section could help cheer me on to pizza pie victory.

Besides, I learned long ago that it was helpful to have your mother along for any experience that might end badly. When you're young, you can cling to her and cry. When you're older, you can simply find some way to blame her. If I ended up vomiting in the barf bucket that the kind folks at Caper's had placed behind me, you could be damn sure it would somehow be my mother's fault.

I arrived fifteen minutes before game time. Experience had taught me that idle time in a bar might result in excess beer or shots of Sex on the Beach. To preserve the space in my stomach, I would not be drinking a drop of alcohol that evening. My priorities were clear.

Once I was seated at the table of dishonor, I glanced around and sized up my competition. Just five of us: me and four near-boys. One clearly had been keeping the bartender busy all afternoon. I doubted he could even maneuver a pizza slice into his mouth. Another appeared either as hammered as the first or at least not as focused on the task as I was. I smiled smugly and straightened in my chair.

The emcee announced the start of the contest. As the crowd's eyes turned upon us, the reality of the moment hit me.

I had worked my ass off (literally) these last several months, trying to get in shape. I still had a way to go. Would this spurt of gluttony set me back on my weight-loss plan for weeks to come? Although I hated to admit it, I also wondered if people in the audience would judge me. After all, I was an overweight, middle-aged woman, not a fit and trim young buck who appeared able to afford such gorging like the rest of the contestants. The idea of stuffing my face in front of an audience gave me heartburn before I took a single bite.

Still, now that I was older, I'd begun to stress less about what others thought about me. And I'd learned that sometimes it was OK to take a detour from your ultimate destination, as long as you felt confident and strong enough to get back on course. I told myself that tonight I'd be a carb-devouring and fun-loving version of Wonder Woman.

We each had our very own cheese pizza set in front of us. My choice would have been anchovies for us all. I was probably the only miniscule-fish aficionado, and I would have welcomed any edge at all. But a medium cheese pizza it was.

We were instructed to tackle this first pizza and then order as much more as we could stomach—in ten minutes.

Ten minutes? I didn't remember reading that in the rules. I hoped for a half hour or so. Being a tortoise-speed eater, I feared I had little chance of victory. But, sweet baby Jesus, this was pizza! I hadn't allowed myself to even sniff a pizza in months. Surely, I could rise—like a nice pizza dough—to the occasion.

The countdown began.

I shoved folded pizza slices in my mouth and masticated like a toothless cow. I repeated my mantra in my head: "I can eat pizza like nobody's business, or my name's not Stanfa."

Sadly, my own Sicilian blood didn't carry the same punch as Rocky Balboa's. By the time I chewed halfway through my first pie, every other contestant was already diving into his second. By my sixth crammed-down piece, I didn't taste— let alone savor—a single bite. This wasn't dining. This was culinary slave labor.

Still, I refused to admit defeat. Following my original plan, I continued to gag down all the cheesy insides, leaving the doughy crusts for last.

And then I heard the emcee give the three-minute warning. I hazily eyed the six thick outer crusts remaining on my plate. I began shoveling them into my mouth, one after another. A logical move, although not a pretty one.

A photographer paused in front of me, as I was mid-chew. I waved him away and attempted to frown at him, but my chipmunk cheeks could barely budge. All I managed was a slit-eyed glare. I tried to mutter, "Go away," which translated only as a forceful "uh-uh-uh" uttered through my stuffed-open lips.

He grinned and snapped a couple of shots, right as a blob of half-chewed dough dropped from my mouth.

Seconds later, the emcee called "time." I forced the last crust into the remaining millimeter of space in my mouth.

And, a full five minutes later, after everyone had congratulated the winner—who managed to wolf down an entire pie and a half—I was still chewing. And chewing. And chewing…

I didn't win the contest, the trophy, or the free pizza for a year. Perhaps I conveniently saved myself from that.

The agony of defeat was short-lived. I might have come in last place, but I left that evening knowing I'd tried something new. I survived the anxiety of potentially being judged by dozens of strangers. And, I'd enjoyed some damn good pizza—well, at least until I didn't enjoy it at all.

While I waddled out the door, "The Eye of the Tiger"

Rocky theme rang in my head. Yes, I'd been a contender. And, although I would never be Rocky, I eventually would be *Rocksy*. (See my college mascot chapter for details about that.)

As an added bonus, I felt confident my diet would get right back on track. I figured I wouldn't be tempted by a frigging pizza again for the rest of my life. Or, as it happened, for nearly two weeks.

Even Wonder Woman had her weakness.

Chapter 6:

CHURCH HOPPING

*A*s I perused my list of accomplished and upcoming new ventures, I noted an emphasis on several of the Seven Deadly Sins, specifically pride (with a hint of sloth, gluttony, and lust). If a higher power was keeping track, this seemed an appropriate time to redeem myself with a spiritual experience.

At this midpoint in my life, however, my only spiritual or religious belief was not knowing *what* I believed.

I wasn't always agnostic. I was baptized and raised Catholic, including eight years of Catholic school. As I grew older though, I began contemplating and questioning not only my own lifelong faith but also organized religion as a whole.

Maybe this uncertainty was a result of knowing so little about most religious foundations, traditions, and services. I decided a logical step toward spiritual discovery was to visit, over several weeks, a variety of churches and temples outside my upbringing.

It seemed inconceivable that, by my fifties, I had never visited a synagogue, not even for a bar mitzvah. I'd recently discussed Judaism with my coworker, Allie, who kept kosher and sent her two young children to a Jewish preschool and summer camp. Raised in Miami with New York City roots, she was now entrenched in Toledo's Jewish community. Although I probably could have wandered into any temple on a Saturday, Allie touched base with her rabbi, who gave my mother and me his blessing to attend a Shabbat service and bar mitzvah.

In my next life, if I happen to come back as a Jewish boy, I hope I possess half the confidence, poise, and remarkable memory that thirteen-year-old Asher demonstrated that day. I smiled as I observed him sing, recite sections of the Torah, and provide warm insights into his young life.

While we felt awed and honored, even as anonymous observers, to be a part of his ceremony, my mom and I were often befuddled and overwhelmed—particularly by the Hebrew language. As I followed along in the printed English program, these translated words touched me most:

"And we shall beat our swords into ploughshares and our spears into pruning hooks. Nation shall not lift up sword against nation; neither shall they learn war any more."

The Jewish faith appeared rich in tradition. Scripture and family played important parts in the service. While my mom and I agreed it was the most beautiful religious celebration we'd ever attended, I wondered if I didn't feel engaged enough to fully experience it.

It wasn't just the Hebrew language that made us feel out of place. The service involved little interaction among the congregation. I had always been an inhibited churchgoer. I preferred to keep to myself in my pew, so I was initially relieved by the fact that no one shook my hand or introduced himself. Yet I was also oddly disappointed by that.

Except for the Christian belief in the role of Jesus, much of the Jewish religion and the services I attended really wasn't such a far cry from the Catholic Church to which I was accustomed. Hinduism, I soon discovered, was markedly different.

A week after my mother and I attended the synagogue, we joined a service at a Hindu temple. We'd researched the Hindu religion and admired the little we knew: its reputation for tolerance and tranquility, as well as its focuses on karma and rebirth. The service itself, however, proved less enlightening than we hoped.

With the exception of the last fifteen minutes, the two-hour service consisted entirely of chanting in Hindi, to the accompaniment of a keyboard and occasional tambourine. No translation was provided in the prayer books. At the previous week's synagogue visit, we could follow along with some of the Hebrew through English interpretations. Here, we were lost in translation.

It was impossible to focus on or find enlightenment in something I couldn't begin to comprehend. While the chanting was pleasant and melodic, even keeping my eyes open was a battle I failed to win. Perhaps my experience was hindered by the fact that this occurred on day seven of my week without caffeine. (See forthcoming story about that.)

While I felt slightly awkward and out of place at the synagogue, here I felt totally out of touch. I never understood what was happening or what was being said during the service, which was not only uncomfortable but unsettling.

I wondered if this was why we continue to cling to the status quo in our life. Even if the familiar—a job, a relationship, or a religion—no longer provides contentment or gratification, it's somehow less stressful than the unknown. What we know almost always seems less intimidating or frightening than what we've never experienced.

Still, as I looked around and saw how content and at peace the small Hindu congregation seemed, I had to wonder if I was missing out on something wonderful. If I had been able to interpret some of the words and meaning behind the songs, it's possible that morning might have been more satisfying.

The last experience of my month of spiritual exploration proved to be the most rewarding.

Friendship Baptist Church, where I'd been invited by my coworker, Yves, was the only Christian place of worship I visited in this pursuit. The basic beliefs of this Full Gospel Baptist Church appeared similar to the other Christian churches—mostly Catholic or Lutheran—that I'd visited throughout my life. The service, however, was oh, so different.

My friend, Cindy, and I were among a total of six white people in that morning's congregation of about five hundred. I cringed as I took my seat. Not only would I feel like an outsider through my bumbling participation in an unfamiliar service, I would also stick out simply through the color of my skin.

Awkward as I initially felt, the racial difference soon appeared irrelevant. Within minutes, we were welcomed through handshakes, smiles, and warm words. We never felt like we didn't belong: racially, religiously, or otherwise. That proved important because, just like my other church experiences, my goal was seeking information, introspection, and also a sense of community. In order to truly feel a part of their celebration, I had to feel I was fully accepted. And here, I did.

We happened to visit on a morning when five people received an "apostolic anointing" to become ordained ministers. The service consisted largely of these individuals providing personal, powerful, and animated outlooks on spiritual issues.

The congregation responded to these monologues with standing ovations and applause, as well as shouts of "Amen," "Tell it," and "That's right, brother!" As someone who was distressed when the Catholic Church began requesting hand-holding during the Lord's Prayer, this level of pew-side participation pushed my personal boundaries by far.

Although I'd strayed from the Catholic Church, what had remained with me was a vague comfort in being a passive observer of Catholic rituals. When I occasionally attended Mass, I could rely on simply listening to the refrains and prayers that seldom changed, week to week or year to year.

Everyone else at Friendship Baptist was accustomed to this active involvement. I squirmed in my seat, reluctant to shout out. Yet I was fascinated by the congregation's enthusiastic engagement. While I wasn't comfortable enough to fully take part, I was surprised that the differences between this service and a Catholic Mass were what appealed to me the most.

And, the music. Oh, the music!

The old-time gospel songs, combined with more modern rhythm and blues, brought the congregation to their feet. My friend, Cindy, danced and sang along with them. I knew few of the hymns, and I couldn't dance to save myself (pun intended), but I smiled and swayed beside her.

My favorite sermon that day came from one of the newly anointed ministers. He talked about the importance of not just attending church services but also of incorporating core beliefs into your everyday actions and decisions. He noted the need to live your life "with The Word on you."

This struck me as the true mission of any religion. It seemed to me that spirituality should not center on a full alignment of formal religious beliefs or be judged by our church attendance: It should be based on how we live our life.

I can't confirm I left that morning with "The Word" on me. But, I did walk away feeling moved and inspired.

Maybe, just maybe, that's the first step in any life-changing journey.

Chapter 7:

I WILL SURVIVE

I'd always secretly imagined myself as a TV or movie star. Since I didn't live in New York City or Hollywood, the possibility of a show auditioning or filming anywhere near Nowheresville, Ohio, made that a long shot. Well, *that* detail along with the fact that my only acting experience was playing Ernie in an eighth-grade production of *Sesame Street*.

Who'd have guessed that one night, while avoiding my mildewing mountains of dirty laundry by scrolling through my Facebook newsfeed, I would spy an announcement about an open cast call for the TV show *Survivor*. No acting experienced required! And, auditions were being held two days later at Put-in-Bay, a tiny but popular summer resort town on a Lake Erie island just a hop and a skip away.

I cancelled all plans for the day (including an important meeting with my new boss), jumped in the car for the hour drive, and took the ferry to the island. If there was one thing I had learned, it was that when serendipity comes calling, you better open the damn door.

While I probably should have worried about my job

security, I agonized instead over what to wear to my audition. I finally decided upon a black T-shirt and black Capri-length jogging pants, along with the running shoes I'd bought a month ago to start training for my planned 5K run—and still hadn't worn. Surely this ensemble would make me appear thinner and more athletic than I truly was. An important impression to make, I figured, since one of the requirements was that contestants be in "excellent physical and mental health." I'd only seen the show a few times, but enough to know this noted mental health stipulation allowed *a lot* of leeway.

Athletic wear, I discovered upon my arrival, was a female fashion faux pas. I was the only auditioning woman not baring her cleavage and shapely, bronzed legs in a bikini or skimpy sundress. The other bad news: I was among the oldest and most full-figured women there.

The good news, however, was my pasty white cankles were as much of my skin as the on-site production crew probably cared to see. I would have to rely on my speech and my charisma.

The online announcement had explained we'd each have a one-minute taped screening to sell ourselves to the producers. The guidelines explained the selection would be based on the contestants with the following traits: strong-willed, outgoing, adventurous, physically and mentally adept, adjustable to new environments, and interesting lifestyles, backgrounds, and personalities.

I figured I met all the criteria, except that little detail of physical and mental adeptness.

With little time for prep, I wrote up talking points that morning, focusing heavily on The 52/52 Project objectives and experiences. While I made the hour-drive to the ferry dock, I attempted to commit the speech to memory. Considering I could seldom remember my ATM or email passwords, I could only hope for the best.

Anyone familiar with Put-in-Bay—the Key West of the Midwest—won't be surprised to know ninety-eight-percent of the people there, at 3 p.m., were fully stewed. I went into the audition stone-cold sober. I figured I deserved bonus points for that.

When my audition number was finally called, I bounced onto the stage, in an effort to demonstrate my youthful exuberance. I caught myself as I tripped and just before I almost landed facedown. Righting myself, I grinned at the woman who appeared to be in charge. One corner of her mouth turned up in what I told myself was a smile.

As the perspiration poured down my face, melting that morning's painstakingly applied makeup, I dove into my prepared speech. I'd spent two hours standing and sweating in the audition line, but it didn't seem anywhere as long as the single minute I stood on that stage.

Concentrating on my speech, I tried to block out the shouting and splashing from the hotel pool. A pool-side resort at Put-in-Bay: Who chose this venue, the *Jersey Shore* producers? Jerry Springer?

Thankfully, I remembered most of my last-minute script. But my memory didn't make up for my ineloquent delivery. As I stuttered and stared at the onsite director, she began rolling her hands in the universal "Wrap up this shit now" signal, long before I reached the most compelling part of my spiel. I stammered some more, wiped a combination of sweat and Maybelline honey beige foundation from my cheeks, and finally murmured something like, "So, I hope you'll please consider me." The semi-smiling director nodded, waved me away, and called the next number.

I walked off the stage, my lips and my legs still trembling. But my confidence was boosted by a couple of young women, Donna and Julieann, who'd become my BFFs during the long wait in line.

Oh yes, you can bet we'd already formed our alliances.

Donna hugged me and assured me I nailed my audition. "Oh my God! You did great! You are *totally* in!" She was so sweet and supportive. Did I mention she was tanked?

She later emailed an action shot she captured of me, mid-audition. And by "action shot," I mean the only moment in which I wasn't standing awkwardly with both hands clenched in fists by my side. Is it possible they'd award extra credit not only for sobriety but also for stiffest pose?

I am patiently standing by for my *Survivor* callback. Surely, the producers are seeking a middle-aged, square-shaped woman who is ready to change her life.

I have big plans for my million-dollar prize, so if I'm chosen, you can be sure I will kick even my closest alliance's ass. When we eventually arrive for the show's filming on another far-off island, I will have a tough time backstabbing Donna and Julieann. But I will do it because I am a gamer. And verbal contracts, even with the sweetest of island drunks, don't hold any water on *Survivor*.

If I never hear from the producers again, likely because they lost my audition tape, I still walked away that day feeling like a player.

And then I stopped at the closest bar for a drink. Or three. Because when you're stranded on an island, especially a place like Put-in-Bay, you do what it takes to survive.

Chapter 8:

CREEPY CRAWLERS

While still awaiting my callback for *Survivor*, I reasoned I should start training by learning to live off the land. Choking down a couple creepy crawlers seemed a good start.

Except for my brief foray into competitive pizza eating, I'd been following a high-protein, low-carb diet for months. I'd grown weary of obscene quantities of cheese and meat— I'd even tired of bacon. If nothing else, eating insects would diversify my protein selections.

The first step was researching how one procured such delicacies. I knew of no mom-and-pop edible bug shops in Toledo. The answer, of course, was the always accommodating Internet.

I scrolled through the selections. I could choose from bare-naked bugs, barbecued, or the chocolate-covered variety. Sure, I wouldn't have that option on any *Survivor* island. Also, chocolate wasn't exactly low-carb.

But the chocolate variety pack proved to be the winner. If there were leftovers, I figured I could freeze them for thoughtful holiday gifts.

The online disclaimer noted, "Sorry, barf bag not included." Not the most practical marketing ploy, but the company wasn't targeting reasonable clientele.

I left the UPS carton on my kitchen counter for three days before I worked up the courage to open it. The "variety pack" included two dozen tiny crickets and worms, half of them covered with milk chocolate and the other half with white chocolate. "White chocolate" was the persona non grata version of *real* chocolate, and would make those insects even less appetizing. I'd save those for gifts.

I scrutinized the treats and called over Son #1 to take a look. He glanced through the clear plastic wrap on a couple of packages and read the labels.

"Eww!" He stepped back. "Why would you order these?"

"I'm going to eat them, obviously," I said. "But I was hoping for more of a variety, maybe some grasshoppers or ants. I hear chocolate-covered ants taste like Nestlé Crunch bars."

I sighed. "And I thought they'd be bigger. I'm kind of disappointed."

Son #1 stared at me. "OK, stuff like your belly dancing and adult bookstore trip were just plain embarrassing. But when I hear you talk like this, you're really starting to worry me."

Several of my friends, however, were eager to get an up-close look. We scheduled an insect-eating party. I assumed they came along to provide moral support, yet this was apparently manifested in their cringing and laughing at me. One friend proved helpful by taking photos, and another videotaped the ordeal. But not a single one agreed to partake in a sampling of my party hors d'oeuvres. I should have made that a requirement.

Tackling the cricket first seemed the obvious choice, since crickets were considered good luck in China. Although I did question whether *eating* them would bring me the same good karma. Either way, I figured a tiny cricket would entail only a couple of quick crunches before it could be swallowed right down the hatch.

The chocolate masked the insect's initial taste and texture. But just like an M&M candy, the chocolate melted in my mouth. Immediately. Once it dissolved, I was left with nothing but bits of cricket.

And by "bits," I mean a leg. Or maybe an antenna. Whichever piece remained, it wedged itself between two of my top molars, and I was forced to dislodge it with the nail of my index finger. I presented the tiny body part to my audience for inspection.

My friends recoiled in disgust, but surprisingly they— and I   stuck around for the second course. Round two was the worm, or "larvae," as it was labeled on the package's list of ingredients. For some reason, "worm" seemed a far more appetizing notion than "larvae." When eating insects, the devil was in the details.

I feared the worm may be an even bigger challenge than the cricket. I anticipated a long and suffering chewing process. The best I could hope for was that it was similar to eating a worm's gummy candy counterpart.

I shuddered, mid-bite, and wildly waved my hands.

"Uh-uh-uh," I squawked through a mouth of unswallowed worm. "Worse than I thought! Not chewy. Crunchy. It's *crunchy!*"

My videoing friend, Joan, shrugged and nodded. "Well, yeah," she said. "Because it's dead and dried up, like the worms you find on your driveway a couple days after it's rained."

This was the precise moment I was captured on camera, mid-gag. I finished off the worm. And I washed it down with half a beer.

Four unopened packages of chocolate-covered crickets and worms remained on a back shelf in my refrigerator. It was unlikely I'd be finishing those off any time soon. Instead,

I offered them as prizes to readers on Facebook, and I found several enthusiastic takers. My followers were clearly of a questionable nature.

I promised to mail out these treasures, but not until winter. I didn't want these chocolate delicacies to potentially melt in transit. They would melt in my reader friends' mouths soon enough.

I suggested they each have a stiff drink before they dug in. And that they have some dental floss handy to deal with any leftover bug body parts.

It was the best way I knew to get a little leg up on the experience.

Chapter 9:

YOU'RE GETTING VERY SLEEPY

$\mathcal{A}$ conversation with friends about nature versus nurture made me wonder if we are who we are either due to our genetics or to our upbringing. Or could there be more to it—something stemming from our far, *far* past?

While I'd always been intrigued by the idea of hypnosis as well as the concept of reincarnation, I couldn't say I was a true believer in either. I decided to test my combined curiosity and cynicism by being hypnotized for past-life regression.

An acquaintance referred me to Virginia Ulch. Ginny was a professional counselor who also specialized in hypnosis, particularly for weight loss and smoking cessation. Hypnosis for past-life regression had proven a successful tool for some of her clients struggling with various issues in their lives.

Other than reading some basic background on Ginny's website, I did no further research, in order to remain objective. Besides, research seemed unnecessary since I doubted I'd actually be hypnotized.

I felt slightly unnerved going in, knowing so little about the experience. All I could envision was the age-old stereotype of having a coin waved before my face and being told I was getting very sleepy. And then, being asked to squawk like a chicken.

Instead, with her office darkened and soft music playing, Ginny offered soothing words to try to steer me toward relaxation and, ultimately, hypnosis. As she recorded our session, she painted an image of a garden in my mind and suggested I find myself sitting among the flowers and fountains.

Gradually, my body began to feel both heavy and weightless at the same time. My mind drifted. Ginny did indeed coax my mind and body into a highly relaxed state.

Was I truly hypnotized? As the first moments passed, my skeptical side was certain I was simply primed for a nice afternoon nap. I told myself I couldn't be hypnotized, since I remained cognizant of Ginny's voice and my immediate surroundings. (I found out through later research that hypnotized people generally do remain aware of these things.)

In fact, I was mindful enough of my environment to realize my left leg was bent awkwardly across the ottoman. I remember thinking it was uncomfortable and that I should readjust my position. But even as I considered this, I just couldn't move my legs.

It was a strange and surreal sensation—like experiencing a dream while asleep and comprehending that it was a dream, yet being incapable of awakening and opening your eyes.

The cynic in me wasn't sure what to think.

"I can't move my legs," I told Ginny. "I don't know. Maybe I can, but it seems like too much effort."

"You can move, if you need to," she said.

Maybe, yet I never managed to convince myself to move my cramping leg. Eventually, I gave up on the idea.

As I grew more relaxed, Ginny asked me to think about

a time and place in my childhood, as far back as I could remember. I let my mind wander and finally pictured myself pushing open the screen door to the concrete back stoop of my childhood home, a place I hadn't been in nearly thirty years. I was about two years old, barefoot, and wearing a dotted swiss romper. In my mind, I stepped onto the porch and gazed out at our backyard.

I saw this visibly, which was no surprise since I'd always had an incredible long-term memory. Even though I clearly described the setting to Ginny, I couldn't provide any other telling details about the scene. No other people present, no significant events that occurred. It was simply a moment in time.

Next, Ginny verbally led me toward a large mirror. "You see many images in this mirror, of different times, places, and people," she said. "Many faces you remember. Choose one. Choose one and go back."

Even though I was presumably hypnotized, I knew what she was implying: One of these "images" would take me back into some subconscious beyond this life—into a previous incarnation.

I tightened my closed eyes. I concentrated. I blew out a sigh of frustration. I couldn't even envision a mirror, let alone see a reflected collage of faces.

I sat quietly for quite a while. Ginny encouraged me to keep searching.

Finally, I envisioned a *scene*. I eventually saw three scenes: visions of three different individuals in three distinctly different time periods and locations.

Was I reliving these moments from my soul's own past, or was I only envisioning these individual episodes with someone else taking part in them? That remained the major question.

My first image was of a Native-American woman. She/I walked alone through fields and thick forests. I sensed this was set a couple centuries ago. I told Ginny it appeared I was on a journey to a faraway place. It seemed I walked for days before finally coming to stop on a riverbank.

As I stood and watched the river run, I accepted the fact that I would likely never find my way to my destination.

Ginny prodded. "Do you see any other people? Do you have a sense of anything else happening?"

I shook my head. "No."

"Is there anything from this life that you should learn," Ginny asked, "to carry over into your present life?"

I contemplated this for several minutes with no revelation. We moved on.

The second scene took place in the kitchen of a small urban apartment, possibly above a storefront, in what seemed to be the early 1950s. I was a fortyish-aged woman, wearing an apron. I sensed there were a couple of small boys somewhere in the home, but not in the room with me.

"Do the children seem familiar?" Ginny asked. "Are either of them the sons you have now?"

I couldn't quite come up with a distinct image of either boy. "I'm not certain. I can't tell for sure." I paused. "Maybe one. There's a boy with wide eyes. He seems... familiar."

Nothing else became clear. Then, I had a sudden flash of this same woman, about twenty years earlier, perhaps in the thirties. Wearing a dress or skirt and high heels, she/I walked down a sidewalk in New York City. Just walking, alone, looking straight ahead. Nothing more to the scene.

"Are you happy with this life," Ginny asked, "either as a young woman or the older one?"

I told her that although this life wasn't particularly exciting, it seemed to be a contented one. The images offered nothing more.

The third scenario was the clearest and most detailed of all. I envisioned myself as a wealthy man or nobleman wearing some type of robe. I sat at a desk in a large house or castle in England and was writing with a fountain pen—the early type dipped into an inkwell.

"Are you a writer?" Ginny asked.

"No. Just writing... something. A legal paper of sorts, I think."

In my mind, I rose to look out an upper-level window. From there, I observed people down below coming and going on horses and in carriages, on the front drive of my large estate.

"Is anyone else with you?" Ginny asked. "Any family, friends, or servants?"

I envisioned servants, somewhere in the house. No one else.

From nowhere, a strange thought struck me. I believed one of the horse-drawn carriages carried a casket.

"I... I think someone died," I told Ginny. "A young woman." I paused, as the scene seemed to illuminate in my mind. "I think she might have been my wife."

With further questioning, we concluded the woman had been very young. She had been weak and sickly for a long time.

"If she was my wife," I asked Ginny, "why am I watching from inside instead of being down there as part of the funeral procession?"

"I don't know," Ginny said. "How do you feel? Are you angry? Sad?"

I hesitated. "Not angry. Not sad, exactly. I feel, mostly, a sense of numb melancholy."

We never determined more about this scene, even while Ginny attempted to coax more specifics from me. While the segment was more detailed than the other two, it was still fuzzy and vague.

Eventually, Ginny led my mind back to the mirror and the garden and then out of that hypnotized or deeply meditative state. I opened my eyes, and the lights came on. I sensed my bent leg was still cramped, and I stretched it across the ottoman.

I squinted at Ginny. "OK. That was pretty weird," I said. "I don't know what to believe about all this. What do you think any of it meant?"

She shook her head. "This was more difficult than many of my regression sessions. It may be because most of my clients point out specific problems or questions when they come in, and they are looking for answers to issues in their current life. Without your having a specific focus, your experience may have been broader and more vague."

As far as how any of these three visions could relate to my current life, Ginny saw only one common thread: I was always alone. I never spoke to or interacted with anyone.

"That's unusual," she said. "It could be significant."

"You're right. I was alone in all of them," I said. "That seems kind of depressing. I really don't think I'm depressed though." I paused. "But, I am alone quite a bit."

I enjoyed socializing, yet I was probably more an "extroverted introvert" than most people thought. I had close relationships with family and friends, yet I greatly appreciated my solitude and independence. I told Ginny that I also had chosen not to enter into any serious romantic relationship in the fifteen years since my marriage ended. And, as I concentrated more on my writing, I was spending an increasing amount of time alone.

Whether or not my seclusion in these envisioned scenes was actually related to my current life, it was at least an intriguing coincidence.

This experience left me with more lingering questions than answers. Was I truly hypnotized? Based on my deep relaxation and my feeling of being either unable or uninclined to change my position, it was very possible. The second, more pressing, question I had was did I really return to three previous lives? I didn't fully believe it. Yet, I didn't disbelieve, either.

The first two scenarios could have been a result of a couple of my lifelong interests: I'd always been captivated by Native American life and by New York City. It seemed natural that I might picture myself in those places and time periods.

The third scene, however, couldn't be so easily explained. I never had any interest in England or in that particular era. I had no idea why I would envision myself there, or why I might summon up the other odd details about it.

Did I truly once live these former incarnations? Or was I just an imaginative writer who simply wrote myself into three fictional short stories? I will question that forever and will never know for certain.

But, like so many items on my 52/52 list, my hypnosis session wasn't truly about the final outcome, the experience's success or its failure. It was mostly about taking part and tapping into something new or, in this case, perhaps something very, very old.

In this life, the one that matters most, maybe that's enough.

Chapter 10:

IF LOVING YOU IS WRONG,
I DON'T WANT TO BE RIGHT

I'd struggled with a handful of bad habits throughout my lifetime. Marlboro Lights, to be sure, were among the worst. I also had a love-hate relationship with carbohydrates, the Internet, and credit cards. (I mean, why pay today for something you can pay for over the next twenty years?)

What I most relied upon to get me through life, however, was caffeine. Caffeine was my go-to, my crutch, my kryptonite. Except, unlike kryptonite, it didn't outright kill me. In fact, I felt sure caffeine was all that stood every day between me and certain brain death.

The day I was to start my newest 52/52 venture, I completely forgot about my objective until late that morning, after I had jumpstarted my body and my brain with a considerable amount—meaning my normal level—of caffeine.

Unfortunately, this particular endeavor had been to give up caffeine. For an entire week.

I started over the next day. I'd like to call it a fresh start, but by 9 a.m. I was feeling anything but "fresh." The exact words I posted online that morning were, "It's barely 9 a.m. Will this Hell Week never, ever end?"

Yeah. It got ugly quick.

I was in the minority of caffeine addicts. I was not a coffee whore. My drug of choice was Diet Coke. My first cracked-open can in the morning progressed into an eight-hour infusion of caffeine and delectable—but allegedly deadly—chemicals. Only midway through did I morph into a pleasant and productive person.

Without it, I was nothing. *Nothing*. Except a blithering mess.

I muddled through that first day, avoiding other people, heavy machinery, and important decisions. Luckily, I had no meetings scheduled at the office. I stared blankly at my computer monitor and let a couple phone calls go to voice mail, doubtful I could carry on a professional conversation. I jotted down very little in my 52/52 journal that night, since the day had been nothing more than a bleak blur.

Somehow, I managed to survive. I crawled into bed, oh, just before the sun set. Only six more days to go, I reassured myself.

Six more days. I buried my head below my pillow. Just kill me now. Or at least before 8 a.m. tomorrow.

By day two, mornings had turned even nastier. As did I. My coworkers whispered among themselves and began taking elaborate detours through the office to avoid me. My friend, Lynn, cautiously peeked in my door and suggested that having gone a single day without caffeine might be *enough* of a challenge.

I contemplated replacing the normal caffeine in my diet with alcohol. It would have made me more amicable at the office, but I had a hunch it might be frowned upon.

So, I persisted with my original ill-advised plan.

Day three was by far the worst. As I huddled over my desk at 3 p.m., I devised an idea to get through the rest of the week. Perhaps I could finagle a prescription for Ritalin and take up chain-smoking. If smoking Ritalin had been a thing, I'd have been all over that.

Sadly, I didn't get my hands on any Ritalin before I got a phone call, on day four, from a local newspaper wanting to interview me about The 52/52 Project. I warned the reporter that I wasn't my sharpest that day. And it was very possible I might fully snap, mid-interview.

Although the interview remains hazy, I can't be certain I didn't tell him, "Shut up and high-tail it over here with a six-pack of Diet Coke!" Thankfully, the reporter knew the art of paraphrasing.

Most unexpected was that I never suffered from the much forewarned caffeine-deprivation headaches. Or maybe I did. Honestly, I endured most of the week through a fog. I could have robbed a convenience store or married a one-night stand in a Las Vegas chapel of love, without being able to recall or being held accountable for my actions.

The biggest surprise, however, was that the week gradually did grow a *bit* easier. I never stopped craving caffeine, but I did manage to get through a one- or two-hour stretch without obsessing about it.

By Day Seven, I was not quite the bitch I was on Day One.

The point was, I proved myself capable, with tremendous struggle and sacrifice, of getting through seven days without caffeine.

I returned to caffeine the following week. However, this weeklong hiatus did enable me to cut back my intake to a level *slightly* less likely to kill a rat in a laboratory test—or at least to slow the process. Before I popped open a can of

Diet Coke, I now gave it more consideration and occasionally poured a glass of ice water instead.

Living without caffeine for a week was one of my most personally daunting experiences. While lots of huge challenges still awaited me, I wouldn't need to rely upon heavy doses of my favorite drug for most of them. I needed only one, totally natural chemical to get through the rest of my list.

Adrenaline, especially when it's fear-induced, is mighty effective all on its own.

Chapter 11:

THE WOES OF WAXING,
NOT SO POETIC

On my way to the salon, I stopped at a red light and pondered why, on God's Good Earth, I had chosen this particular impending fate. Never, on my true bucket list, would I ever, *ever* include undergoing a Brazilian wax.

Personal humiliation, accompanied by excruciating pain, was likely the mother of all boundary-pushing challenges. The waxing of my nether regions, along with my legs, could take this year's goal of going outside my comfort zone to an entirely new level in more ways than one.

I'd been told "southern" waxing had become the norm of the under-thirty crowd. For most women of my generation, however, it remained a disturbing thought, much like a gynecological exam combined with botched Botox.

When I made my appointment, the receptionist brushed over my Brazilian wax. I was happy to ignore the subject. She mentioned only that the hair on my legs should be about the length of a grain of rice. Hmm. During the recent chaos of packing up and moving twenty years' worth of hoarded belongings from my old house to my new condo, my legs had been sorely neglected. When I arrived at the salon a couple days later, my once rice-length leg hair more closely resembled al dente spaghetti.

We soon encountered bigger problems. After I'd stoically endured most of the waxing of my left leg, my esthetician, Rebekah, stepped back and frowned.

"Wow," she said. "Your leg looks like a road map."

Probably I should have remembered, before I was in the midst of having every hair below my waist ripped from my body, that I had a condition my allergist called "dermographism." My highly sensitive skin welted up under the slightest scratching or pressure, to the degree that you could literally write on me with just the firm brush of a fingernail.

I glanced down at my leg. A swarm of mutant killer mosquitoes would have left less damage.

I winced but reassured Rebekah this was no problem. My dermographism didn't generally pose much of a issue. Neither did all my allergies, thanks to a simple routine of a daily antihistamine pill, two nightly spurts of nasal spray, and biweekly immunotherapy shots—which gradually pumped me full of everything that hated my immune system. In exact controlled doses, what doesn't kill you apparently *does* make you stronger.

The wax Rebekah was using, she noted, was composed primarily of pine oil. "You're not allergic to that, are you?"

Pine? I pondered this. My host of allergies includes dogs and cats (thank goodness I only had a total of five of those at home), dust, mold, weeds, and grasses.

And most trees.

I shrugged. What the hell.

"I have an EpiPen in my purse," I told her. "Just jab it into my thigh if my throat swells shut and I stop breathing."

Strangely, this did not put her mind at ease. Yet, we carried on. After all, I had a new item to check off my 52/52 list. Death by waxing could be a new experience for both of us.

Neither an allergic reaction nor any ungodly pain from the leg waxing proved lethal. Not that having every hair ripped from my legs wasn't painful. The worst part was the waxing of my shins, where the thin skin was more sensitive. For a single moment in my life, I wished my thick ankles were even fatter.

But then came the experience I had dreaded most—the waxing of my "Cupid's Cupboard." This seemingly sweet woman began yanking sections of tiny hairs from my most delicate body region. Oh, sweet Jesus, did it burn!

Call the Ohio Forestry Division! We had a major bush fire down in the valley!

I cringed and whimpered, but the most painful aspect proved to be the mental anguish. While I lay naked and spread-eagle in front of this stranger, who squinted and frowned as she scrutinized territory that had remained unexplored and untamed for far too long, my dignity suffered most.

If someone tells you that lying naked with your legs hiked over your head (while a salon technician studies your nether regions) may not be the most humiliating thing you could ever endure, don't believe it.

"Spread your legs a little wider," she said. I complied. And I died a bit more.

While she studied my "vajay" for over half an hour, I tried to focus on other, more pleasant thoughts. As Rebekah ripped off strip after strip of hair, I clenched my teeth and contemplated what I might make for dinner. Maybe a grilled steak or broiled salmon. I cringed. No, fish was definitely out of the question.

Rebekah tried to put me at ease by making small talk. I was stunned by her story about a client who, after years of this process, had grown so desensitized to the sting of both physical pain and humiliation that she fell asleep during it. Clearly, one brave—or sick—woman.

As Rebekah inched her way through the remainder of my Brazilian, she said I had a couple options for properly finishing up the "back" region. One was to roll over and get on all fours, in a crawling position, upon the table. The other was to continue lying on my back and then hold both legs in the air, as if positioned for a backward somersault.

These were my options? It was a lose-lose situation. I flipped a mental coin and chose the backward approach. I grabbed my ass and hiked my legs into the air.

And while I found myself in this most humiliating of positions, she told me the story of another client who drove in for her regular appointments from an hour away. This woman told Rebekah she wouldn't get her hoo-ha waxed in her own hometown because she wanted to ensure she was never forced to make eye contact with someone who had viewed her this particular way.

Good point. Rebekah was pleasant and professional, but after this encounter, I prayed I'd never meet up with her in my local supermarket's produce aisle.

She paused. "Are you OK?"

"Uh-huh. Great. Almost finished?"

"Almost done waxing," she said. "But I'm a bit of a perfectionist. I'll want to go back and see if I've missed any stragglers. And then I'll tweeze them."

If the thought of a Brazilian wax caused me any amount of unease, the idea of a Brazilian *tweeze*—a hair-by-hair pubic plucking—prompted me to nearly jump off the table and run out the door, my skivvies in hand. But before I could flee, Rebekah commenced yanking. Holy hell. I would never again look at a pair of tweezers without recoiling.

I left the salon, smooth as silk, except for the lingering welts over the lower half of my body.

This experience left me wondering why women would put themselves through this ordeal, willingly, on a regular basis. Were there any true benefits?

Sure, it might make wearing a bikini more aesthetically pleasing. As a couple of my younger readers noted, there might be some erotic motives, too. Given my current celibate life, however, those were left only to my imagination.

My Brazilian wax escapade—my first and most likely my last—didn't end up being the most frightening of my year's new experiences. It would, however, win out as one of the most uncomfortable and mortifying ones.

At least by a hair.

Chapter 12:

JUST SHOOT ME

While taking on an unbucket list, it's important to learn to roll with the punches. While most of my experiences were planned challenges, I hadn't expected to be hit in one of my most vulnerable points—shot with a camera lens.

I despised the camera. And, from all physical evidence, the camera didn't seem fond of me. Fortunately, as my family's primary photographer, I'd been comfortably absent from a couple decades of family photos.

There was no hiding behind the camera for this one though. When a newspaper interview asked for a professional photo, I was forced to add "enduring my first-ever author photo shoot" to my list. I was obliged to be the solo, overweight, middle-aged model with thinning eyebrows.

Mortifying.

A bit of advice about professional photo shoots: It's best to not schedule one while you're in the midst of moving, after you've packed away nearly your entire wardrobe. Or to have this photo session scheduled the very morning you discover a volcano has erupted on your chin. I was fifty two years old. Must I endure crow's feet *and* acne?

I pushed these futile worries aside and instead agonized over items more under my control: my hair and makeup. During the two hours I attempted to pretty-up, I cringed and wept. I cemented my hair with hairspray, did a double-take in the bathroom mirror, and then crawled back into the shower to start from scratch. I finally picked an outfit from the mountain of already discarded clothes on the floor. I applied brown eyeshadow and a double-brush of mascara and, to appease my mother who often referred to me as her "Amish daughter," I even swiped on some lipstick.

After all that prep work, my talented and obliging photographer, Alex, saw me through a couple hours of self-conscious grimacing and sweating. He managed to leave me with at least one photo in which I thought I appeared presentable: the one in which I posed with Ringo, the Wonder Retriever. Like Lassie, my pooch managed to save the day.

They say a picture may be worth a thousand words. This experience, however, was hardly worth half that.

Chapter 13:

HAIR TODAY—GONE TOMORROW

"S o," my hairstylist asked, dipping my head under the faucet. "Are we just trimming it up today?"

I'd obsessed over this for weeks. Whenever I spied an attractive woman with great hair—a college student with a thick flowing mane, a model with a cute pixie, or an actress with a fabulous bob on a TV legal drama—I would think, "Wow, if only I had hair like that, I bet I would look just as hot!" Chopping off my shoulder-length hair, far shorter than I'd ever worn it, evoked images of Anne Hathaway in *Les Misérables*. I only hoped it would entail less suffering, pain, and horror.

"Not this time," I told my stylist, who'd been doing my hair for twenty years. "I'm thinking something different tonight. Something short. Really short. The shortest I've ever worn it."

I attempted to explain exactly what I had in mind, biting my bottom lip as I considered how this monumental decision could potentially ruin the next eight weeks of my life.

But Pam simply cocked her head, glanced at my hair,

and nodded. I reassured myself that this woman with my head—with practically my *entire life*—in her hands, was a paid professional. She made her living by making women beautiful. Surely, I would live to have no regrets.

Forty-five minutes later, she brushed the clippings off my shoulders and removed my apron. I gathered up the kind of courage generally reserved for a job interview or a root canal, and I peered into the mirror. I looked... gorgeous!

Well, not all of me, perhaps, but at least my hair. Yes, that looked amazing.

I beamed. "I love it!"

"Yeah? Good," Pam said, with not an ounce of the desperate relief I was experiencing. I didn't know what calming and confidence-building drugs all hairstylists must be required to consume, but I definitely wanted in on that shit before my next appointment.

I hesitated as I grabbed my checkbook. "So, you think I can do it just like this, myself, right?"

"Oh, absolutely," she said over her shoulder, as she motioned to her next client. "Just make sure you use plenty of product."

I contemplated the generic use of the word "product" for mysterious hair goo, as well as the word "plenty." Hmm. Was that a tablespoon or a quarter cup? I'd prefer if she provided an exact measurement. Using my own judgment in the care of my hair had never proven successful.

"And when you're blow-drying," Pam continued, "be sure you hold the dryer nozzle underneath the roots of each section of hair as you lift it up, like I did."

"Uh-huh." My mind raced to recall that particular step of tonight's appointment. This memory was fuzzy, since I spent much of the hair-drying segment shouting about the injustices of parenthood. And the injustices of my job. Or both. Who needs a therapist when you have a hair stylist?

"And then, don't forget," she added, "to spray it again."

Again? Wait. Was I supposed to have already sprayed once before this step? I bit at the cuticles of my newly painted nails.

"That's it, really," Pam said, as she began shampooing the next client's hair. "Except you'll probably need to scrunch it a bit. Just a tiny piece at a time. Then, take a look and decide whether or not you want to use a curling iron on any section. But with the right amount of product and more scrunching, you should be all set. Unless you need to spray it again."

On the drive home, I repeated this set of instructions to myself, over and over. It was an all-consuming lesson. I nearly ran a stop sign, slamming on my brakes just short of T-boning a minivan as I murmured my new mantra, "Product, dry, lift, spray, scrunch, curl, spray, scrunch again."

After a sleepless night, I rose early. I ran methodically through every step of the process. My fingers began to ache from repeated scrunching.

I finally stepped back and surveyed myself in the mirror. I squinted. *Huh.* Was this how it looked last night? Perhaps I was not objective enough. I scrunched and sprayed one last time, shrugged, and continued getting ready for work.

Just as I headed out the door, my visiting son—who for twenty-plus years had appeared oblivious to every single one of my hair styles—stopped in the hallway to stare at me.

"Um, hey, Mom." He cleared his throat. "Your hair looks a little, well, funny."

I fought a swirling stomach of despair, as I realized that even this most lowbrow of opinions might be fully on-target. But I had no time for further reflection; I was already late for work.

I shuffled to my car. I spent my drive time peeking in the rearview mirror, scrunching some more. For the next eight hours, I hid inside my office—with the door closed.

Before going to bed that night, I showered and washed

out the copious quantities of product and hairspray. I collapsed in bed with a wet head.

The next morning, I peeked in the mirror. At the sight
of my bed head, I sighed. I didn't have the energy to repeat
the process all over again. In fact, I barely recalled the first
two steps of the process. And I was fairly certain an entire
bottle of product wouldn't be enough.

I cocked my head. Maybe it wasn't so bad just like this,
I considered. Though short and splintery, and a little flat
in a couple places, it had a tousled, carefree kind of look. I
looked sort of like Meg Ryan in whatever-the-hell that one
movie was. She didn't fare so badly. Until that whole supposed plastic surgery fiasco.

I rubbed in a bit of product, scrunched a few spots, and
called it a day.

That afternoon, I peeked in the mirror again. I wasn't
certain whom I saw in the reflection, but it sure didn't look
like me. Wow, was it short. It was nowhere near my normal
look. But, I was slowly growing to like it. I wasn't ready to
submit my photo and application for Ms. America. But I no
longer felt compelled to crawl, sobbing, into a corner of my
closet either.

Was the new hairdo more or less attractive than my
long-standing style? Most friends and family were compli-
mentary. I wondered if it was truly the look of the new cut
or simply the idea of change itself—something different to
acknowledge about someone—which appealed to them.

Embracing change in our own life, however, is more
challenging. Especially when it results in not only feeling but
also *looking* so different. It's difficult to notice, let alone eval-
uate, changes in our own character or personality. But alter-
ations in our appearance jump out at us every time we simply
look in a mirror—the good, the bad, and the ugly.

I went with the new style for several months until,

through pure procrastination, my hair grew out. When I finally arrived at the salon, returning to my old look seemed anticlimactic. Yet another major change seemed risky.

Pam stood over me, with scissors in hand. "So, what are we doing today?"

I glanced up at her, shrugged, and said, "You're driving. Just go for it."

She winked at me, and the cycle of haircare chaos began all over again.

This time, I kept "plenty of product" on hand. It might never be the answer, but it was at least a damn good guess.

Chapter 14:

OUT ON THE STREET

I spied Linda as I pulled into the suburban shopping center. She stood in the median, looking disheveled with scruffy hair, grungy T-shirt, and sweatpants. A stuffed backpack was hitched across her shoulders. She held a cardboard sign reading, "Homeless and Hungry." And, in smaller scrawled letters, "Anything helps! Thank you!"

Wary and suspicious of begging strangers, I had passed by people like her for years. While I sometimes felt bad enough to wonder about their situation and their welfare, I rarely stopped to offer a dollar or even a warm smile. It was easier to not become emotionally involved or financially invested.

But this afternoon, as I bit my bottom lip and glanced back at the line of cars trailing me, I paused. I leaned out my window and offered to buy this woman lunch.

Linda hesitated briefly, before nodding. "That would be great. Thanks."

We met at the entrance to a casual chain restaurant, just across the parking lot. After I paid for our order, I found a corner table in the back, where I hoped we'd have some privacy. But the restaurant was busy. A group of teenagers sat across from us, two of them in shirts bearing the logo of the private high school my youngest son attended. They eyed Linda, likely recalling her standing with her sign by the side of the road. Their sideways glances, either out of curiosity or discomfort, persisted for a half hour.

Linda sat across from me, both of us awkward as we faced each other. How to make small talk with a homeless stranger? We started out with the safest of topics: the weather, the traffic, the food. And Linda gradually opened up.

She was a local girl, or woman, to be exact. At a closer look, I decided she was probably in her late twenties. She told me she was homeschooled, until her parents could no longer afford the curriculum. I knew much of that was now provided online for free, but was likely not so accessible when she was younger. She'd gone on to get her GED, testing above the average. In her early twenties, she scrounged up the funding to take classes at a nearby business college, where she received a degree in entrepreneurial business.

"My dream is to open my own pizza place," she said. "I'd like to have a sit-down restaurant, with twenty-four-hour delivery. I'm really passionate about the pizza industry."

"Passion is good," I said, nodding. "Passion leads to setting goals."

But Linda said she never found a position in which she could really use her education or skills. She worked a number of jobs, and now, at the age of twenty-nine, she found herself out of work again.

"My last job was cleaning rooms at a motel. I kept bringing home bed bugs, which upset the people I was staying with, so I had to quit."

She recently applied for federal assistance, but this process took time, she explained. Plus, there was a glitch with her paperwork. She was still waiting. She'd applied for work through a local temp agency and was hopeful she might find a job that way.

"Meanwhile, I keep looking. I've applied at all these places," she said, waving a hand across the window at the line of restaurants along the busy roadway. "Right before you came along, a guy stopped to tell me IHOP was hiring, so I'll head over there next."

Why was it so difficult for her to find work? I glimpsed her old, unkempt clothing and her stubby hair. Was it her appearance? Or was it something else?

She saw me glancing at her head and she ran a hand across her scalp. "This probably doesn't help," she said. "I had to shave my head when my kids came home again with a bad case of lice. I know I look odd."

Linda had two sons, ages three and four. Seven months ago, their father quit paying the meager child support he once provided, although she knew he had a job that paid him under the table. He didn't visit. Occasionally, he called to ask how the children were doing. She was angry with him but tried to keep some peace, since she wanted her boys to have a relationship with their father.

"I want to say to him, 'Really? Today, all of a sudden, you wonder how they are? Did you think about them last week or last month? Do you really care?' But he's their father, and I'm their mother." She lifted her chin, with defiant pride. "And so I tell him, 'They're terrific kids. And we are doing the best we can.'"

If things got really tough, Linda moved around to look for work. She hesitated to constantly move the boys, especially to places she didn't think were safe or appropriate. She relied on a couple close and responsible friends to temporarily keep them.

"All that's important is that my kids are safe. I do what

I need to, but I try to not let it affect them. Your children come first. That's the way I was raised. The children always come first."

"Do you have parents?" I asked. "Could they help?"

She shook her head. "My mom has had mental health issues my whole life. She worries a lot. If she knew what I was going through, well, it wouldn't be good for her. I try not to tell her much."

Her mother's mental illness was a telling detail. That, along with Linda's mention of being "homeschooled"— which I now guessed meant her education had more likely been neglected—made me conclude Linda hadn't managed to come first for her own mother. She never mentioned a father.

I studied her. I knew mental health was a family issue, affecting children either through heredity or through environment. I gazed at her wide-set, clear eyes, set off by her pale skin. A half hour spent with someone was not nearly enough to know what all was at play. Did she have her own mental issues? A lifetime of hard knocks? Or was it possible drugs were involved? No, I didn't think *that* was the case, and I was fairly savvy to that.

She seemed to read my mind. "I haven't given up on finding a job, and I've tried to find other assistance, for me and my kids," she said. "But most seem to be shelters that focus on homeless people with addiction problems. They want to get people like that off the streets, so they can get clean. I understand that. But I think sometimes people like us get left behind."

I knew organizations existed to help people like Linda. They *must*. But, as I sat across from her, I couldn't conjure up the name of a single one, other than a downtown Toledo soup kitchen. If I—a well-educated woman with Internet aptitude and community connections—couldn't name any, how was someone like Linda supposed to find the help she needed?

"I just try to remain positive," she said. "I pray a lot. I

know God wouldn't give me anything I couldn't handle. I'm sure things will get better. They always get better, you know?"

I forced a nod as I swirled a spoon in my chicken soup. I would have liked to honestly agree. I wanted to believe. Yet, I wasn't so sure.

Linda said begging on the street didn't come easy. "I don't like to be out there, asking for help. But I do because I feel like I have few options right now. And every little bit helps. If I get a free meal like this, any money I get can then go toward my boys," she said. "I just accept what I need or what I get, gladly, and then I move on. Sometimes the police tell me to leave. But honestly, I try not to be greedy. Other people need help, too."

Most people who drove by her didn't want to help though. The majority simply ignored her. Others leaned out their car windows and yelled, "Get a job!"

"I'd like to tell them I'm trying," she said. "But I seldom get that chance."

Some people went beyond shouting out their contempt. Once, a man stopped, handed her a package, and said, "You'd better eat this, or I'll be all over you!"

She said she pulled the foil off the paper plate to discover a pile of regurgitated food.

"I don't know how he could do that." She lowered her head and then glanced back up. "How could he look me in the eye and hand that to me?"

I shook my head, trying to imagine how that experience might affect a person. I realized I wasn't the only one taking a chance that afternoon. A war-torn and weary Linda had taken a chance on me, too.

As we finished our lunch, she looked down at her plate. Half her barbecued chicken remained. "I think I'll take this home, if it's OK with you," she said. "I have some bread. This will make a nice sandwich for one of the boys."

We headed outside. I reached into my purse and handed her five dollars. "Sorry," I said. "I don't carry much cash. I generally just use my debit card." First-world problems. At least for some of us.

Linda smiled. "Every little bit helps. And really, you've already helped a lot."

We shook hands, and I climbed into my minivan. I watched her cross the parking lot. We waved at each other as I drove away. I pulled onto the highway, headed back to my condo in the suburbs.

I never got Linda's last name. I looked for her for months afterward, searching the faces of every panhandler I passed, those strangers for whom I now more frequently stopped to offer a couple dollars and a simple "Good luck to you."

More than one reader told me I was scammed, manipulated by Linda through some made-up story. Yes, I knew scammers existed. Without hearing their testimony and without knowing their true story, I couldn't be judge or jury in every case. All I knew was that offering a few dollars now and then wouldn't hurt me a bit, yet it could help someone who truly may be down on her luck.

I never saw Linda on the street again. I hoped that, just maybe, she'd finally found a job. That she and her two sons found a safe place to live, together, for good. That her story had a happy ending. I wanted to believe that I'd someday find myself eating in a pizza parlor and Linda would stop by my table, smile, and ask, "How was your meal today?"

Over that half hour on a summer afternoon, I offered Linda a willing ear, a warm meal, and a five-dollar bill. In return, she opened my mind to the struggles of people around me. She gave me a lifetime of angles and attitudes to consider.

As trades go, this one hardly seemed fair.

But sometimes, life isn't.

~ FALL ~

Chapter 15:

A MATCH MADE IN HELL

Since my divorce, I'd made little effort to meet men, let alone find another potential life partner. My last official date was as distant as my memory of wearing stilettos. Coincidence?

I liked men just fine. I enjoyed talking with and looking at them, and all the better if they happened to look back. But, my long-term investment in a relationship was something entirely different. Independent living agreed with me: no dirty boxers to wash, no obligation to cook dinner when all I craved was a Diet Coke and microwave popcorn, and no TV for entire days if I wanted. It's possible this male stereotype was unfair, based on a few married girlfriends' complaints or maybe my memory of raising two sons.

By putting myself out on the dating battlefield, I wondered if I could discover something that might be missing from my life.

As I stared at the computer screen, I considered all the new experiences I'd endured over the last several months. Couldn't I audition for *Survivor* again? Or maybe have another

Brazilian wax? Either option would have been preferable to filling out the application on Match.com.

QUESTION NUMBER FOUR: "WHAT'S YOUR BODY TYPE?"

I labored over this for a half hour, sighed while scrutinizing myself in the mirror a couple times, and then came back to it. Probably, "slender" or "trim and athletic" should be ruled out. Other options included "big and beautiful," "curvy," "full-figured," "heavy-set," and "stocky." Huh. Were these not pretty much the same? Which was more appealing: "full-figured" or "big and beautiful"? And maybe it was the PR professional in me, but why would I label myself "stocky" when I might be considered "curvy"?

Curvy, it was.

QUESTION NUMBER FIVE: "WHAT'S YOUR SIGN?"

Thank God! A question I knew how to answer. And apparently, one so imperative that it must be addressed on the *first* page of the application, four full pages before any questions about a person's religious, political, or societal beliefs.

QUESTION NUMBER 5,674: "WHAT ARE SOME OF YOUR FAVORITE LOCAL HOT SPOTS?"

I chewed my bottom lip as I mentally ran through all my favorite haunts. Somehow, I doubted the local bookstore or Dollar General qualified.

After working on my profile for nearly an hour, the only terms I conjured to describe my character were "fun," "well-read," and "open-minded."

I considered adding "decisive," but I wasn't quite sure.

Finally, I clicked the button, making my Match.com application live. I uploaded a recent enough photo and finished my profile:

More Humor, Less Drama: Humor writer looking for someone to make me laugh. Must love books and animals, since I have a houseful of both. Will watch baseball and basketball with you, if you'll watch Downton Abbey and Doctor Who with me. Happy to cook if you're willing to clean up. Looking for intelligence, sincerity, and kindness. Perfection not expected, but surely not discouraged.

Good thing I proofread it just before clicking the finish button. I had mistyped "kindness" as "kinkness." I smirked but then cringed as I considered the kind of replies a perceived misspelling of "kinkiness" might have elicited (although, probably dozens more responses than the profile of a woman looking for kindness).

As the weeks passed and I found no decent prospects, I revisited the profiles of men who had viewed or liked my listing. Here, I swear, are a few *totally unaltered* profile snippets:

some ne that free trustworthy truthful one woman man willing to take a chance again on life willing to share their life with movie dinning out have fun fishing camping walking in the park fle market watching the sunset not over weight good nature woman

realy dont know what to say never done this befor wasaired foe 25 yares she died 2 years ago like to go to dirt track races and camping but bean a long time cence i non that and out and listin to music sometimes

looking for a casual relationship at this time wanting to have lots of fun sharing things. having great sex together would be wonderful...looking for a friend with benifits type relationship

What? Yes, perhaps I was a grammar and spelling Nazi, but... still. I knew I'd be red-lining even a freaking grocery list written by most of these men, let alone any love letters they emailed me. And the third guy, *who mentioned three times in his profile that he was looking for great sex*, didn't include a single photo. His listing said he was "recently separated." I was pretty sure he meant, *"momentarily separated,"* as in he was currently sequestered away with his laptop in the bathroom while his wife was making dinner in the kitchen.

If any of these dating options were going to evolve into a face-to-face encounter, I would clearly have to learn to speak gobbledygook, agree to a friendship with "benifits," or take up camping. After my recent camping experience, I never expected camping would one day appear the least of all evils. Oh, the humanity!

A week passed before I revisited the website. I scrolled through the tabs to discover a handful of men had "winked," "liked," "favorited," or "shown interest" in me. Decoding the significance of this jargon proved as problematic as deciphering the posted profiles. The old-school method of hanging out at a bar and having a drunk and desperate guy ask, "Can I buy you a drink" began to sound better by the minute.

I schlepped my way to the kitchen and stared blankly into my pantry, managing to ignore an ancient half-eaten bag of Fritos. The open pantry door impelled an orchestra of yowling from my four cats, who were all sprawled in their usual fashion across my mahogany dining room table.

Perhaps *this* was the real reason I hadn't had a date in so long.

I tossed the cats some treats. And then I hugged my dog, Ringo the Wonder Retriever, in an attempt to convince myself I wasn't a crazy cat lady.

The next evening, as I finished off the stale Fritos and the last season of *Parks and Recreation*, I summoned some courage and signed back in to Match.com. Wait, what was *this*? I paused the TV show, while nearly choking on a corn chip. Someone of actual interest had visited my profile!

This guy appeared attractive, well-spoken, and authentically single. As a bonus, he was a *Doctor Who* fan! He was the first guy I had any real inclination to contact.

While he was nearly perfect, the one caveat was that he lived nearly three hours away. Hmm. I had noted on my profile that I was only interested in men who lived within fifty miles. But, what did a bit of a road trip matter, especially since I was just seeking a single date?

And if we ended up hitting it off? As I considered the idea, a long-distance relationship didn't sound half-bad. We'd enjoy infrequent romantic dinners and conversation, plus the occasional dessert *(wink, wink)*. I'd face no fear of losing my independence—and no daily depositing of dirty boxers on my bathroom floor. Plus, since a three-hour commute would prevent him from spending much time at my place, his note about being allergic to cats might prove almost irrelevant. I wouldn't mention my cat colony quite yet. We'd cross that cat hair-covered bridge when we got to it.

Sure, he hadn't formally liked, favorited, or winked at me, but he had at least made the effort to click through to *look*. Maybe he was a bit shy and just needed some encouragement. At a reader's strong-arming, I finally "winked" at him. And then I sent him a direct message. I told him I was new to this computer dating stuff but I enjoyed reading his profile and thought we might have a great deal in common. Would he be interested in an online dialogue?

Holy mother of God! What did I do? Just kill me now!

I scoured the Match website for the "undo" button without any luck. My message was locked in and sent. All I could do was wait. I distracted myself, and soon felt normalized, by reading a series of inane and nasty comments on Yahoo News.

Before I checked my email the next morning, I show-ered, shaved my legs, moussed my hair, and put on a full face of makeup. Not that I expected to meet up with my mystery man that very day; I simply wanted to look good while he might be reading my email.

That evening, I finally got a reply. Sadly, my online love interest declined my invitation to connect. He explained he was "looking for something different." Seriously? If he only knew me better, he'd quickly discover I was *different*, indeed. I had to admit I was disappointed, but I told myself there were other men out there, surely one of them a better match.

As the weeks passed though, I realized I'd hit the bottom of the barrel. Only two more guys—*two*—viewed and "liked" my profile over the next two weeks. Considering my cumulative options, they looked pretty good. As good as they *could* look, considering neither posted a photo. Were they both married or perhaps both on the FBI's most-wanted list?

I knew several people who had luck with online dating. A few of my friends had met their husbands this way. I con-sidered either tweaking my profile or settling for meeting a questionable guy. But, if truth be told, I wasn't seeking more than a single date for my year of new experiences. Was this endeavor worthy of further pursuit? I wasn't even looking for a serious relationship. And if I *were* looking for a long-term romance, why would I pretend to be someone I wasn't or settle for less than what I wanted?

I would have liked to say I managed at least one date on Match.com—though preferably not with a married man, a serial killer, or even an avid camper. I wasn't sure I would survive any of those.

When my last suitor wrote that "*Shivery* is not dead," I realized my odds at online dating success were shaky at best.

Maybe it was me and not them, but three months after registering on Match.com, I bid it a not-so-fond adieu.

I remained Dateless in Toledo. But when I signed off for the last time that evening, I dined happily, alone, on microwave popcorn and Diet Coke. I never once touched the TV remote. I laughed at my own jokes and took a bit of pleasure in my own company.

For now, at least, it appeared I had found my perfect match. And it was me.

Chapter 16:

FROM MEETLESS TO MEATLESS

As an animal lover, I was proud to say I walked the walk in many ways: I donated to a number of animal causes and rescued more than my share of homeless pets and injured wild creatures.

Yet, I had been raised on bacon and eggs, baloney sandwiches, and meatloaf. Even as an adult, I planned most family dinners around an entrée of meat. My favorite way to celebrate a special occasion was by splurging on surf and turf.

While I vilified cruelty to animals, I continued to eat them every single day.

Changing a steadfast lifestyle would be a struggle, I was sure, but attempting to go vegan—at least for a week—seemed a natural and noble challenge for a hypocritical humanitarian like me.

I began by questioning the vegans and vegetarians I knew. What were their personal motivations: health or humanitarian reasons? *Humanitarian*, mostly. What plant-based foods rocked their world? *Beans and legumes.* (All good, aside from lima beans, which clearly belonged in a separate food category I labeled, "Puke Foods.") What animal-based foods did vegans miss most? *Cheese. And bacon.* (Duh.)

My research gave me confidence. I'd been a born-again virgin for years; I figured becoming a born-again vegan couldn't prove more difficult. To soften the blow, the day before I undertook my animal-free diet, I scarfed down a BLT at lunch and then prepared a seafood smorgasbord dinner of mahi-mahi, crab legs, and seared scallops. Best to get all those taboo favorites out of my system in one spurt of hypocritical glory.

While losing weight over the past eight months, I had followed a low-carb, high-protein diet. Meat had been my mainstay. Cheese had been a God-send. Although I'd successfully lost thirty pounds while enjoying chunks of cheddar, strip steaks, and bacon, it wasn't without sacrifice. I'd missed carbs. I'd missed them so, so much.

I figured the best thing about eating vegan, besides taking no part in the cruel factory raising or death of animals, would be the ability to partake in potatoes and pasta. They might not be my weight-loss friends, but damn if I wouldn't allow myself a carb binge—with little guilt—while I could.

By day two, I realized the biggest downfall of a vegan diet was going without dairy products. How could I make a proper Greek salad or eggplant parmesan without cheese? And forgoing eggs, which were ubiquitous in baked goods? *Sigh.* Yes, a vegetarian diet was one thing, but vegan would be a challenge, indeed.

I eyed the vegetarian section in the grocery store. Were those pale slabs of tofu any tastier than they looked?

I decided a variety of beans, nuts, raw veggies—along with Mediterranean and Mexican meals—would comprise my daily diet. These were some of my favorite foods anyway, so eating them wasn't a sacrifice.

The week's major win? I made a huge pot of chili using my

normal recipe but replacing ground beef with textured vegeta-
ble protein. I even used less of that than planned. (I accidentally
dumped half of it down my shirt during preparation.) And I
could barely taste the difference in the final dish, especially when
I scooped it up with whole-grain tortilla chips. I later served the
chili to my two sons, who never noticed the switch.

I ate french fries, the first fries to meet my lips in months.
(Heaven.) And, as I ate pasta the next night, I discovered I
could enjoy spaghetti with marinara sauce while barely missing my homemade meatballs. (Barely.)

I learned several other things while living as a vegan:

- If dining vegan-style at a Mexican restaurant, it's
  best to ask—*before* you've finished dinner—if the
  refried beans were made with lard. I hoped guilt by
  accident didn't count.

- If you're awake at 3 a.m. questioning whether you
  ever refrigerated the colossal containers of tabouli
  and garlic hummus you bought the previous day,
  rest assured you will find them the next evening
  in the back seat of your hot, odoriferous car. You
  will be forced to toss them and improvise that next
  night's dinner. Thankfully, Diet Coke and popcorn
  are both within vegan guidelines.

- Beans are definitely your friend. I ate them all: black
  beans, kidney beans, navy beans, garbanzo beans
  (but not lima beans, those pasty little bastards). Perhaps it was best I had no hot Match.com dates lined
  up, considering the quantity of beans I ingested.

Being a vegan for a week proved to be among the easiest
of the new ventures I'd experienced so far. I figured I was

overdue for something slightly less challenging or frightening. Besides, three things played to my advantage.

First, my only dinner party that week was a cookout that I hosted. I made grilled portabella burgers, corn on the cob, and vegetarian baked beans, with frozen mushed banana "ice cream" for dessert. If I'd been a guest someplace where my host was serving up cheeseburgers, deviled eggs, and potato salad (with mayo, which I had never considered was made from eggs), I may have failed. A person can only be so strong.

It also helped that I attempted this in autumn. Farm-fresh produce in early fall was as abundant in Ohio as our chirping cicadas. (No, although I had recently choked down a few crickets, I wouldn't be eating cicadas. They weren't vegan-friendly.)

And, finally, after my recent low-carb, high-protein diet, I had consumed enough meat over the last eight months to last any normal person beyond a lifetime. That week, I hardly missed it.

From a humane standpoint, I knew forgoing meat forever would be rewarding. For me, however, it was not realistic—at least not yet. I couldn't imagine a life without occasionally indulging in a New York strip or a sweet, buttery lobster tail. Or, without *cheese*. Oh, the wondrous meals prepared with cheese! Eggplant parmesan or a humble but *fabulous* grilled cheese sandwich! Vegetarian diets were one thing, I thought, but vegans take the challenge to a whole new level of crazy. Cheeseless for life seemed an ungodly burden to bear.

I returned the next week to a carnivorous lifestyle. My backslide was not without guilt but was at least accompanied by a bit of redemption. I succeeded in making some permanent switches in my diet. I incorporated far more meatless meals, explored other tofu and soy options, and began buying eggs only from pasture-raised chickens. I began dining at restaurants that offered these alternatives.

And, I eventually gave up pork. After reading several stories about the intelligence and social traits of pigs—not unlike dogs—this seemed like a natural first move toward a vegetarian lifestyle. I'm still working on eliminating all other meat from my diet. Personal evolution, even for a hypocritical humanitarian, can surely be achieved through baby steps.

But I gave myself some credit for these small changes. I celebrated my victory with a glass of pinot grigio. I was pretty sure not a single animal was harmed in the making of that.

Chapter 17:

RIDING SHOTGUN

When I called to inquire about riding along on a Toledo police officer's shift, I expected to be turned down with a polite, "No way in hell, thank you very much." As much as I anticipated a dead end, after explaining my project and undergoing a simple background check (thankfully, my youthful escapades had gone undocumented), I was given the nod. I continued to be amazed at what I could gain permission to do, if I simply asked.

I assured my local readers they could sleep soundly that night: I would be keeping the streets of Toledo safe.

The officer randomly assigned to me could have been handpicked as my BFF. In the small world that was northwest Ohio, I discovered she was only a few years younger than me, had grown up in the same part of town, and graduated from the same high school. Her father and my former husband's late father had been police partners and *best friends*. What were the odds? We also shared some personality traits, most notably a similar sense of humor.

And, the clincher: Officer Sheri and I shared the same name, although her parents were apparently unaware of the correct spelling.

The one glaring difference? I was a chicken shit hoping to feign eight hours of courage, while she was a legally licensed badass.

I had never sat in a police car before, not even in the backseat while clad in cuffs. While riding shotgun in the squad car that afternoon and evening, I was pumped with both benevolence and bravado. Oh, the respect and power I possessed, even if by proxy! When heavy-footed drivers spied us and pressed their brakes, I grinned at their reactions. When young children waved as we passed, I smiled and waved back.

"Yeah, the kids are usually pretty sweet," Sheri said. "But last week, I waved at a little boy—maybe six years old— and he flipped me off."

Clearly, the concept of respect wasn't something only earned; it was also learned.

Minutes later, we received our first radioed-in call. When Officer Sheri suggested I get out of the vehicle to enter a small bungalow in a lower middle-class neighborhood, my pumped-up bravado burst wide open into panic.

I wasn't sure all my training—and by that I mean a full amount of *none*—had prepared me for a custody dispute between a husband and wife in the midst of a tumultuous divorce.

"I hope this isn't a repeat of my last experience like this," Sheri said. "The guy punched his fist through the front door."

I crept out of the patrol car and glanced at the father, standing with his arms crossed, next to his SUV. He glowered at us. Was he angry in an "I'm-calling-my-attorney-in-the-morning way" or angry in an "I'm-taking-care-of-this-right-now-with-the-.45-in-my-glove-compartment way"?

If things got really ugly, I figured I'd duck for cover behind Officer Sheri. She was tall. She was tough. She was the only one wearing a bullet-proof vest.

We spent more than a half hour questioning each of the parents and attempting to engage in thoughtful and calming discussions with their two frightened children. Finally, Officer Sheri's good sense and sensitivity safely resolved the situation. At least for that night.

At the next call, with a few hours of successful law enforcement under my belt, I climbed out of the car more confidently. It was another domestic dispute, this time between a woman, her eighteen-year-old son, and the young man's stepfather. At least I might know what to expect this time.

My courage was quickly snuffed out by the ubiquitous smell of alcohol in the party garage where the parents were watching football. I soon discovered that even more frightening than mediating the heated conflict of a divorcing couple was finding oneself in the middle of a family fight involving enraged drunks.

According to the boy's mother, her son had withdrawn to his basement bedroom for his nightly ritual of smoking: both cigarettes and weed. This disrespect of house rules infuriated the mother and stepfather, who made it a point to sit at the bar in their attached garage to drink beer and smoke their own cigarettes. After we talked with the young man, my gut feeling was his recurring routine of retreating downstairs was usually preceded by the parents' nightly drunken rage.

As Officer Sheri questioned the parents, the mother admitted the stepfather once had been charged for hitting the boy. The episode left bruises, but she quickly noted that her son, who was thirteen at the time, "deserved it."

I was simply a ride-along civilian. I had no authority or any training in these matters. I stayed silent, while protectively folding my arms across my chest and shooting my partner concerned looks.

I wasn't certain a definitive right way or wrong way
existed for handling this kind of situation. My anxiety and
heart rate soared. If firearms were stored anywhere in the
house, I prayed Sheri would prove quicker on the draw.

We left an hour later without a punch thrown or a gun
fired. While Officer Sheri managed to defuse that night's
conflict, I doubted it would be the family's last.

Parenting is a universally complicated and difficult occupation. I'd experienced, firsthand, my own trials of raising sons as
a divorced mother. I was empathetic about the challenges. Yet as
we drove away, I felt distressed for this not-quite-a-boy, not-quite-
a-man. He showed signs of being rebellious, unambitious, and
self-medicated, but I felt certain he'd also spent most of his life
neglected and abused. I feared he never stood much of a chance.

In between my panic during these two domestic calls,
which Officer Sheri referred to as "fairly routine," our day
was punctuated by the still lingering paperwork from a
non-injury traffic accident earlier that afternoon. The only
noteworthy part of this minor incident was that the young
man appeared polite, apologetic, and mostly concerned
about disappointing his parents. As I told him I thought
they'd understand, I wanted to hug him. I hoped his parents,
after seeing him uninjured, would do just that.

After Sheri was forced to spend yet another chunk of
time finishing the accident form, she leaned toward me and
apologized.

"I'm sorry this accident report is dragging on so long,"
she said. "It's a brand new form, and it's the first time I've
had to fill one out. Sorry if the day's been kind of boring."

Boring? I reassured her that was not the case.

"Here's a thought," she said. "How would you like to go
on a drug raid tonight?"

Was she joking? A first-time patroller taking part in a raid? *Holy Toledo!* I had hit the crime-fighter lottery!

I bounced in my seat. "Absolutely!" I answered. And then I hyperventilated.

Officer Sheri had all the connections to make it happen. A few hours later, we found ourselves at the downtown Toledo building where the SWAT team and vice squad met covertly to plan raids.

Sheri and I took seats in the back, and I gawked at the SWAT team. My admittedly sexist stereotype didn't miss its mark. Every SWAT guy was toned and exceptionally attractive. Each was attired in a pair of black cargo pants and a form-fitting black T-shirt, with the ensemble later completed by a dangerously intriguing armored vest. For those readers familiar with the *Stephanie Plum* series by Janet Evanovich, just picture the character Ranger. And then swoon.

But this was real life, not fiction. What lie ahead that night was a serious and potentially dangerous reality, not an adventure scene within a romantic comedy. I dismissed my daydreaming so I could focus on the plan at hand.

The team leader presented a layout of the targeted house and discussed what we might expect that evening. They'd thoroughly researched and rehearsed their plan. They were familiar with the neighborhood, the home's occupants, and the level of danger.

I learned in my crash course that, depending on a particular raid's perceived level of danger, metro police categorized raids into two types: the "Knock" or the "No-Knock" variety. My own experience that night would best be classified as the "Knee-Knock" kind.

Our caravan of vehicles—vice squad car, SWAT van, and the patrol car carrying Sheri and me—entered one of the roughest parts of town.

I knew the area, especially since it had been featured for

weeks in the national news as the neighborhood of a missing toddler. Just hours earlier that evening, while Officer Sheri and I were in the midst of filing that accident report, Toledo Police had finally found Baby Elaina's body in her family's garage—only a couple blocks from the house we were about to enter.

As we grew close, we shut off our headlights. We stopped in front of the targeted house.

If I'd felt trepidation about leaving the patrol car during our earlier domestic disputes, it came nowhere near my fear of even cracking open the car window in the midst of a night-time raid.

The SWAT and vice guys knocked once before pushing in the front door and rushing inside. At Officer Sheri's encouragement, I crawled out of the car.

Minutes later, we heard the shout, "All clear!" This was only vaguely comforting. Sheri had to nearly pry my hands loose from the side of the police car.

I followed her closely, nearly a shadow behind her back as she headed toward the front porch. Sure, we'd been given the word that it was safe to enter, but I knew twists and turns in these kinds of events were always possible. A second perpetrator could round the corner of the house at any second, grab me, and hold me hostage.

I'd watched my share of crime TV shows.

As we made our way into the house, my eyes spun across the room. I spied the suspect sprawled facedown on the threadbare carpet, his cuffed hands behind his head. A few feet away, a tiny auburn-haired girl sat on the couch, watching *The Little Mermaid*.

While the SWAT team and black-hooded vice squad tore apart every cupboard and closet in the filthy and disheveled house, the little girl chatted casually about the movie with one of the SWAT guys and me. She appeared oblivious to everything happening around her. Apparently, for this smiling, blue-eyed kindergartner, the night's events were nothing out of the ordinary.

I gazed down at her, unable and unwilling to comprehend a childhood that could result in such nonchalance in this kind of situation. If I'd ever questioned the parenting mistakes I'd made, and I knew I'd made plenty, I was overcome with gratitude that my children's lives had never come anywhere close to this.

As heart wrenching as it was to watch this tiny girl sit there amidst this chaos, the saving grace was she made it through the night with no physical harm. As did the raid team, Sheri, and I.

And the girl's father? I figured he got really lucky, especially after he yelled, "Give me a break. I'm doing the best I can!"

One of the SWAT guys bent over him and said, "The best you can do? This is the best you can do? You're dealing dangerous drugs, with your six-year-old daughter sitting right here. No, you're *not* doing the best you can. Just shut the hell up."

Besides fearing for my own safety and the welfare of all the people on site, I had also remained worried all night about a dog that was presumably in the house. Having prior knowledge of the dog, the SWAT team had mentioned at our planning meeting that they were prepared to shoot it, if necessary. I understood the safety issues presented by a charging and vicious animal, but my heart sunk at the thought of shooting a possibly innocent pup who may simply be a victim of circumstance.

Thankfully, even the cowering half-grown boxer, who had the fortune to be locked inside a cage when we entered, survived the night.

While the team finished its search and wrapped up other details, Officer Sheri and I headed out the door. I beamed at the SWAT team and said, "You guys are my heroes."

As apparent by the subtle round of eye-rolls, The Avengers weren't impressed by my adoration. I shrugged this off. What mattered was the perp had been apprehended. Justice was served. And, most important, to quote *Doctor Who*: "Everybody lives!"

I'd think about the families, especially the children I met that night, for months to come. No police officer could solve all the issues they would likely continue to face.

On my drive back home, I called my mother and my two sons to say I was safe and I loved them.

And then, I made a detour to Dunkin' Donuts. Apparently, Officer Sheri and I had been far too busy that day to stop there. I celebrated my survival—and my very loving, if sometimes imperfect, family life—with a hot mocha and a chocolate-frosted doughnut.

The next time I rode shotgun with a police officer, I'd be certain to request a doughnut stop, along with a bullet-proof vest.

And I'd be damn sure to wear a pair of Depends.

Chapter 18:

A COULDA-BEEN OR A WANNABE

I 'd been a professional singer most of my life. By "professional," I mean the kind who belted out Jackson 5 tunes while driving alone or before my car-captive children grew old enough to object.

I never participated in a choir nor tried out for a high school musical. In fact, my only public singing appearances had entailed swaying on top of a bar booth while I bellowed the song "American Pie" along with the jukebox.

Inexperienced a singer as I was, I always dreamed I could have been another Barbra or Adele, if only I'd given it a shot. I wondered if, deep down, I had what was necessary to take my vocals to the next level. Even if I didn't achieve phenomenal success, I wanted to believe I could at least keep a tune.

By never pushing myself to test my talent or open myself up to that possibly personal—or very public—failure, I kept that hope alive well into middle age. I believed in this latent talent of mine. I truly *wanted* this.

And so, I finally gave in to facing my fears and risking disappointment by attempting to discover if I was a coulda-been or just a wannabe. This 52/52 venture, taking singing lessons with a professional voice instructor, would either lift me up or smack me down.

My friends and family, who'd all heard my rendition of "American Pie" and yet only complimented me on knowing every line of the lyrics, seemed to be betting on my failure. *Whatever*. They wouldn't get a dime from the royalties off my first hit single.

If I was completely honest though, any humor or courage I tried to embrace while facing this item on my list masked my true apprehension. As I stood before my instructor at my first lesson, I visibly trembled. My feelings of self-consciousness, exposure, and vulnerability could best be likened to standing naked in front of a total stranger. As it so happened, I would experience that, literally, a couple months later.

We started off the lesson with breathing exercises. My teacher, Joan, waved her arms below her breasts, urging me to breathe from my diaphragm. I last contemplated something called a "diaphragm" during my twenties, when I researched birth control methods. I felt fairly certain *that* wasn't what this music maestro had in mind.

I tried to conjure up tenth-grade biology images of the human body. Even after Joan poked the bottom of my rib-cage, indicating the location of this muscle, I still couldn't master the art of breathing or vocalizing from it. This was the most basic tool in singing, yet it continued to elude me.

My savvy instructor sensed my frustration. Possibly because by my fifth attempt, I clenched my hands and shouted, "Aargh! I can't do this!" She assured me this ability would come, in time. I hoped she was right. Secretly, I pondered the possibility that I didn't actually *have* a diaphragm. Maybe, when the doctor performed one of my C-sections, she inadvertently plucked out this essential singing organ.

Joan handed me printed directions for breathing exercises, which noted that I should place my hands on my diaphragm and "pulse short hisses for 30 seconds."

Right. I hissed a "thank you" right back at her.

We moved on to singing scales.

Warming up by singing scales, Joan told me, was the best way to exercise my voice and also learn to control it.

After hearing me through a few rounds of "Do-Re-Me," she cocked her head. She nodded. "Well," she said. "You're very *loud.*"

I would assume this was a compliment. After all, she didn't openly cringe or cover her ears. Regardless, singing scales and practicing breathing techniques hardly seemed a true measure of one's vocal talents. She promised we'd move on to actual singing during my second lesson.

Hearing her mention a second lesson buoyed my confidence. If she considered me hopeless, surely she wouldn't even *suggest* that I return.

I researched dozens of songs to perform at my next lesson. They had to be ones with which I was well familiar and which weren't too vocally complex. Eventually, I decided upon "You've Got a Friend" and "Moon River." They had always been two favorites in my car-ride repertoire. As a bonus, both appeared to be within what Joan had concluded was my "tight" vocal range. If "Moon River" was good enough for Audrey Hepburn to pull off as an Academy Award-winning song—even with her own reportedly narrow range—it was good enough for me.

Over the next week, I listened to recorded versions of both songs and practiced them every available chance: while driving in the car, chopping vegetables in the kitchen, and sitting in my office—behind closed doors.

I arrived at my second lesson with the lyrics and sheet music for both songs in hand. If I had been nervous about my first lesson, I could only describe my feeling about this next class as something along the lines of "totally freaking mortified."

I'd like to say my voice instructor stopped me halfway through my song and shouted, "Stop right there! Get thee to *America's Got Talent*, STAT!"

At the opposite end of the spectrum, she could have shaken her head, eyed me with a pitying gaze, and mumbled, "Stop. I might suggest—nay, insist—that you never sing another note." Maybe that would put a simple end to a ridiculous lifelong notion. After all, there is something to be said for closure, however disappointing it may be.

But, no. My second lesson just rather sputtered and fizzled and went—nowhere.

I didn't believe my singing skills that day proved at the far end of abysmal, but I had a hunch I didn't display great promise either. My teacher's physical and verbal reactions were best described as ambivalent, erring on the side of "Hmm."

Joan suggested I continue practicing "Moon River" and that I inquire among local jazz vocalists to see if one might be willing to work with me on it. She didn't mention that I return to her for a third lesson.

"So," I finally asked, "should I come back for another lesson with you, too?"

She shrugged and smiled. "Sure, you could," she said. "Why don't you think about whether you'd like to do that and get back to me," she said.

Although she didn't officially answer my question, I concluded the decision was already made.

I told myself not to take this personally. After all, I had explained to her my series of one-off ventures for The 52/52 Project. Perhaps she assumed I wasn't in this with any long-term desire or serious commitment. In addition, I discovered during that second lesson that Joan was formally trained as an opera singer. My interest in modern music was outside her focus and expertise. She wasn't even familiar with the song "You've Got a Friend," which I considered a contemporary classic. Maybe she didn't feel we were a good musical match.

Perhaps another teacher might have said, "Whoa! Move over, Carole King! Girlfriend here just killed 'You've Got a Friend!'"

Or maybe my promise of talent was iffy, at best.

The real question came down to this: Was vocal training something I wished to continue? Or, should I tell myself I gave it a shot and simply ought to move on?

I put my singing lessons indefinitely on hold. Even if I never resumed them, I told myself I hadn't failed. I sang in front of a professional while knowing I was being appraised. I gave this performance my serious all without my usual escape mechanism of hamming it up.

The year still held many new opportunities for me to expand my horizons. I would laugh and scream and even sing through some of those.

Yet I would never manage to vocalize a sound of *any* sort from my damn diaphragm.

Chapter 19:

REVOLVER

I'd long been an advocate for gun control. Since the first time I became aware of a school shooting, by a San Diego teenager in 1979 who offered the simple explanation of "I don't like Mondays," the subject of guns appeared black-and-white for me. Too many guns possessed by too many people, and too many resulting in tragedies. In fact, was the gun invented with any purpose except to kill?

Still, I found the issues of gun possession and gun control teeming with questions. Why did people own them? How did they get them? What was the appeal of owning the most dangerous kinds, the sort most often used in shooting sprees and murders?

Years ago, when a close family friend in Indiana invited me to accompany him to a shooting range, I politely declined. I believe what I said was, "Um, no. Not gonna happen, ever. But thanks anyway."

Spending a couple hours at a shooting range with my lifelong friend, Kent, who subsequently had become a gun dealer, fell *way* outside my personal limits. But several months into my year of new experiences, I contacted him and finally agreed.

My first up-close encounter with firearms had taken place only weeks before, during my police ride-along and raid. I gained a deeper understanding of the need for and use of guns in law enforcement. But as far as the Average Joe's desire and right to own a pistol or semi-automatic weapon? I figured my shooting range experience would either solidify my stance or broaden my thinking about that.

As a .38 Special recoiled in my shaky hands, I feared the afternoon was just as likely to result in a premature end to my 52/52 journey.

Note: A year later, while I edited a story about this experience, news hit of a nine-year-old girl who inadvertently shot and killed her shooting range instructor with an Uzi submachine gun: a nine-year-old girl, whose parents took her to a shooting range and allowed her to handle a powerful weapon, as a fun vacation outing.

As I reflected upon my own first-time shooting experience, I wasn't so certain that couldn't have been me. My coordination had forever been my weak point, and I possessed no more experience than this young girl.

The biggest difference may have been that the gun expert accompanying me that day was a skilled, trustworthy, and lifelong friend. Kent and his young adult son, Bryan, understood my uneasiness, and they mastered the art of patience by answering my litany of questions and trying to alleviate my worries.

That professionalism proved even more essential as they taught me the proper way to stand, hold and handle a gun, and shoot. More than trying to sway my opinion or ensure I had a good time, their primary focus was on my safe handling of a gun.

I attempted to put aside my nervous misgivings and

focus on every aspect of the experience. I tried my hand at shooting a .38 (a revolver), plus a .22 and a CZ-P01 (both semi-automatic pistols).

With the .22, I hit my target nine out of ten times. The .38 proved the toughest to handle. It weighed too heavy in my hand, and even with my legs positioned to balance my strength—as Kent instructed—the gun resulted in a recoiling I couldn't quite control.

That was a hell of a lot of deadly power I held in my shaky, inexperienced hands. And knowing that most people wielding such weapons possessed more physical control and shooting expertise than I did gave me no additional comfort, especially when I considered how easily an estranged spouse or school shooter could aim and hit a mark.

Kent's preoccupation with safety proved just as important for him and Bryan as it did for me. Maybe we just got lucky.

The most surprising outcome I was forced to admit? Target shooting was a blast. It invoked my childhood memories of shooting a water pistol at balloons on an amusement park midway. Each time I hit the target, I smiled with satisfaction. I felt pretty pleased with my prowess.

"See?" Kent said. "You get it now, right? This is a sport." Yes, I could see how many people viewed target shooting as a sport. And I was intoxicated by what only can be described as the thrill of the hunt.

Still, I found that momentary exhilaration a bit disturbing. Each time I felt the force of the gun in my hands and then felt gratified by the holes ripped through the torso of my human-shaped paper target, my reaction dropped from delighted to unsettled.

If I, a presumably rational person, found pleasure in hitting a paper bullseye, what kind of satisfaction or thrill might an unbalanced individual anticipate by the thought of shooting a *human* target?

Kent and I engaged in a great deal of discussion that day about guns: their recreational use, the constitutional right to bear arms, and the need for average citizens to defend themselves. Even after we left the shooting range and continued our conversation over bratwursts and a couple of beers, our opinions differed. We managed to be respectful and polite, as it should be with the oldest and truest of friends.

Unfortunately, in the wider world, politics and passion make calm and logical discussions about such issues far less possible.

I came away that day with a much greater understanding of target shooting as a form of recreation. But, I didn't sway from my discomfort with the "constitutional right" to bear arms. I wasn't so sure current gun laws—especially with the modern, more deadly types of guns—were what our forefathers had in mind when that law was written more than two hundred years ago.

What I learned and experienced also didn't change my unease about masses of people owning guns for safety purposes. While I could cite dozens of examples of guns being used in domestic quarrels or mass killings, or accidentally killing children, I could name very few instances of a person successfully using them for protection.

Kent told me he assumed everyone in Indiana, an open-carry state, carried a gun. Carried openly or not, loaded guns were out there everywhere: in automobile glove compartments, pockets or purses, and—as I found out during my visit that day with Kent's elderly father—in the side pockets of living room loungers.

I didn't anticipate a couple hours at a shooting range would fully change my stance on guns and gun control. That might forever be a more in-depth and intense debate than I was equipped to win.

Many responsible people, like these longtime family

friends, owned guns. Yet many irresponsible or unstable people had easy access to guns, too. For me, that remained the
real and troublesome issue.

I succeeded in pushing my boundaries that afternoon
with a more opened mind—while my fists were tightly closed
around the butt of a gun. Through this experience, I gained a
bit more understanding.

Acceptance was far more elusive.

But if my goal was simply aimed at going outside my
comfort zone, I clearly hit my mark.

Chapter 20:

GET THEE TO A NUNNERY

I had an aversion to guns most of my life. And, ever since my first-grade teacher Sister Mary Estelle refused me an emergency trip to the little girls' room, resulting in an ill-fated accident at my desk, I'd remained wary of nuns, too.

By the time I graduated from eighth grade at St. Patrick of Heatherdowns, I'd had enough of nuns, and they of me. Most of my Ursuline order teachers—and my lay teachers, for that matter—would never have guessed I ultimately turned out responsible and nearly respectable. I wondered if I might view them differently, too, if given the opportunity to know them on a more level playing field, now that I was an adult.

Would spending twenty-four hours at a convent be a hoot or a horror? Or might it simply provide me with a whole new insight?

Sister Lourdes was my first cousin once removed. She was the second-youngest of my very Catholic great-uncle and great-aunt's ten children, and one of three daughters to become a nun. (One later left the sisterhood, married, and raised a family.) Sister Lourdes was twenty years older than me and left Toledo for a convent in Joliet, outside Chicago, before I was born. We'd never even met.

We knew each other only through a sprinkle of comments on an extended family website. Yet after a few emails about my including a visit to her Joliet convent for The 52/52 Project, she appeared enthusiastic.

It would be awkward, I was sure. After all, we were virtual strangers. And there was the little detail that she was a nun and I was a middle-aged pagan child.

In one day and night, I gained more understanding of nuns than I did through my eight years at St. Patrick's or my lifelong and intermittent relationship with the Catholic Church.

INSIGHT NUMBER ONE: NUNS HAVE LIVES OUTSIDE THE CHURCH. Somehow, in my Catholic schoolgirl mind, I had assumed that when nuns weren't busy putting me in a classroom corner for my irreverent attitude and nonstop talking, they spent the remainder of their waking hours in the church, praying—quite likely for my depraved soul.

When I accompanied Sister Lourdes for her weekly bowling league, I discovered she competed nationally and placed second in the state for the over-seventy division the past year. I watched her joke and interact warmly with the rest of the local women. "Sis," as they called her, appeared to be just another one of their bowling buddies.

In between her throwing strikes and spares that night, we chatted over a beer and a plate of cheesy fries. I figured that was as close to decadent as nuns got.

Afterward, Sister Lourdes and I headed back to the convent. I grew uneasy as we sat down at the communal kitchen table. Without the diversions of a crowded bowling alley, I wasn't sure what to expect. Maybe a marathon prayer session? Instead, Sister Lourdes and her neighbor, Sister Odelia, taught me how to play dominoes. We laughed and made small talk, like old girlfriends, while they totally kicked my ass at the game. Neither of *them* used that particular language, but somehow I doubted they would think less of me if I did.

INSIGHT NUMBER TWO: NUNS DON'T ALWAYS JUDGE US. Those choosing religious vocations may adhere to a different way of life and set of beliefs. Yet that doesn't mean they all judge or condemn our words, actions, or lifestyles. All of the nuns I met there, the working professionals and the elderly ones residing in the convent's affiliated nursing home, were nothing but warm and welcoming. I never pretended to be someone I wasn't—and I was likely a sinner by official definition—but they never made me feel like one.

After a question about my marital status, I hesitantly discussed my divorce. I wasn't certain if Sister Lourdes agreed with my explanation, but she listened and nodded in empathy. It struck me that while we often seek total affirmation of our beliefs and decisions, some people agree politely yet insincerely. Empathy signifies understanding. It is perhaps the most supportive reaction of all.

We agreed divorce was never ideal. When I told her I thought it may have been the right decision at the time, Sister Lourdes grasped my hand. She reassured me that my ex-husband and I had done what we thought was best and that we appeared to manage a better job in co-parenting our two sons than many people did. She was glad I went on to find happiness on my own.

Did I need reassurance about a decision made more than a decade ago? Yes, somehow I still did. I hugged her afterward.

Throughout our visit, Sister Lourdes and I touched

on several other provocative issues, including birth control, abortion, and gay marriage. I wasn't eager to go there, since several of my left-leaning beliefs didn't coincide with those of the Catholic Church.

I didn't anticipate we'd agree on everything. However, based on her subtle comment about the "negative and extremely conservative" thoughts that people expressed on the Internet, I concluded she was less black-and-white about some things than I expected. I wondered how many other religious professionals saw both sides, or at least acknowledged some gray areas, of these issues.

We didn't dwell on these controversial topics for long. Inevitably, Sister Lourdes would segue into a humorous anecdote, and the conversation would leave us both laughing.

INSIGHT NUMBER THREE: NUNS CAN BE PRETTY DAMN FUNNY. Here are a couple quips from Sister Lourdes:

While we studied old photographs of the Sisters of St. Francis, she pointed at a photo of the nuns' traditional habits from the sixties, featuring that era's fully concealing robes, long veils, and tight headbands. She mentioned this was the dress code when she first entered the convent.

"I'll bet you don't miss that," I said.

She laughed. "Oh, God, don't you know it."

Later, as she made an abrupt left turn into a parking lot, veering across a line of fast oncoming traffic, I jumped up straight and clutched the sides of my seat. Sister Lourdes grinned over at me, shrugged, and said, "Meh. They're aiming at *your* side of the car."

This sense of humor was not an anomaly among her religious order. When I met the congregation president, Sister Dolores, she asked if I was visiting because I was interested in joining. I stammered some awkward response until Sister Lourdes finally cut in and explained The 52/52 Project.

"Oh," Sister Dolores deadpanned. "So, I guess I should toss that application I had waiting for you."

INSIGHT NUMBER FOUR: WE'RE NOT SO DIFFERENT, ANY OF US. What set these women apart from even the most religious lay people I knew was a primary commitment to serving God. As a midlife agnostic, I wanted to better understand that. I asked Sister Lourdes why she became a nun.

She shrugged and said, "I never had a desire to do anything else. I knew this was what I wanted to do since I was in the eighth grade. When you love the Lord, you love the Lord."

I contemplated this later that night, as I lay in the small convent bedroom that held simply a twin bed, dresser, nightstand, and table light. I opened the Bible, the only other object in the room, and paged through it. It was difficult to grasp such lifelong dedication to a spiritual being and belief that still left me questioning so much.

I can't say I came away from my experience with any element of these women's commitment to their faith. I remained a lapsed Catholic and agnostic. That may or may not ever change.

However, my time at the convent did change the stereotype I'd held for so many years. The Sisters of St. Francis were real and ordinary people in so many ways. They bantered and laughed. They cried. They experienced frustration with their jobs and with the daily life occurrences that plague us all. They found enjoyment in everyday things. They even managed to find joy when it seemed most elusive.

That proved evident on my last evening in Joliet, when I attended a wake and prayer service for their friend and colleague, Sister Alcuin Kelly. I sang hymns with them and listened to their uplifting stories of their ninety-three-year-old friend's life and work. Perhaps it was these memories that made a normally grief-filled occasion less sad. Or perhaps it was due to their unwavering belief that death led to something far more beautiful than life itself.

As Sister Lourdes pointed out, the Sisters mourned death, but more important, they "celebrated life."

It's unlikely my time at the convent ensured my own spot in heaven. That remained debatable, even if such a place truly exists. I wanted to believe this afterlife was real, but too many questions remained in my mind. Maybe I would never find my way to a conclusion about any of them.

Heaven or no heaven, I did conclude that hanging with nuns could be one *hell* of a good time.

Clearly, they weren't all replicas of Sister Lourdes. Regardless of her vocation, this delightful woman might have been one-of-a-kind. In many ways though, she and her colleagues altered my lifelong views of nuns.

As a thirteen-year-old Catholic school girl, I never would have dreamed it possible. But God knows I wasn't that girl anymore.

Chapter 21:

OLD FOLKS AND NEW FRIENDS

Like many people, I generally squirmed my way through visits to hospitals, hospices, and nursing homes. Attempting to comfort or make small talk, especially with individuals in irreversibly failing health, made me uneasy and anxious.

I'd always admired people who chose to work or volunteer with sick and elderly strangers. While I liked to consider myself a caring and strong person, my shoulders were not nearly broad enough for that.

And so, I slumped and forced a smile as I followed Sister Odelia—or Sister Odie, as she was known—through the doorway of Our Lady of Angels (OLA) in Joliet, Illinois. The nursing facility was affiliated with the Sisters of St. Francis, and many of the residents were retired religious professionals.

Sister Odie, who served as OLA's coordinator of music therapy, was recovering from rotator cuff surgery. She required assistance with her daily responsibilities, especially transporting immobile patients. Aiding her in the physical tasks was no issue; I could handle pushing a wheelchair. The idea of personal interaction with residents and patients was a different story. I wasn't sure how I would react to the physical frailties or, even worse, the failing mental states and dementia of the people I encountered.

When Sister Odie asked me to round up the members of OLA's chime choir, I felt a rush of relief. Anyone able to play a musical instrument must still be somewhat physically apt and mentally sharp.

I knocked on the half-closed door to Sister Bernadette's room and then peeked inside.

In her youth, Sister Bernadette had likely been a petite woman, probably close to my height. Age and some progressive form of bone or maybe muscular disease had rendered her a disquieting figure. With her head bowed down to her chest and her chest bent nearly to her thighs, she was less than four-feet-tall.

More than her physical appearance, what took me aback was our ensuing conversation. Sister Bernadette's condition forced her to literally cough out her words in short, halted utterances. Reluctant to ask her to repeat herself, I leaned in closely, laboring to understand her words. I simply nodded and semi-smiled at what I couldn't comprehend, which was nearly everything.

As I wheeled Sister Bernadette to the music room, I shook my head. My very first resident encounter and already I'd failed. It was too soon to give up though. I had hours ahead of me and a couple dozen more people to assist.

All the residents I met had their own challenges and distinct personalities. In one short day, I grew to know and appreciate each of them.

Paulette had a neurological condition. She cried easily and often, for no obvious reason, but music seemed to comfort her. Within minutes, I developed a special soft spot for her. A smile from Paulette meant everything.

Father Louie, in his eighties, was a smart-ass retired priest who kept me laughing. As I led him from his room, I had a difficult time maneuvering his wheelchair, which seemed to have a bad wheel. "Wow," he deadpanned, as I bumped the wall while rounding a corner. "That was a close call. We almost didn't make it." Father Louie never let me forget this. On the way back to his room, later that afternoon, he leaned his head back toward me and murmured, "I hope you're a better driver now."

Two of the residents were each over a hundred years old. One was completely nonverbal, but she managed to communicate through gestures and facial expressions that she wanted to sit through both chime choir and the subsequent music therapy session, as well as the dice game that followed in the activity room.

Chime choir proved difficult. This wasn't due to the residents' physical or mental challenges. I soon realized the weakest link was *me*.

I tried to follow along with the written music and my marked parts, but I didn't know several songs and could also never figure out when it was my turn to "chime" in. The residents were patient with me, providing lots of encouragement even when I couldn't keep up.

I didn't recognize a few songs during that afternoon's music therapy session either. One of the participants offered to sing them first, to give me some guidance. Once I was trained and we were each provided with a musical instrument, our informal concert began.

Surprisingly, it wasn't a Catholic hymn or a forties tune that proved to be the resident fan favorite. The most popular song? "YMCA."

Even those in wheelchairs stomped, clapped, or moved their arms along with this apparent classic. The Village People had nothing on this geriatric crowd.

I watched Sister Odie interact with the residents. She

was extremely organized, if not a bit strict. I soon realized this diligence was necessary to keep the group involved and on track. And she clearly wasn't lacking a soft side. She told me later how she loved her work and how music therapy truly seemed to help the residents.

"It's important to keep them engaged, to be active participants in life," she said. "They need that now more than ever. That's why I'm here."

A few of the residents echoed that same thought. Activities like music therapy and chime choir made them feel sharp and purposeful.

"You know," one of them told me, "some of the other residents never even leave their rooms. Some can't, and some choose not to. I feel bad for them. Activities like this mean so much to me."

I passed by rooms of other residents who were either too physically or mentally impaired, or else too despondent, to participate in OLA's activities.

I mentioned this to Sister Odie. "That has to be disheartening," I said.

She nodded and said that some of the residents, including a couple members of the chime choir, were "slipping." Her expression grew sad, yet she shrugged. "It's inevitable. I just stay focused and keep doing my work. I help as many as I can."

When you work in a nursing home for so many years, you are forced to witness many people, including those you've come to know as close friends, decline physically and mentally. I admired Sister Odie's matter-of-fact strength. It was a necessary trait in order to encourage each of them to thrive—and for her to carry on.

When I approached Sister Bernadette to take her back to her room, her face lit up. I realized that throughout the entire day, I had never seen her without a smile. She grasped my hand, peered up at me, and whispered something. I didn't understand what she said, other than one word: "happy."

It didn't matter if I couldn't comprehend everything she said. I understood what she was feeling. Hugging her, I told her I was so happy to have met her. And I meant it.

Even given all my initial misgivings, Sister Bernadette and so many of the nursing home residents made me smile that day. They also gave me inspiration and hope—through their continued determination, vibrancy, and wit.

Maybe the opportunity and ability to enjoy life doesn't need to end when our body and mind begin to fail. If we remain open and positive, perhaps more pleasure and purpose lie ahead.

I had already managed to change and enrich my life a bit at age fifty-two. I could only imagine what I might pull off by the time I was one-hundred-and-three.

Chapter 22:

ZIP-A-DEE-DO-DAH

I'd lost count of how many times I found myself mid-step into a new situation speculating that it wasn't such a terrific idea after all. Yet I'd never passed the point of no return and still been consumed with such fear that I prayed there was some way, *any* way, out.

Not until I was strapped upside down into a harness, dangling seventy-five feet above the ground, with only an inch-thick cable to save me from crashing to my death.

I'd never been afraid of heights, per se. I could stand and gaze out, with only minimal heart palpitations, from the observation platform on the top of a high-rise building. If my feet were planted firmly on a stable surface that wasn't moving, and if the odds appeared slim that I'd find *myself* moving—in a fast downward spiral—only then was I good to go.

But I'd been plagued by a lifelong aversion to *falling*. It's that physical feeling of falling—specifically, the sensation of your stomach rushing up into your throat as you dropped.

Dear Lord. *That.* If the subsequent thump on the far-below ground didn't kill me, I knew I'd suffocate. The autopsy would find my stomach lodged tight in my windpipe.

I learned to just say no to rollercoasters and to cope with air travel by downing a pre-flight Bloody Mary. One drink usually sufficed to soften the blow of my presumed impending death.

The idea of zip-lining, suggested by a thoughtful friend who knew my fear all too well, gave me nightmares and day terrors for a week. My friend, Murf, and her eighteen-year-old daughter, Leah, appeared giddy about joining me. I figured Leah, a college freshman, still possessed that teenaged sense of naïve invincibility. But Murf, whom I'd known since grade school and who clung to her comfort zones as tightly as I did? I could only assume her middle-aged mental faculties were slipping.

We'd signed up for a zip-lining excursion in the gorgeous Hocking Hills region in southern Ohio. The company's website listed a handful of options, each ensuring a beautiful experience we'd "want to do again and again." I suspected this PR spin held as much real promise as a plastic cup of poisoned purple Kool-Aid. But I succumbed to the zip-lining cult, nonetheless.

Based on the brief descriptions, we chose the Super Zip option over the full Canopy Tour. The listed specs indicated that the Super Zip was the cheapest and shortest ride: perfect for our budget, our schedule, and my hope to minimize the duration of agony.

Upon our arrival, however, we discovered the Super Zip was also the highest, steepest, and fastest zip-line of all.

Final score? Research: zero. Stupidity: infinity.

Imminent death laughed in my face.

We had little opportunity to contemplate the true terror of our half-assed planning while we plodded across the first of three steep rope-and-wood bridges leading up to the tower platform. We were too busy cringing and cursing as the sharply inclined bridge swayed with our every step. The website never mentioned precarious bridges. Probably, I just glossed over that section. As I do.

If I didn't fanatically study every footstep while clenching the rope railing, I knew I was certain to roll backward, knocking down both my friends in a deadly game of human dominoes. Fear was one thing; but I was a pansy with piss-poor coordination.

By the second and higher bridge, even our fearless leader, Leah, paused. She steadied herself while gripping the railing, and suggested it wasn't too late to back out. We huddled up, gave each other a pep talk, and stumbled onward.

We managed to cross the final bridge, reached the tower, and then climbed a few flights of steep steps to the top platform. By then, we'd already experienced ample thrills and chills for the day. Surely, *now* we could turn around.

At the top of the tower, however, Leah regained her courage. If she hadn't been there, I undoubtedly would have scrambled back down. As I watched the people in front of us being snapped onto cables and sent flying through the air, my stomach rolled in waves. I came damn close to tears.

But the line moved quickly, and in only a few minutes we found ourselves next up for this suicide launch. The zip-line crew told us we had two options. One was to sit upright in a harness-type swing. This comfortable, almost nonthreatening position was the one I had seen in online photos and the same one a few of my readers had experienced and enjoyed.

The other option was to sprawl facedown, with our arms and legs extended, dangling vulnerably in what the crew called the "superhero" position.

Seriously? I was so not Superman. Super Chickenshit summed me up more accurately.

I hugged myself and murmured that the sitting position looked less terrifying.

The zip-line cable guy, a twentyish rugged sort who probably bungee-jumped and hopped out of airplanes every day before breakfast, shrugged. "Do you want less scary or do you want less dangerous?"

He held up a simple strap harness. "This is what you wear in the sitting position. With the superhero position, you wear that, plus *this*, too." He held up a military looking vest with an assortment of straps, buckles, and hooks.

I didn't have such a great history with safety harnesses and cables. More than thirty years ago, I had been talked into repelling down a cliff, right here in Hocking Hills. Halfway through my descent, I realized the harness and cable were entwined within my T-shirt. Every step I took down the face of the cliff yanked my shirt higher. By the time I noticed this, my shirt was already hiked above my belly button. My choices were to either slip out of the harness and fall to my death, or to keep descending. So, the crowd eventually got a peep show, I plopped safely onto the ground, and I gave up that repelling shit for good.

Embarrassment, however, was the least of my concerns while zip-lining. I wrung my hands as Cable Guy explained my two options. Seriously? Did I look like a moron? Yes, give me two safety harnesses! Give me twenty!

All three of us opted for the double-harness superhero version.

As I secured my helmet and was hitched into the mega-harness, dying remained a fairly big concern. And vomiting, before I ever took this dive, also seemed inevitable. Apparently, I would crash to my death while puking. Talk about a lose-lose situation.

I wasn't the only one petrified. "Oh my God, look," Murf said, holding out her hand. It was visibly shaking.

But while she and I contemplated our mutual terror, a grinning Leah was swooped away from the platform.

We watched as Leah took flight, and then Murf swiveled her head back at me. "That's my *daughter* out there," she said. "I need to follow her. I have to go!"

Oh, the mighty pull of maternal love.

As my friends were whisked off through the treetops, I knew I had to see this through, too. It was do or die. Or, more likely, do *and* die.

I assumed the position. Lying stomach-side down, I was hooked onto the cable. My feet managed to locate the back edge of the platform, and I flexed the toes of my shoes securely around it. I'd be damn certain to guarantee I wasn't going anywhere any time soon. What had I gotten myself into? Apparently, it's easier to scribble an obscure idea on a to-do list, many months in advance, than it is to finally find yourself in a ready-set-go position.

Cable Guy asked me twice to pry my feet from the platform. I begged him three times to check all the buckles and hooks.

Once I loosened my ankle grip from the back edge, I was yanked upward and then forward, just enough for my head to extend past the platform and hover in thin air. The zip contraption paused, sadistically, right there. My body swung, upside down, from the cable. I eyed the ground far below for a mere moment before I squeezed my eyes shut.

I took a deep breath. I told myself I wasn't *really* doing this. I tried to step outside myself, to pretend I was simply observing someone else in a scene in a movie. I'd done this before, say, during a Brazilian wax, and surprisingly, I'd found it could work.

Cable Guy counted down quickly: "Three, two, one."

The cable yanked me off the platform, and I flew through the air.

I started off slowly before picking up speed. I awaited that sickening free-falling sensation I expected to endure just before death. But, oddly, it never struck me.

As I soared through the sky, I finally opened my eyes. Zip-lining was much like the flying dreams I'd had all my life—the same spread-arm position, same treetop vantage point—and surprisingly, the same exhilarating sensation. I began to feel secure in the harness, growing confident I wouldn't fall to my death after all.

I soon determined, however, it was the *trees* that would kill me. Huge branches loomed just inches from my body. It was a jungle out there, and I couldn't avoid it. No helmet or double-harness would save me when I smacked straight into a tree.

Yet, as I passed through the forest, I tried to reason with myself. Not *one* of the riders before me had been whacked by a branch, and it was doubtful the trees had repositioned themselves in the last few minutes.

I slowly relaxed. I half-smiled. And then, I began to wave my arms, as if I were indeed a superhero or else a bird. I was flying! If not an eagle, maybe I at least was an ostrich.

I glanced around at the hills and valleys and trees below. From this bird's-eye view, the autumn foliage proved to be a gorgeous sight, indeed.

As I approached the landing platform, I remembered to pull in my arms and tuck my chin to my chest, as we'd been instructed. I swooped down, and a crew member guided me to a soft landing.

No vomiting. No crash landing. No sudden death. A triple bonus.

"So, what'd you think?" he asked me.

"Once I relaxed, well… Wow! It was really kind of fun!" I couldn't believe these words came from my mouth. The horror of all my expectations aside, I actually had enjoyed the experience. Not the portion leading *up* to the flight. Or the moments of being strapped into the harness. But I rather fancied the flying part—and especially the not-dying part.

Leah was eager to head back out, as soon as we landed. Murf, who wasn't so certain that dodging a tree wasn't just a lucky break, announced she would never, *ever* go zip-lining again.

Me? I still needed some recovery time from the pre-flight trauma. But I knew it was at least possible I might return to fly through the trees again, another day.

Our adventure in Hocking Hills didn't end on that landing platform. It culminated in an unexpected phenomenon at the bottom of a cavern.

With a few hours of daylight remaining, Murf was eager to hike one of the park's trails. Leah and I were far less enthusiastic. The rain had started right after we finished zip-lining, and it showed no sign of ending. After we sat for a half hour in a shelter house, my relentless friend finally convinced us to head out. We set off on a muddy trail, with rain hoods, a single umbrella, and only one of us possessing a good attitude.

About a half-mile along the trail, we encountered a group of people ascending a makeshift set of stone stairs cut into a cliff.

"It's beautiful down there," one of them told us. "You really should check it out."

I glanced down at the narrow, winding steps that were slick with wet fallen leaves. Leah and I exchanged frowns. We'd already zip-lined, hiked, and oohed and ahhed at the scenery. Whatever lay at the bottom of those stairs, even if it were hidden treasure, could not be worth the effort.

Despite our misgivings, Murf—the friend who once convinced me to let her drive my mother's car on the sidewalk in her college town—soon talked us into slogging down the steep and slippery steps.

We maneuvered our way downward, Leah and I grumbling and grasping the rocky walls for stability. As we neared the bottom, Murf paused ahead of us.

"Wait. Do you hear some kind of music or singing?" she asked.

Yes, we heard singing, growing stronger with each step we took.

We reached the bottom of the stairs, which opened into a huge cavern. We gazed around to discover the cave was filled with Amish people. Dozens of men, women, and children in traditional Amish clothing surrounded us. Most were seated upon the huge half-circle of rock floor, while the rest stood behind them.

Every one of them was singing.

My friends and I listened, mesmerized. I'd never heard such perfectly harmonized singing, not in any church choir or Broadway chorus.

As they finished the last refrain of "Amazing Grace," I felt compelled to break into applause. But clapping seemed somehow inappropriate or even sacrilegious: an inadequate and anticlimactic response to the magical moments we had just witnessed.

Just as the crowd began to disperse and we started to walk away, a man at the center of the cavern stood. He began playing the bagpipes. It was a haunting and soulful song. Everyone stopped and turned around to listen. As the music echoed through the cavern, my friends and I shook our heads and exchanged glances of silent disbelief.

Among all the experiences in my life, this unplanned one may have topped the list as the most sublime and surreal. And by far, the most beautiful.

While talking with a few of the Amish folks afterward, we learned that not only was it our first visit to this cavern, it was their first time too. Their singing was spontaneous. And the bagpiper? He wasn't even with their group. It was pure serendipity that we all landed at that spot, on that day, at that exact time.

As we left the park, my friends and I reflected upon how taking a chance, how following even a seemingly insignificant whim, can affect your life. If we hadn't decided to take that trip to Hocking Hills, if we hadn't dismissed our misgivings, and if we hadn't headed down those treacherous stairs to explore that cave, we would have missed out on this fleeting life experience. And we agreed, this was one of the most amazing moments we'd ever experienced.

Was it chance that led us down those slippery, rocky stairs that day? Or was it fate?

All I knew was the familiar road we choose to travel, over and over again, may seem the safest and most comfortable. But we need to force ourselves to look beyond, above, and even far below that well-worn path.

That is often where we discover the most remarkable music in the soundtrack of our life.

Chapter 23:

ROCKING IT AS A
COLLEGE MASCOT

$\mathcal{P}$ossessing no athletic ability whatsoever, along with a lackadaisical interest, had always hindered me as a sporting enthusiast. I figured I simply hadn't found my personal athletic niche. Hitting the field as my college alma mater's mascot, thirty years after I graduated, could be my final chance to find superstar glory.

"Rocksy" was The University of Toledo Rockets' female counterpart to UT's original mascot, "Rocky the Rocket." Not that Rocksy was any less of a big deal. The beloved Rocksy appeared at hundreds of campus and community events. She was selected each year through an arduous audition process, and her identity was kept top-secret.

Through my superhuman journalistic skills, I managed to track down the real Rocksy. Maybe I was given special dispensation or perhaps she just needed a breather, but her consent proved once again that even the oddest requests in life may be granted—if we simply pose the question.

The last time I'd engaged with the public while in costume was during a high school gig as a local mall's Easter
Bunny. It was a short-term but lucrative job, paying five dollars an hour, almost twice the minimum wage at the time. All
went swimmingly, until a terrified toddler peed on me.

I recalled this important detail as I arrived for my Rocksy
debut at a UT soccer match. I'd engage with every youngster
there, but I wouldn't allow a single one to sit on my lap.

The true Rocksy, whose identity I pledged across my
Rocket-shaped heart to take to my grave, met me before the
start of the match. I suited up in my costume: a midnight blue
and gold belted dress with a wide skirt, tights, helmet mask,
and clown-sized boots. I blew out a sigh of relief that this costume, designed for collegiate women, somehow managed to
fit me. Meanwhile, Real Rocksy offered some coaching.

Only a small handful of UT folks knew a switch had
been made that day, and she warned me I had a reputation
to maintain. Rocksy, she told me, was known to be sassy and
a bit of a troublemaker. Huh. Didn't seem too far a stretch
from my normal reputation.

I learned that Rocksy also had a sly, somewhat sexy
signature saunter. I rehearsed a few prances in the hallway
outside my changing room. Real Rocksy watched me before
subtly suggesting I might need a bit more practice.

Most crucial of all, she told me, was that I remain constantly in character. That detail proved to be one of the most
challenging bits.

First off, Rocksy was apparently mute. Poor girl was incapable of uttering a single word. This was *not* part of my standard modus operandi. At least not according to the teacher
who reprimanded my chatty twelve-year-old self in front of
my entire seventh-grade class with, "Miss Stanfa, for such a
tiny person, you have the biggest mouth I've ever heard."

Throughout my entire Rocksy performance, I found

myself forced to keep my mouth completely shut. Go ahead and smirk, Mrs. Mills, wherever you may be.

An unseasonably hot autumn day added a whole new element to my ability to stay in character. That afternoon's temperatures soared to one thousand degrees, with one hundred percent humidity. Approximately.

By the time I jogged out the door, having morphed into my new blue and gold Power Ranger persona, I was already a hot mess under my costume. I sneaked away several times to pry my helmet mask loose and wipe the streaming sweat off my face.

I didn't allow the oppressive heat and humidity, or my incapacity to speak, to crush this opportunity to make my mark on NCAA mascot history.

My always suffering sports-enthusiast father had often teased me, rightfully so, about my lack of sports knowledge. My ignorance about sports was so open-and-shut that he was fond of saying I didn't even know "whether the ball was pumped or stuffed." (Side note: A soccer ball is pumped. A golf ball is stuffed. See, Dad? There's hope for me yet.)

My lack of soccer know-how proved to be no true handicap that afternoon. I simply followed the cues. If the crowd on my side of the field cheered, then I cheered. I cheered *silently*, of course, but with great physical gusto, throwing my arms in the air, hopping, jumping, and dancing. And the crowd would hop, jump, and dance with me.

Who would have guessed the power of my latent cheering skills?

I mingled with dozens of UT fans and found myself greeted with hugs from all the children and even a few adults. I slapped lots of hands in high-fives and posed for pictures. Members of the Blue Crew, UT's mysterious and masked spirit organization, welcomed me into their secret fold for the day and even loaned me their cowbell.

I befriended a cute little dog, too, although I refused to let the nervous pooch sit on my lap. Not only was I pee-wary, but Real Rocksy had forewarned me that my costume wasn't waterproof.

In fact, it was a powerful rain storm that ultimately cut short the soccer match and my promising mascot career. When intermittent sprinkles finally swelled into a monsoon, I pranced past the crowd. I waved and blew kisses at the UT Rocket faithful as I dashed toward shelter, where I would return to my alter ego of a mild-mannered writer.

Maybe I wasn't totally objective, but I thought I rocked it that afternoon. I honed my cheerleading skills, helped lead the team on to two goals, and made new friends. I managed to entertain a large crowd while not uttering a single word, leading me to realize that I occasionally might be better off just keeping my mouth shut.

My performance went so well, I felt certain Rocksy was one step closer to taking top-billing over her boy Rocky— with one *small* caveat and a couple missteps.

As I tumbled in the hallway, thankfully out of sight from my new fans, I realized it was impossible to score a mascot's sassy saunter when you're a clumsy middle-aged woman wearing clown shoes.

Being Rocksy was a trip, in more ways than one.

Chapter 24:

MUCH A DOO-DOO
ABOUT NOTHING

My doctor first suggested a colonoscopy when I turned fifty, but the advice was hard to digest. I disregarded it as a crappy idea. Two years later, The 52/52 Project gave me a kick in the ass. I decided to add this moving experience to my list. I'd get it behind me.

Why did I wait so long to eliminate this burden? I'm guano get to that. I had a number of reasons, but the biggest one was Number Two.

I hope I'm not being too cheeky.

The afternoon before my scheduled appointment, the doctor's office called to pull the plug. They found themselves in a pinch. My colonoscopy was cancelled, and nothing that night would be running as expected. I was shit out of luck.

"Butt wait," they said. "Fortunately, our schedule isn't totally backed up." Just two weeks later, I was squeezed in.

I had been carrying a heavy load, and it was time to relieve myself of this duty.

I'd been warned about the cleansing preparation, a detrimental downslide that would leave me on the skids. I eyed the prescription drink that would get things moving. I raised my glass. As I gulped it down, I joked, "Bottoms up!" Haha—what a gag!

Considering what followed, the nasty-ass drink was only a drop in the bucket. The rest of the evening went right down the drain. It wasn't a straight fifteen-hour stretch of gallops to the bathroom, more like occasional trots, since it came in spurts.

Although I'd always loved a good party, tonight I was more of a party pooper. And this bash was a blowout.

I stomached the events of that night, which continued into early morning, with a lot of grumbling. Why had I agreed to this when I knew deep down in my gut that it wasn't likely to be a good run? I felt like a stool.

The evening went down the crapper. Fortunately, I did not di-a-rrheal and ghastly death.

The medical procedure itself proved to be pretty dope, thanks to a bit of Propofol (Michael Jackson's drug of choice). I couldn't beat it, so I simply turned the other cheek.

Next thing I knew, I was awake, missing only a polyp that was nipped in the bud. The final test was eliminating the air that had been pumped into my stomach. I managed to pass this, too. Yay, me! My own horn wasn't the only thing I tooted.

At the tail-end, I had to say the experience was much a doo-doo about nothing. Several of my readers wrote that I encouraged them to get their asses in gear and schedule their own appointments: Perhaps I started a movement! (Wait, did that last sentence require a comma or a colon?)

And, next time I am told I need a colonoscopy, I won't be so quick to poo-poo the idea. In hindsight, compared to my big pile of new life experiences, this shit came easy.

Chapter 25:

HONK IF YOU PRETEND TO

LIKE MIMES

*A*s I headed out to a busy shopping center, clad in full mime costume and makeup, my sister, DC, suggested I carry a sign reading, "Pretend to Honk If You Like Mimes." Clever, sis, but when it came to silent street performers, most people I knew had nothing nice to say at all. A more appropriate sign might be, "Honk If You Pretend to Like Mimes."

I had never had an affinity for mimes either. They'd always struck me as strange, intrusive creatures who never told you what they were thinking. I steeled myself for feeling awkward, out-of-place, and unloved—much like adolescence.

Popularity be damned, at least I knew I *looked* fabulous. My costume included a navy and white-striped Parisian boat shirt, red suspenders, white gloves, and a beret. And my face paint, applied by a talented family friend, Rachel, who was well-versed in stage makeup, rendered me nearly professional.

But looking good wasn't good enough. I would need to pull off a theatrical routine, acting out a series of stories told entirely through body motions. Being silent for the duration of my performance would be a real effort, considering the women in my family struggled to stay quiet for more than, say, two minutes. Sure, I had managed to remain silent during my Rocksy routine, but that performance had taken a secondary stage to a soccer match. As a street-side mime, I'd have to hold an audience all on my own.

So I spent the previous evening in a hotel room, studying mime routines and tutorials on the Internet. I found over 270,000 Google hits for "mime skit." At the time, one of the most popular pantomime trends appeared to be something called "twerking." Apparently, that got a real rise out of an audience.

I doubted I could pull off twerking. Besides, as I approached my venue—the popular outdoor shopping center of Kentucky's Newport on the Levee—I knew I should focus on a more kid-friendly routine. Dozens of families wandered about, many headed to the Newport Aquarium. It was time to dive in, even if the humiliation killed me and left me sleeping with the fishes.

I danced, mime-fashion, toward my first victims, a couple with their two young sons. They paused as they spied me. I stopped in my fancy-footed tracks, just as apprehensive as they were about my next move.

I then realized this wasn't just about taking on a weird lark of an experience; it was about *succeeding* at being funny and crazy and clever. If there was one thing I'd learned in the past several months, these new life experiences didn't mean much if I didn't give them my all. I wanted to master being a good mime, a skillful mime, a classy mime. Wait, a *classy mime?* Was that an oxymoron?

I straightened and took a deep breath. I bent my arms,

reached my palms out, and attempted the most famous mime skit of all, the illusion of being inside a box. It wasn't much of a stretch: I suddenly felt trapped as hell. I could fail on the spot, and there would be no way out but skulking away. Silently, of course.

The boys smiled. I felt a rush of adrenaline.

Next, I pretended to eat an apple and pull out a worm. Although I'd studied this routine online, it was met with cocked heads, squinty eyes, and frowns from my audience. Clearly, this mime move was a ball of confusion.

Ball of confusion? A new idea struck me. I improvised and pretended to toss a baseball at the older boy. He didn't grasp the motion, so I pounded my invisible bat on an invisible home plate. His eyes lit up, and he pitched the pretend ball back. I swung and stumbled in circles.

The boys laughed. Even their parents, who'd been observing with grim faces, grinned. My impromptu baseball swing was a hit.

I relied heavily on the baseball sketch for the rest of my gig. It proved popular, as did my faux swimming in front of the aquarium entrance. Another routine that went over well was pulling string out of a person's ears and using it as a jump rope. I proved way better at fake jump roping than I ever was at the real thing. While my grade school jump-rope skills never made me any fast friends on the playground, these kids were enchanted with watching me hop and trip over a pretend rope.

The comments from the kids made my day. My favorite came from a little boy who turned to his mother, laughed, and said, "She's sure having a hard time talking." Oh, if he only knew how I struggled to *not* talk.

My nearly ninety-minute routine exhausted me. Given the nonstop hopping and twirling and keeping my mouth shut, it proved a far more physical ordeal than I'd expected.

The physical exertion wasn't the biggest surprise. I was amazed by how much the children, and even many adults, enjoyed my performance. Dozens of people stopped to watch, and some went out of their way to veer across the plaza to interact with me.

Oh, sure, a few adults brushed past me, trying to not make eye contact. I chased after them. A few children shrieked and hid behind their parents. I chased them, too. But my observing niece, Cori, rushed over and suggested I shouldn't be *quite* so aggressive. Apparently, a stranger chasing small children is frowned upon.

The greatest surprise of all was that I actually proved decent at this. Maybe my Rocksy appearance had given me just enough confidence as a silent, costumed crusader. Perhaps I simply embraced my weirdness. Or, maybe the passersby and I agreed in an unspoken understanding that, deep down, we're *all* weird, really.

My afternoon of miming served as a lifetime reminder that the craziest, most random ideas often prove to be the most memorable. Sometimes, experiences like those leave us smiling—and speechless.

Chapter 26:

BARING IT AT THE BEACH

When visiting a nude beach, I figured a sunbather should bring along three things: plenty of sunscreen, an extra-large towel and, of course, her seventy-five-year-old mother.

Sure, the last item seemed a wildcard. But, when each of my *formerly* fun sisters vetoed this side trip during our family vacation in south Florida, my mother hesitated only briefly.

"Just be sure to mention we both kept our clothes on," she said.

"Um, maybe I didn't clarify that," I replied. "I'll be going au naturel, too."

"Oh." She pondered this. "Well, then please don't sit near me. I saw you naked as a baby, and I don't really care to anymore."

Huh. So, my mother recoiled at the idea of seeing her own daughter naked yet hardly flinched at the thought of viewing dozens of strangers letting it all hang out? As I considered the scenario, I decided I wouldn't wish to sit next to her on the beach if *she* were naked either.

Apparently, awkward nudity is something best reserved for total strangers.

We made the one-hour trek down to Haulover Beach, near Miami, on a windy, overcast afternoon. As we approached the warning sign on the beach that noted, "Attention: Beyond this point you may encounter nude bathers," I reminded my mother about the rules of Nude Beach Social Etiquette that I'd researched on the Internet. The first was to keep your eyes on the other sunbathers' faces and not on their other body parts.

"Do not ogle or stare," the website instructed. "Nude sunbathers expect eye contact if they choose to be spoken to." Sound advice, although I was certain neither my mother nor I was eager to strike up a conversation face-to-face, or face-to-other-body-part, with anyone.

Just a few feet within this legal and "special" area of the beach, we encountered a man—sans even a Speedo—walking in our direction. I had little trouble not ogling him since I was preoccupied with helping my unsteady mother negotiate, with her cane, across the mounds of sand.

But we were immediately interrupted by his deep voice, prompting both of us to look up. "This sand is hard to walk on, isn't it?" he said.

My mom paused, leaning on her cane, and nodded. "Yes, it is," she replied. She smiled at him. He smiled back. I grabbed her arm and pulled her away.

We trudged about three feet farther before she leaned in and whispered to me. "Did you see how good I did? I made really good eye contact."

I snorted, calling bullshit. Neither of us had maintained full contact with the man's two blue eyes. No matter how much we tried, how could we avoid his third eye, when it was right out there, only a few inches away?

Next, we passed by a bronzed Adonis. Fortyish. Dark, wavy hair. Holy Mother of God! Was he standing at half-mast?

I yanked my mother's arm once again, before either of them had a chance to speak.

We continued on a bit and found a sheltered place, next to a stack of rental lounge chairs, for my mother to settle in. I headed down the beach. As I plodded across the sand, I glanced around. The winds were high and the sky was slightly ominous, so the beach wasn't nearly as crowded as advertised. Although it was publicized as a family-oriented nude beach, I didn't spot a single child. I saw very few women, either.

Ninety-five percent of the sunbathers were men. Some lay spread-eagle on the sand, their hands behind their heads. Several roamed the beach, in what I could only assume they believed to be their untethered glory.

It was a blustery day. All around me, dozens of winky-dinks waved in the wind. I didn't wave back.

I lowered my head, hell-bent on finding the perfect spot to drop down—and to drop my drawers. About three miles away from anyone else, I figured, would be just about right.

I finally gave in to the futility of privacy. Privacy—at a public, nude beach—was probably an oxymoron. And considering how stupid I was feeling for ever believing I could go through with this experience, "moron" was the operative word.

Spreading out a towel, I plopped down. Still wearing my swimsuit and cover-up, I opened a book and pretended to read while contemplating my next move and questioning my sanity. I realized I could only end this by ripping off the Band-Aid quickly, and that meant peeling off my swimsuit. And so I did.

I promptly covered myself with a second towel. It was windy! It was chilly! I needed that towel! But a gust immediately whipped the towel into the air. It landed neatly folded over my face, leaving the rest of my body fully exposed.

I sprang up to spread the rogue towel back over me, but then the towel beneath me also went awry in the wind. I silently swore and attempted repeatedly to unfurl it, with no success.

Finally, I heard a voice say, "Here, let me help you with that."

Swiveling my head, I saw a young man kneeling directly behind me. "I noticed you struggling," he said. "Here, let's just put one of your sandals on each edge of the towel to anchor it down."

I forced a smile, looking only at his two brown eyes while praying he'd make proper eye contact with me, too. Especially in this close encounter.

"Oh, uh-huh. Good idea," I murmured. "Thank you."

Once the bottom towel was secured, he returned to his spot several feet behind me. I lay back down and held my second towel on top by extending both arms firmly over it. I stared at the sky. Finally, I pulled the top towel off. I squeezed my eyes shut. I adopted the logic of a two year old: If I can't see anybody, then nobody can see me.

I sucked in a deep breath, both to steady my nerves and to flatten my stomach.

Nude sunbathing, I tried to tell myself, was much like sleeping in the buff. There were no clothing constraints or elastic pinching, and the breeze provided a soft, cooling sensation much like a bedroom ceiling fan. Totally conducive to relaxation.

Right.

I heard the voices of people passing by and I flinched any time I heard a pause in their conversation. Wait. What were they doing? What were they looking at? A couple helicopters flew over me. I prayed they weren't taking aerial photos. Or *areola* photos. Amidst my terror, I managed a snicker.

Fifteen minutes later, my mother texted me from her secluded post a few hundred yards away. "I think it's starting to rain. Want to go?" No, it wasn't raining—probably just sea spray from the wind. But, *hell* yes, I wanted to go. I hesitated.

"Fifteen more minutes," I wrote back. I figured forty-five minutes on the beach and I could call it a day.

"OK, whenever you're ready," she texted. "*So* much to tell you. I've been taking lots of notes." As I suspected, having my mom along raised the entertainment bar a notch or two.

I closed my eyes again and endured another fifteen minutes of emotional duress. Time passed more slowly than it ever had in the history of the universe.

Finally, I yanked my swimsuit back on and quickly gathered my things. I also gathered my courage and looked behind me. The young man who'd assisted me with my towel sat a few yards back, fully clothed and reading a textbook. A pile of other books and spiral notebooks lay next to him. He glanced up and smiled. I nodded back.

For a college student like him, I figured any beach was a nice alternative to the campus library. I pictured him penning a term paper about awkward middle-aged women who visited nude beaches, probably an assignment for his abnormal psychology class.

My mother shot me a look of relief when I returned. She rolled her eyes and gestured to her right, just around the stack of lounge chairs. It seemed our friend, Adonis, showed up there just after I left.

"Do you mind if I sit right back here behind you," he'd asked her, "to get away from the wind?"

She'd replied, "No, you're fine." She told me, later, she had smiled to herself, thinking, oh yes, you *are* fine, indeed!

But he'd gone on to spend the rest of our stay parading around her. She'd squirmed a bit in discomfort and then grew annoyed. She had no issue with viewing his endowment; she just wasn't keen on how intent he was on her admiring it.

As we prepared to leave, Adonis immediately stood up, walked over to us, and preened some more. I think we would have found him more attractive if he'd left a tiny bit to our imaginations. Although Adonis would be pleased to know "tiny" wasn't a word either of us would *ever* associate with our memory of him.

While we made our escape, my worldly mother reminded me she'd been to another nude beach, years ago, in St. Martin. She said the Europeans seemed much more nonchalant. They appeared comfortable, and far less demonstrative, with nudity. The Americans down here in southern Florida? Not so much.

Some people might go to nude beaches to flaunt their stuff. Others, like me, visit out of one-time curiosity. Maybe a few simply prefer the freedom and the full body tans. I'd take the tan lines, thank you very much.

Our day trip to Haulover Beach proved to be quite the sideshow. With a great amount of trepidation and a long-lingering sand wedgie, I took part in it, from top to bottom. I gave myself some credit for that.

In the end, the person most mortified was Son #1, who caught wind of the experience upon my return home.

"Wait, you and Grandma went to a nude beach?" His eyes widened in horror before he tightly closed them, attempting to shut out the image. "I could have gone my whole life," he muttered, "without knowing that."

I rolled my eyes. The boy knew nothing about humiliation. Just wait until he was fifty-two and had lived to tell a few more tales. By then, I'd have a few more stories myself. I doubted, however, that they would include any additional nude beach experiences.

And, next time I whined about trying on bathing suits, I'd remind myself *anything* might be better than nothing at all.

Chapter 27:

DINING IN THE DARK

𝓝 othing delighted me much more than eating a nice meal out. So why was I apprehensive about going to dinner one evening while vacationing in southern Florida? Maybe because I was still nauseated by that afternoon's naked outing at the beach. Or maybe because this particular restaurant served you a mystery meal and advised you to not use any sharp implements—since you'd be dining in total darkness.

"Dark dining" was a new trend, suggested to me by my friend, Toni. Only a few places in the United States offered it, but an online search led me to Market 17 in Fort Lauderdale. I reasoned my mother and I could stop there on our way back from the nude beach near Miami. How challenging could dark dining be after the afternoon escapade I just endured? I only hoped I hadn't lost my appetite.

I wasn't sure how to envision this experience, especially since I wouldn't be able to see a thing. My research, however, noted that without sight, our other senses are often amplified: particularly the abilities to smell, feel, and taste.

Our server seated the two of us, alone, in a private back room. I wondered if she'd overheard our replay of the nude beach excursion while we'd waited in the fully lighted restaurant bar. I assured her I wasn't a serial nudist. She laughed and eyed me nervously, disconcerted rather than comforted.

She went on to explain that the rest of the restaurant featured normal dining, and while they used to group all "dark diners" together in one separate room, all the voices in the dark room tended to confuse everyone. It seemed a wise change in protocol, especially since my mother and I were the easily confused sort.

We wouldn't be befuddled by a menu, even if we *had* been able to see one, since our server said she would be choosing our four-course meal for us. We were allowed some input: Our waitress inquired about any major food aversions or allergies. No food allergies, we told her, but we were both quick to mention our mutual loathing of lima beans. (Do I need to explain this again?) I added liver and onions to my no-fly list, and I noted I didn't eat veal either, for humane reasons. (Vegetarians: No need to relay how inhumanely other food-providing creatures are treated, too. I know. But, after my recent vegan week, I had not yet given up pork and I was still taking a vegetarian lifestyle one baby cow step at a time.)

Our server reassured us she'd be serving none of these repugnant items. My queasiness eased. As long as I wasn't served filet of cat, I promised not to complain.

The waitress left to place the order for our first course, and the lights went out. I leaned across to my mother, nearly butting heads in the pitch black.

"This is weird, sitting here in the dark," I said.

"What?"

"I said, 'It's weird sitting here in the dark.'"

"You're going to need to speak slower and louder. I'm not wearing my hearing aids."

I rolled my eyes in the darkness, knowing she couldn't see my response. "You're not wearing your hearing aids?" I yelled. "Why?"

"I didn't want to get sand in them at the nude beach."

I rolled my eyes again. Terrific. Apparently, I'd be dining that evening with Helen Keller.

"You should probably put them in," I shouted. It was more a command than a suggestion. She poked around, finally located her purse on the floor, and spent five more minutes digging through it. Miraculously, she managed to find her hearing aid case in the dark.

"Got it. That wasn't so hard," she said. "Now, I just need to find the little pack of batteries."

Sigh. I refrained from my usual sarcastic retort. Although sarcasm would have mattered little since she couldn't hear a word I said.

Inserting the batteries was a more intricate process, one for which my mother insisted she needed light. She reminded me that she and her friends always carried a flashlight. Just as she fished one from her purse and switched it on, our server appeared with our first course.

"Uh-uh," she scolded us. "No cheating."

"Please," I implored. "For my sanity."

The waitress, who was wearing night-vision goggles, waited patiently as my mom adjusted her hearing aids and shut off her flashlight. Then, the server announced she was placing our plates directly in front of us. She left the room again, and I reached my hands out in the dark to locate my food.

Finding my plate was only part of the battle. The next challenge was *getting the food into my mouth.*

We started off the meal the proper way, by attempting to spear our food with a fork. Fortuitously, neither of us stabbed ourselves. But we brought our forks up to our lips countless times only to discover we'd either turned the fork sideways or else our food dropped off entirely.

Fellow dieters: Dark dining is a damn good weight-loss plan. You can cut your calorie intake in half simply by missing half the food on your plate.

Since forks were little help, we took to eating with our hands. Our server reassured us this was typical for dark dining. It proved far messier, yet no one was there to witness it or complain.

With her night-vision goggles, the waitress could see just enough to place our plates on the table. The most difficult task, she told us, was filling our water and wine glasses. Still, she never spilled a drop. At least as far as we knew. My mother, not known for her daintiness or grace even in an ordinary dining situation, feared she wasn't faring as well— with her food or her red wine.

"When we get home," she said, "I'll probably have to throw away this white jacket I'm wearing."

When the food did make it to our mouths, the next puzzle was deciphering what we were eating. Who knew how much we rely on the sense of sight while dining, especially when we haven't even chosen the meal? Without being able to see our food, figuring out what we were eating proved a tremendous test.

During our four courses, our speculations were only somewhat on target. Some of the individual ingredients were easy to guess. Throughout the evening, I noted curry, onions, and whole almonds with little difficulty.

By the texture and shape of the first course, I guessed at first it was overcooked baby carrots, although far less sweet than I'd expect. After a few more bites, I concluded it was some sort of dumpling. Our waitress later confirmed it was potato and chive gnocchi. Gnocchi/noodles. Poh-tay-toes/poh-tah-toes. I gave myself half a point for accuracy.

The second dish consisted of round slices of a mysterious substance I thought might be eggplant, yet the rind had an almost meaty taste. My mom and I were fully confounded. We learned it was "wahoo," a kind of fish, cooked rare. I'd have failed that challenge even in bright light, given multiple-choice options, or after phoning a friend for help.

The third course: easy-peasy. By the smell, taste, and texture, my mother and I both agreed it was beef. Our server corrected us. No, it was actually venison. And so, I added eating deer, something I'd never had any inclination to try, to my list of new experiences. My deep apologies, Bambi.

The last course, dessert, resulted in a scoop of ice cream upon a flourless chocolate cake. My mom and I eagerly devoured it, pleased that we'd closely called this one—we'd both guessed brownies.

Throughout our dark dining experience, I noticed I did concentrate much more on the aromas, textures, and flavors of each dish. And, certainly, the sense of touch proved to be important. The old adage "Don't play with your food" was justifiably ignored all night.

As far as the meal itself, my mother and I agreed it was good, but not fabulous. Given the gourmet courses we were served, a true connoisseur might have appreciated the food more than we did. Maybe we were lowbrow diners. Or per haps we needed to *see* it to believe in it.

On the drive back to our hotel, my mom said dark dining had been interesting. Out of that day's two experiences, however, she thought she enjoyed the nude beach more.

Huh.

Clearly, you're never too old to try something new. Or to learn something new and slightly unsettling about your mother.

With some things, maybe it's best to remain in the dark.

WINTER

Chapter 28:

I'M JUST A SINGER
(IN A ROCK AND ROLL BAND)

*F*ollowing my two professional voice lessons, I disregarded my instructor's dubious endorsement of "Well, you're *loud*," and made plans to jam on stage with a band anyway. Given the iffiness of my ability, it was shaky territory. Still, I figured I might pull it off as long as I followed a few hard-and-fast rules:

- Rehearsing with the band
- Singing backup only (singing lead would wait until my musical career exploded)
- Looking hot, with a great haircut and an ultra-cool black leather outfit
- Being one or two sheets to the wind (three sheets to the wind *might* backfire)

It was a decent plan. But, as the saying goes, if you ever want to make God laugh, just tell him you have a plan.

I received an invitation to perform with the Rolling Bones, a terrific Rolling Stones cover band in New York City. My band contact, Charlie, appeared excited about my appearing with the group, although he hadn't yet heard me sing. Minor details.

I was awaiting confirmation about the show date when I attended a huge party hosted by my friend, Joan U. The occasion was the annual rivalry football contest between The Ohio State University and The University of Michigan. I was lukewarm about football, but I always enjoyed a good party.

More than a hundred guests filled a large barn to watch the grudge match on a projected screen. Joan and her husband, Bob, arranged for a post-game live performance by The Danger Brothers, a popular Midwest band.

As parties go, it was top-notch: a fun crowd, fabulous food, and terrific music. The booze was flowing freely, too, but I had decided to stick to nursing a single Bloody Mary all day. I was having such a great time that I even gathered the nerve to join my sister, Lori, and some of her friends on the dance floor. I had never been much of a dancer, at least not while sober, so I gave myself some credit for courage.

During one of the band's breaks, I spied Son #2 talking to Joan. They hadn't met before, so I was pleased to see him being such a gracious guest. From a few feet away, I caught a few words of their conversation: "My mom... The 52/52 Project... singing with the band."

NOOOO!!!!

I rushed over. "No, no, not today!" I shouted. "Yes, singing on stage is on my list, but I can't do it today," I explained to Joan. "I need to work with a band on planning a song. We need to rehearse a couple times. Plus, I'm wearing this old sweatshirt and jeans tonight, and I had to cancel my already overdue haircut last week. I can't go on stage looking like this. I need to be prepared for the whole thing. Besides, I'm already working this out with another band. So, today is definitely *not* the right time."

Joan smiled and nodded. "Got it. I understand."

I gave Son #2 the evil eye before slinking back to my seat.

Joan climbed on stage, and I held my breath. Thankfully, it appeared she was only announcing a couple birthdays of people in the crowd. I blew out a sigh.

And then the keyboardist called me up.

Shit.

I contemplated my response. Which scenario would be more awkward and humiliating? I could either go through with this unforeseen challenge or else chicken out in front of a hundred strangers who were all staring at me in anticipation.

The choice was a given.

I plodded, zombie-like, toward the stage. I passed my grinning son. "I didn't even get to rehearse," I hissed at him. "And I'm totally *sober*."

My 52/52 life flashed before my eyes. My *Survivor* audition, mime performance, and nude beach experience. Sure, I had endured them all without a drop of alcohol. But this? I hung my head. Why did I stay sober at the most inopportune moments?

The keyboardist smiled at me. "So," he asked, "What would you like to sing? Any special song? Any particular band?"

I stared blankly at him. Sure, I had several favorite bands and songs. Put on the spot, however, my brain neurons failed to connect. I came up with—*nothing*. I managed to muster up a thoughtful, "Umm."

He forced another encouraging smile and then apparently sized up my age. "How about something by the Beatles?"

The Beatles! Yes, my rock and roll saviors! I couldn't tell you what I had for dinner last night (probably microwave popcorn and a Diet Coke), but I still knew every song lyric in the Beatles' complete discography.

"But I can't sing lead. Not alone. Not today," I whispered to him. "You need to sing with me." He nodded and winked at me, and my hyperventilating slowed to a few lingering gasps.

In honor of the evening's birthday boys, who were also standing on stage, the band launched into "Birthday." The keyboardist shoved a microphone into my hand. The music jumped into the song's familiar opening, "Da-Da-Da-Da-Da-Da-Da-Dah."

There was no turning back. I turned to face the crowd.

"You say it's your birthday," I yelled into the microphone. "It's my birthday, too, yeah."

I glanced down at the mic. Wait, was this thing on? Or had the band, wisely, turned my microphone off? Although I was shouting the song, all I heard were the instruments. I wasn't sure anyone else could hear me either. Which would possibly be to their benefit.

All I could do was continue singing.

I smiled out at the crowd. Many of them were dancing and grinning back. I grasped my microphone, belting out the next words: "We're gonna have a good time!" I strutted around the stage and sang some more.

As I sang and danced, I pondered what the hell was happening. I had never sung on stage in front of an audience before, and my two singing lessons had proven less than encouraging. To top it off, I was *dancing*. Dancing wasn't my thing, by any means, mostly because my moves tended to mimic an electrocuted crab. Dancing on the floor that afternoon with my sister was one thing. But dancing—and singing—on stage?

Why wasn't I a nervous wreck? Why did I feel so at ease with all this? Why did it suddenly feel so *right*?

In the strangest and scariest of times, perhaps you simply feel the moment and find the courage. And at that moment, I felt like a rock star.

As the first stanza ended and the music continued, however, I grew confused. I'd forgotten that this song had a strange musical arrangement. I bopped about and smiled at the audience, but I couldn't recall when the song's vocals should jump back in again. Did I miss my cue? Should I be singing right now?

I didn't hear the keyboardist singing either, so I pranced, limply, for a while longer before glancing back at him. He was pointedly eyeing me while his mouth moved with the music.

Damn.

Apparently, it wasn't just my voice I couldn't hear. I couldn't pick up the vocals from any of the microphones.

I collected myself, recognized the part of the song we had reached, and quickly chimed in. The keyboardist looked almost as relieved as I felt.

The remainder of my performance may have lacked a bit of my original gusto and confidence, but I got back in the game and finished the song. I even ended with a smile and a bow—and a smattering of applause.

I walked off the stage with a feeling of near triumph.

I learned later that the earpieces worn by singers are actually a kind of monitor allowing them to hear the full scope of what the audience is hearing. Without such an earpiece, I could only hear the instruments around me and not the vocals, which is why I found myself momentarily lost, even in a song I thought I knew so well. If I'd rehearsed with the band, or had any musical background at all, I might have known this and made it through the song snafu-free.

A few people in the crowd stopped me to say I did great. It probably helped that most had been drinking all day. Yet, even Son #2—and lord knows our children can be our biggest critics—told me he was proud.

Sure, I would have preferred a foolproof performance over my flawed one. What struck me, regardless, was other than that one mid-song mistake, I had felt perfectly at ease singing with the band. Even unprepared, in front of a huge crowd of almost all strangers, I'd endured little stage fright. I'd pushed past all malfunctions and misgivings, and although I almost certainly didn't sing from my diaphragm, I did sing with my soul.

After living through months of frightening and sometimes humiliating new exploits, had I grown braver? Become more desensitized to fear? Or, perhaps, was I simply destined to perform on stage?

I'd go with all of the above.

I still had many new experiences to undertake. After that night, I knew I'd face each one of them with more courage than I had imagined.

My journey wasn't finished yet.

Who says it's over when the fat lady sings?

After my Big Fat Greek Party, I wanted to enroll at Marquette University and pledge Sigma Chi—fresh off its double-secret probation.

As I embraced my weirdness during my mime performance, the passersby and I seemed to agree—in an unspoken understanding—that we're all weird, really.

After our day of visiting a nude beach and then dining in the dark, my mother told me she enjoyed the nude beach more. Perhaps lighting is everything.

It was a blustery day at the nude beach. All around me, dozens of winky-dinks waved in the wind. I didn't wave back.

When I accidentally caught the bouquet while crashing a wedding, I was happy to hand it off to a more enthusiastic recipient. I applauded from the background before making my escape.

I headed out for the day in pajamas, slippers, and a headful of curlers. Breakfast was at a restaurant called Chowders 'N Moor, a fitting name for a fish out of water.

Channeling my inner Ferris Bueller, I jumped in line and marched in the St.
Patrick's Day parade. Waving to my would-be fans, I pondered how to sing
"Danke Schoen" in Gaelic.

As we prepared for the New Year's Day Polar Plunge, I told my nephew, Cole, he was brave. Silently, I toyed with the idea that he was just genetically inclined toward poor decision-making.

Awaiting my racing experience, I watched the cars tear around the track. I convinced myself it appeared almost less hazardous than a Detroit freeway.

When I debuted as The University of Toledo's mascot, Rocksy, UT's mysterious and masked spirit organization—the Blue Crew—welcomed me into their fold and convinced me I needed more cowbell.

The Blade, *Amy Voigt, 2014*
After bathing Sam the white rhino, I added "I gave a rhinoceros an erection" to the list of things I never thought I'd hear myself say.

Chapter 29:

YOU CAN RING MY BELL

*E*very December, on my first couple passes by storefront Salvation Army bell-ringers, I smile and toss them a buck or two. Then, I spend the rest of the holiday season trying to slip past without making eye contact.

My seasonal avoidance disorder wasn't without a bit of guilt. After years of this routine, I decided to make amends by making it my mission to collect a bucketful of cash for the Salvation Army.

I hoped all I had to do was ring my bell, flash a sweet smile, and offer a warm holiday greeting. What I didn't want to do was plead or beg.

To my relief, I learned I couldn't directly ask anyone to contribute. This policy was *so* fine with me. Although I worked full-time for a fund-raising organization, my occupation entailed overseeing more general communications; I wasn't required to actually ask people for money. As a bell-ringer, I would somehow need to find a subtle way to *inspire* people to give.

My Salvation Army contact did offer a few suggestions to encourage giving. With this advice in mind, I bought ten dollars worth of candy canes and Hershey Kisses. Wearing a Santa hat and a big smile, I headed out to my station at a nearby Kroger store.

I rang a bell for three hours, and I came away learning a few things about human nature.

First, bribery works. The adults with children in tow nearly always contributed something. Were these parents trying to set a good example through their giving, or were they only desperate to stifle their nagging children? When I asked if I could offer their youngsters some candy, most admitted this was precisely why they had stopped by my station—because their children had spied the candy and begged for a piece.

Still, I discovered that not all the youngsters were simply greedy. A few handed me money from their own pockets or Hello Kitty wallets. In return, I allowed them to ring my bell and gave them an extra dose of sugar. Hell yes, I did. A sweet gesture deserved a sweet reward.

I also learned that some people can't or won't give, no matter what. Even when I offered my brightest smile and warmest greetings, several folks went out of their way, literally, to avoid me. I couldn't judge those who hugged the opposite perimeter of the lobby as they entered, just to evade me. I did the same thing every year.

Maybe a few of them were simply having a bad day. Perhaps some didn't give because they chose to help the poor in other ways or through different organizations. (The Salvation Army had received some bad press recently, but I like to think my fundraising initiative helped several needy people.) In addition, for all I knew, some of these Kroger customers might have fallen upon tough times, forced to become recipients themselves of charitable contributions.

Most adults, even those who donated, shook their heads at my offer of candy. But a few approached and asked for a piece without dropping a single cent into the kettle. While I wanted to call them out on this, I pushed aside my inner Scrooge, held out the candy bowl, and wished them "Happy Holidays."

Even some of the non-contributors still provided a laugh. As an elderly man in an electric scooter passed, I rang my bell and shouted, "Ho-ho-ho!"

He glided by, without pausing, and retorted, "Don't say that on a downtown street corner. People might get the wrong idea." Good point.

Finally, I learned the more I gave of myself, the more others gave too.

I began the evening by simply smiling and offering holiday greetings to customers. By the end of the night, I found myself dancing and beating the bell against my hips, in rhythm to a silent version of "Jingle Bell Rock."

A few people grinned and said, "Are you dancing to the music in your head?" Spurred on, I eventually gathered the nerve to whisper the tune, and finally I belted it out. Embarrassing? Yes. Effective? That, too.

The smiles multiplied. Several customers glanced at me and said, "Well, you sure seem happy!" It seems people's hearts are warmed by the sight of a jolly old elf. Once I became more enthusiastic and more engaged, so did the customers. And when a Facebook friend, Linda, showed up with a cowbell for me to use, the contributions began to pour in.

Apparently, I needed more cowbell.

Toward the end of the night, one customer gave me a side-glance and raised his eyebrows as he passed. I sighed and paused in the middle of my song and dance. He was *so* not enthralled. Clearly, I looked ridiculous.

But just before he reached the exit, he stopped and

looked back. He returned to stick a wad of greenbacks in the bucket. They didn't make it all the way through the slot, so after he walked away, I reached down to push them in. I didn't count the bills, but I did get a good look at the one on top: It was a ten.

When my shift ended, I estimated half the people who came in and out of the store dropped at least something in the kettle. My gig proved far more successful than I expected. A couple weeks later, I received a letter from the Salvation Army. They reported I helped raise $141.52. If my third-grade math skills hadn't failed me, that amounted to about $47 an hour—putting my fund-raising gig well above the national $30 average.

Yet the success of the evening wasn't measured only by dollar amounts. The most rewarding moment of the evening was when an elderly woman stuck a couple ones in the bucket.

"Thanks so much!" I said. I held out my tin of candy. "Would you like a treat?"

She shook her head and smiled. "No, thank you. Being able to help *is* my treat."

That sentiment was worth every minute I spent ringing my bell—and worth more than every bill in my bucket.

Chapter 30:

CRYING OVER SPILLED PAINT

My former husband and I built our dream house when our marriage seemed everlasting and our children were babies. It was the house my two now-grown sons considered our family home and the one where I thought I'd babysit my grandchildren and live out my golden years.

Twenty-one years later, reality and practicality finally led me to sell it. The day I moved, I walked through every room. I stroked the stairway's mahogany handrail, envisioned the crib in my youngest son's bedroom, and fought tears as I walked out the front door for the last time.

I moved out and moved on. Six months later, I watched through my new condo's kitchen window as a plow attacked the mountains of snow on my sidewalk and driveway. I sat back and grinned. Although I had trouble letting go of my family home with all its memories and its aborted future, I decided condo living had its perks.

While living in a condo allowed me freedom from several maintenance responsibilities, I was still waiting for my

BFF handyman, Jerry, to tackle some home projects not han-
dled through my condo association. After months of waiting,
I began to fear he may never show. With my office closed for
the day by a Level Three Snow Emergency, I propped myself
on the couch and stared around at all the shit that apparently
wasn't going to fix itself.

My idea of a do-it-yourself job had never encompassed
more than changing a light bulb or hanging and rehanging a
picture until it looked nearly straight. I possessed little interest, and virtually no aptitude, in DIY projects.

One of the items on my handyman's forgotten list was
sanding and re-staining the trim on a fifty-year-old bar built
by my great-grandfather. It sat, dusty and dilapidated, in my
new basement. I'd already bought sandpaper, brushes, and
a couple cans of mahogany stain, to save Jerry a trip to the
hardware store. The Old Sherry would have waited a decade
to pay someone else to pretty it up. The New Sherry, far
braver and a tad less bright, shrugged and said, "How hard
could it be?"

I talked myself out of an afternoon of Netflix and
Bloody Marys, and I headed downstairs.

Within forty-five minutes, I sanded away the entire top
layer of graying wood. The natural wood soon shined, begging me to finish its facelift.

Buoyed by this success, I reached for a can of stain. I
glanced back at the bar. My face dropped as reality hit me.

Staining inch-wide strips of wood on a piece of antique
furniture seemed a somewhat *intricate* project for someone
with my limited—and by limited, I mean nonexistent—painting skills. I'd never even painted a damn wall.

In my defense, I moved into my first house when I was
eight months pregnant and was advised that painting was hazardous. I bought my second house newly constructed and
freshly painted. By the time I bought this condo, with several

nicked and blotchy walls, I simply put "wall touch-up" on the absent handyman's list.

So, before I began the complex work that day of re-staining the bar, I decided to take baby steps into my DIY career by first touching up a few walls. I rummaged through a collection of rusty cans of paint left by the previous owner and found a can of blue for the living room. I didn't bother with a drop cloth, which I had heard was helpful. After all, I was applying tiny brush strokes to just a handful of blemishes.

After covering a half-dozen spots on my living room wall, I stepped back to examine my work. Hmm. The newly painted areas looked awfully dark. But I'd heard paint light-ened as it dried. Wait. Or, did it darken?

Minor details. One room was finished!

Perusing the old paint cans for beige, I paused as I spied a second container of blue: a lighter, strangely familiar shade. Quite like the color of the wall I just touched up with dark blue.

Sigh. My late father, a former color approver in a vinyl production factory, was surely shaking his head in disgust.

I went over the spots in the living room with the correct color of blue, and touched up the beige on two other walls. I then lugged the original blue can into the guest bedroom, which appeared to be a true match. I slapped the paint onto several bad spots, blending in the color.

"Our House" by Crosby, Stills & Nash played in the background. I hummed along. Now that I was getting the hang of it, painting wasn't so stressful. It was actually sort of soothing! Why had I assumed it would be so difficult?

As I reached down to dip the brush into the can, my eyes spied a sprinkling of blue paint on the tan carpet. Upon closer examination, it appeared less of a sprinkle and more of a widespread spray. In fact, most of the carpet's perimeter was now tie-dyed tan and blue.

Racing to my computer, I Googled "removing paint from carpet." I spent two hours attempting every household paint-removing remedy listed—vinegar, nail polish remover, WD-40—to no avail.

I told myself not to panic. I had saved a hundred bucks doing my own touch-up work. How much could a couple new area rugs, to cover the damaged carpet, cost? At worst, I'd probably break even.

And, if I managed my original goal of re-staining the bar, I figured I'd be way ahead.

I headed back downstairs to tackle that project. In just over an hour, I applied a layer of stain to every bit of wood trim on the bar. Oh, and I'd learned something from my mistakes—I laid down an old sheet as a drop cloth.

After finishing the first coat, I appraised the bar. It looked fabulous! It would need a second coat, maybe even a third. But I'd just learned the raging snowstorm had already closed my office again for the next day. Plenty of time to finish the project and then glow in my success.

Stepping back, I noticed a strip I missed. I dipped my brush into the can, which I'd placed for convenience on top of the bar. As I turned away, my right elbow hit something. Peering over my shoulder, I watched in seemingly slow motion as the entire contents of the overturned can rushed out in a thick, mahogany waterfall, spilling all over the top of the bar and down the sides.

Clearly, staining a single piece of furniture was far more complex than painting the ceiling of the Sistine Chapel. Michelangelo never once had to worry about a paint can spilling upon that ceiling.

I surveyed my destroyed masterpiece in horror. I had already removed the drop cloth, believing I was finished. A half-dozen spills had gushed their way down, exploding onto the carpet.

I added buying a third area rug to my to-do list.

The bar wasn't such an easy fix. I blotted up the sides, hoping I could cover all the stain inconsistencies with additional coats. Next, I studied the pool of stain on top. It was already drying into a splotchy pile of goo. I knew it couldn't be rectified with blotting or disguising it with a third or even fourth coat of stain. The only solution was to cover the bar top with tile.

A tiled top *might* be beyond my DIY skills, however. I hoped Jerry could handle that job. I'd pay him well for this, quite gladly, if only he'd return my calls.

Meanwhile, I had a second snow day awaiting me. Perhaps I would spend it applying a couple more coats of stain to the bar's possibly salvageable trim. Or else I'd let my handyman finish that, too.

Plopping back on the couch, I called Jerry, who promised—on his life—to come the following week to take care of all my remaining homeowner problems.

I hung my head. I'd lived independently for years. And, through this year of new experiences, I had begun to learn I was capable of far more than I thought possible. Surely, I must possess *some* handy skills.

I spent the next hour shopping online for area rugs. Oh, I knew my way around the Internet, for sure. While I surfed the web, I fixed myself a tall Bloody Mary. At least I was handy as hell at fixing *something*.

And, I didn't spill a single drop.

Chapter 31:

UNPLUGGED AND AMISH

While The 52/52 Project had begun to broaden my world, it simultaneously cemented me to an electronic one.

As I planned and reported about events in my life, I grew even more obsessed with my three email accounts. I mainlined Facebook. My iPhone, offering instant notifications, never sat out of reach. And, still old-school enough to actually *talk* on the phone, I generally spent my drive time chatting, particularly on multiple daily conversations with my mother. Sure, I could ignore her calls and messages. But mothers only call again. And again. At least that's what my two sons claimed.

A few months prior, during an attempted three-day break from my computer and cell phone, I instead found myself binging on *Downton Abbey*—an entire streamed season in a single weekend. I went from the electric frying pan straight into the fire. Yes, I was an electronic addict.

It was time to give unplugging from electronics my all.

So, I began one of the most personally daunting items on my 52/52 list: going unplugged for an entire week. Seven days of no phone, no radio, no television, no Internet, and no email. The only phone and email exceptions I chose to allow were communications for my day job and, if truly necessary, personal or family emergencies.

I comforted myself in the thought that I could still receive parcel and post. I prayed someone would send me a box of Little Debbie Nutty Bars, a twelve-pack of beer, and— several long letters.

How bad was my addiction? Before I unplugged, I scheduled a Facebook post to appear midway through my hiatus. Although I wouldn't be able to read the comments for another week, I clung to the idea that this somehow kept me connected to my Internet alliances.

I had it bad. Real bad.

DAY ONE

I pulled out of the driveway and picked up my phone for my usual morning conversation with my mother. *Oh. Right.* This was it. My new unplugged life, for an entire week. *Sigh.*

By the time I arrived at my office, a half hour later, I already felt incomplete. Isolated. Amish. For the next week, I'd apparently be living the life of Ma Ingalls in *Little House on the Prairie.*

I busied myself with paperwork and reports. Just before noon, I checked my office email account and opened a colleague's message. I clicked on the embedded link and on auto-pilot began perusing a delightful collection of new books.

Crap.

I'd made it through the first twelve hours, half of those while asleep, and already I'd failed the test. I wandered ten yards down the hall to remind my coworker, Lynn, that I couldn't read personal emails. Good friend that she was, she consequently saved dozens of Internet goods for me and, on

the eve of day seven, she emailed me an entire week's worth
of personal reflections and web links. Lynn may have needed
an intervention, too.

Minutes later, I picked up my office phone and was
greeted by the voice of Son #1.

"Hey, Mom."

"What's wrong?"

"Um, I thought I could call you at work."

"Only if it's an emergency."

"Well, I do need to talk to you." He paused, and I braced
myself for some sort of dire and distressing news.

"My band is scheduled for a late show Friday night. Can
you watch the dog overnight?"

Deep sigh, reprised.

Two hours later, I received an office email from the editor of my university faculty-staff newspaper, who was writing a story on The 52/52 Project and needed photos. Verrry
iffy territory. But, this was a work-related publication, I told
myself. With a deadline! So, I clicked through to Facebook,
where most of my photos resided.

A glaring red flag greeted me: "14 NOTIFICATIONS!"
Triple sigh.

I averted my eyes, copied several photos to my hard
drive, and emailed them to the editor. I closed out of Facebook without reading a single notification. I applauded my
willpower.

On the drive home, I also resisted the temptation to call
my mother for our usual en route conversation. I gazed down
at the car radio. I'd endured an entire day without any tunes.
The absence of music was soul-crushing.

As my mind was forced to wander, I found myself
thinking about Tom Laughlin of *Billy Jack* movie fame, who
I learned had just died. I spent the drive attempting to recall,
and finally successfully belting out, every line of "One Tin

Soldier." Given the meager amount of ways to temporarily occupy myself, I concluded this was thirty minutes of my life well spent.

After dinner, I sat on the couch and stared at my closed laptop and black TV screen. Unplugging was triple the challenge when one lived alone. How did hermits occupy their time? I was pretty sure most of them spent their evenings talking to themselves and staring into the abyss.

I perused the last three day's newspapers, even the sports pages, and read three chapters of a novel. "I love to read," I announced aloud to no one. Considering I still had my books, how bad could the week really be?

DAY TWO

I awoke to two missed calls from Son #1. (I did allow myself to check my cell phone for missed calls and messages, in light of true emergencies.) Not a single voice mail from him. That was no surprise since neither of my sons would stoop to leaving a voice mail—even if their apartment had burned down and they were left standing on a street corner with their remaining handful of worldly possessions.

But one of my sons calling twice before 8 a.m.? Something terrible had obviously transpired. My heart raced. What would Ma Ingalls do if she were frantic with worry about one of her grown children? I figured she would make a quick stop on her trek to the water pump—or to the office—to ask Grandma Ingalls to text him.

As my mother opened her door, her eyes lit at the sight of me. She reached out and grabbed me in a bear hug. "I've really missed you," she said. Understandable. After all, it had been almost thirty-six hours since our last phone call.

She promised to check in on her grandson and assured me that one of them would call me at the office if it was a true emergency. A half hour after I arrived at work, Son #1's number popped up on my ringing office phone. I fearfully picked up the handset.

"What happened? What's wrong?"

"Oh, hi, Mom. Hey, I wanted to let you know our show is actually Saturday, not Friday. Still OK for you to take the dog?"

DAY THREE

I didn't receive a single phone call all day from any family members. I loved them. I missed them. But I had to admit that not having to mediate their daily lives or coordinate any family matters, even for the upcoming Christmas holiday, was liberating. Still, how could they possibly be surviving without me?

And I did feel disconnected from the rest of the universe. What were all my cyber friends up to? And, what sort of horrendously delightful diatribes were Internet trolls posting in comments on Yahoo news stories? I missed those, too.

On the drive home from work, I stared at my iPhone lying on the front passenger seat. I had turned off all email and Facebook notifications. What exactly was I supposed to do at red lights?

That night, I worked on a draft of a story by pen and paper before retiring to bed hours earlier than usual. I tossed and turned, while visions of Facebook danced in my head. I even, almost, missed Twitter. Yes, I'd hit an all-time low.

DAY FOUR

Without my usual background music at work, I hummed my way through the morning. Later that day, I heard faint strands of the *Wicked* soundtrack streaming from a coworker's office. Would it be cheating to ask her to crank up the volume?

No phone calls the entire day. Son #1 must have concluded we were all set for dog-sitting.

Heading home from the office, I passed a discount mattress store. The only vehicle in the parking lot was a food truck, the concession type you generally see at a festival or fair. The truck banner advertised corn dogs, lemonade, and elephant ears. And, not just the usual sugar-coated fried confections but also "Dietetic Elephant Ears!"

Dietetic elephant ears, offered by a random festival food truck in a desolate mattress store parking lot, in the middle of winter? I grinned and reached for my iPhone to take a picture of this bizarre sighting.

Damn.

OK. No iPhone photos allowed. Well, I'd at least make a note to write about this oddity later. I grabbed my phone again, to leave a recorded memo on my favorite dictation app.

Double Damn.

DAY FIVE

I needed to check the upcoming weekend's schedule for the zoo's annual Christmas light show. An impossible task, without a phone or Internet. I would have to take a wild stab at the hours and beg off as being blameless if the zoo was closed when my family and I arrived.

I also needed to find a new recipe for our family Christmas dinner that weekend. My normal online resources were out of the question. Apparently, I'd have to open one of the four dozen cookbooks gathering dust on my kitchen shelves.

On my way home from work, I passed by my friend Cindy's neighborhood and decided to stop for an impromptu holiday visit. She didn't answer when I rang the doorbell. The rules forbade me from tracking her down by calling her cell phone from mine. Seriously? Who made these damn rules anyway?

As I left and rounded the corner, I happened to pass her approaching car and flagged her down. We managed a visit,

after all. Could I help it if she had music playing in the background? I caught a glimpse or two of something on her TV
screen. It was the best of times, out there on the wild prairie.

DAY SIX

Son #2 arrived in town for the Christmas holiday. At least I
could only assume he did, since he'd been instructed ahead
that he couldn't—and indeed he *didn't*—call to say he safely
made the five-hour trip from Milwaukee. I worried about his
wellbeing, but I never allowed myself to pick up the phone
to check on him. A terrible, inconsiderate, and rule-abiding
mother I was.

After a mid-morning meeting, I returned to my office to
find my friend, Murf, in the midst of leaving a note on my
desk. She'd stopped to ask me to meet for drinks after work.
Yes! I was in! Except, while we were at the bar, who would
let out Ringo the Wonder Retriever, who'd been crossing his
furry legs all day?

Murf convinced me it wasn't cheating if *she* called Son
#2 to see if he'd arrived home and could manage dog duty.
He told her he was only an hour away and would stop home
to take care of Ringo before a scheduled eye appointment.

What he couldn't handle, however, was paying for his
appointment and new glasses. Through two missed calls and
a subsequent text message that appeared on my phone screen
(EMERGENCY—it began), I discovered he needed a credit
card number. I was forced to call him back. I told myself this
was a matter of medical emergency and financial hardship.
As well as a small matter of my not planning ahead.

With no access to phone calls or text messages, poor Ma
Ingalls probably always planned ahead. Me? I just thanked
God I had only one day left of this shit.

DAY SEVEN

My right ear had throbbed for three days. In a curious turn of events, as I'd gone unplugged, my ear canal had plugged right up. I'd stuck it out, blaming it on a temporary allergic reaction and refusing to call the doctor. By day seven, as the pain increased, I figured I'd already used up my medical emergency excuse the day before with Son #2.

I glanced at Ringo.

"Quick, Lassie," I shouted at him. "Run and fetch the doctor!" Ringo blinked twice at me, not budging from his usual reclining position on the couch.

I struggled through my last disconnected day in an even bigger fog, since I could only hear out of one ear. I drove home from work, resisting all temptation from electronic evil by burying my iPhone at the bottom of my purse.

Just knowing I'd be reconnected at midnight made the evening bearable.

I fell asleep, dreaming of my four BFFs: Verizon, Google, Pandora, and Facebook.

DAY EIGHT

I woke the next morning. It was Christmas Eve day! Not only a day off work, but the day I could finally rejoin the great world around me!

My first move was to telephone my doctor, who agreed to call in an antibiotic with no office visit necessary. My next call was to my mother. If there was anyone happier than me to see this week conclude, it was her. She said she'd been waiting for my call since dawn.

Next, I raced to my laptop. I clicked on the Facebook icon. I was greeted by a yellow warning on my monitor: No Internet connection.

Clearly, this was some kind of momentary cruel joke. I tried again. And again. After several repeated attempts, I turned on the TV. No cable either.

I continued to stare at my computer monitor, clicking "Internet Settings" over and over and over. The flickering snow on the TV seemed to mock me. Oh, the brutality of life: to be finally granted permission to use technology—only to have that access technologically denied.

Clearly, I was on Santa's Naughty List.

After checking with my neighbors, who said they were experiencing a similar problem, I called my cable and Internet company. Three times. Each time, they reassured me it was a short-term problem. *Short-term* was a relative and disturbing description. I called a fourth time and was told, nonchalantly, to just sit tight. Bastards.

Hours passed.

Finally, twelve hours after what should have been the end of my weeklong ordeal, my electronic nightmare came to an end. When the word "connected" popped on my computer screen, I embraced my laptop. I emailed both my sons to alert them of my full freedom, checked my other email messages, and then clicked over to Facebook.

As I scrolled through a week's worth of postings, I cranked some Christmas tunes on Pandora and slipped a disc into my DVD player. Oh, the Grinch! What would Christmas be without the ability to watch one of my favorite holiday movies?

I related more than ever to that ornery old recluse.

I could only imagine how much happier he and Ma Ingalls might have been, if only they'd been Facebook friends.

Chapter 32:

FROZEN

After my nude beach ordeal, I promised I would never again complain about cramming my full-sized, middle-aged parts into a bathing suit. Except I never considered I'd soon be donning one on New Year's Day—in frozen Ohio—while plunging into the icy waters of the Maumee River.

As I shivered in a swimsuit on the snow-covered riverbank, it's possible I complained once or twice. Or maybe fifty-two times.

I'd lived nearly my whole life in northwest Ohio and spent the last twenty-five years in Waterville, only two miles from the setting of what's believed to be the country's oldest annual Polar Plunge. I'd never wandered over to even watch because, baby, it's *cold* out there! And those people who jumped into a frozen river in January? They were certifiably ca-ray-zee.

But, considering how far up the insanity meter my life had spiked over the past months, crazy seemed very *murky* territory. So, at the high point of the day's heat index, just before noon, I plodded down to the river for a mid-winter dip.

The temperature hovered around sixteen degrees, with a windchill of five.

That wouldn't stop me or my fifteen-year-old nephew, Cole, who had agreed to join me. As we plodded through several inches of snow toward the riverfront, I pounded him on the back and told him he was brave. Silently, I toyed with the idea that the poor guy was just genetically inclined toward poor decision-making.

A few hundred people gathered along the shoreline. Although my sister, Lori, and brother-in-law, Mike, didn't make the plunge, they did come along to provide their son and me with moral support—and, more important—with towels and a pre-heated escape vehicle.

While we waited, Cole and I attempted to stave off frostbite by wearing sweats and winter coats over our swimsuits. We were among the minority in this logic. Many of our comrades showed up shirtless, wearing only Speedos and flip-flops. One guy arrived in a bathrobe and Viking horns. Another wore nothing more than a threadbare pair of tighty-whities.

I rolled my eyes and pointed out the collection of circus characters to Cole. We laughed and laughed until Lori reminded us that he and I were active members of this freak show.

We waited, shaking on the shore, for nearly five years—or five minutes, if one must be technical. Finally, the announcer instructed all swimmers to prepare to plunge. Cole and I stripped down to our swimsuits. As our exposed skin turned pink, then red, then purple, we found we'd hurried up only to wait *another* five years.

"This isn't so bad," I mumbled to Cole, as we hugged ourselves and huddled together. "I'm not really *that* cold, are you?" The words escaped through my mouth into a frosty cloud in the air. He shrugged, his teeth chattering in response.

Before I realized the deep freeze had short-circuited the wiring from my brain to my mouth, the first wave of a hundred people in front of us suddenly raced into the river.

We'd been cautioned it would be safest to wait for the first running rush of aquanuts. We stood by for a few moments, watching and listening to the screams of swimmers splashing into the river. What we hadn't considered, however, was that we would be plowed over when that same group immediately fled back toward shore.

As we attempted to maneuver past the oncoming frantic and frozen mob, I discovered polar plunging was, literally, a slippery slope toward madness. The crowd had compacted four inches of snow on the riverbank into a slick, icy hill. I sported an old pair of treadless sneakers that I planned to then toss in the trash. Perfect to wear in a mucky river. Not so advantageous when running down a frozen hill.

As I went air-born on the icy embankment, Cole—who was wearing his football cleats—grabbed my hand and steadied me.

Holding hands, we jumped into the water.

As we stood in the river, lying on the shore with a broken tailbone suddenly seemed the more comfortable alternative. My legs turned to ice. And then, no sensation at all.

"I can't feel my legs," Cole said.

"Legs?" I mumbled. "What legs?"

The shallow water reached just above our knees. We agreed that couldn't count for a done deed. We needed to immerse ourselves in the full experience. Besides, I reasoned I might be better off once my entire body was as numb as my legs.

We crouched down until we were sitting on the bottom of the riverbed. As the water enveloped me, it deadened every nerve in my body. My brain went hazy. I gazed up at the two rescue squad trucks on shore. I prayed the EMT squad had already picked me out as the weakest member of the pack and was closely observing me, ready to swoop in for a rescue.

And then, as quickly as we'd raced into the water, Cole and I ran back toward the shore, our legs kicking up shards of ice.

I learned later that the water registered at a balmy thirty-two degrees. Damn toasty, compared to how the *air* felt once we exited the river. Did I mention it was cold? No, *cold* is how you feel when your furnace hasn't kicked in yet in November. Or when you are forced to make a wintry walk from your heated office to your car. Or, perhaps, when your parka and mittens don't soften the sting of a two-minute ride down a toboggan hill.

Exiting a glacial river into the arctic air? This was way, *way* beyond cold.

I blinked to shake off the icicles hanging from my eyelashes and attempted to dry off with a beach towel. I studied the nylon leggings I'd donned that morning. They had provided an extra layer of warmth during our wait and our brief dip. Regrettably, I'd slipped them on *beneath* my swimsuit—instead of wearing them over it. They were now impossible to remove without flashing the crowd. They clung to my legs, trapping a layer of frigid wetness from my waist to my ankles.

In the car on the way home, Cole reached down to take off his cleats. His shoe strings were frozen into solid knots.

As we slowly thawed, our bodies exploded into pins and needles. It would take two days before our body temperature felt normal.

I languished for fifteen minutes in a steaming shower, drank a cup of hot mocha in front of the fireplace, and reflected on the highs and lows—literally—of my day.

What struck me as most inconceivable was that three hundred other people had also gone for a winter dip that day. I wasn't sure if this was reassuring or just plain frightening. Many of these crazy folks had wandered away from the riverfront, chatting about returning next year.

Me?

It would be a cold day in hell before I *ever* jumped in another frozen river.

Chapter 33:

TURN ME ON

Video may have killed the radio star, yet I figured no video would be necessary to kill my new, midlife radio career. All it would take was two hours of stuttering, stammering, and awkward silence.

I'd been asked to appear on *The Theme Park*, an eclectic two-hour show on WXUT/88.3 FM, the radio station of The University of Toledo. The hosts, Tim and Vicki, had been doing this weekly show together for twelve years. They were old pros, but they had never invited a guest host until now. If I bombed, I was sure to be both their first and their last.

My ability to entertain a radio audience on an early Saturday morning wasn't promising. Weekends found me seldom dragging myself out of bed before ten. I managed to slurp down one Diet Coke on the drive to the station and finished off two more in the first hour. Still, I felt undercaffeinated and foggy. I hoped my fear-fueled adrenalin would carry me through.

Tim and Vicki started out the show with a few songs and then, after a quick introduction, Vicki turned to me. "So, tell us about The 52/52 Project," she said.

It was a logical opening question, one which most interviewees would have anticipated and been prepared to answer. However, my mouth simply dropped and hung open.

"Umm," I managed to reply. Vicki and I stared at each other in a moment of dead air. She smiled encouragingly. I shook off my knot of nerves, gathered my wits, and followed up with another, far more thoughtful, "Umm."

But my co-hosts' expertise soon helped calm my anxiety. Their easy conversation brushed over much of my stuttering and stammering, and it filled any moments of silence that would have stretched on if I were left to my own devices.

And, the two of them were so freaking fun—and funny!

Since it was primarily a music show, interspersed with their delightful banter, I wasn't forced to fill the whole two hours with additional clever variations of "Umm." Thank God. If I failed to help entertain their audience, at least their listeners would be in good on-air hands.

As suggested by the show's name, each week of *The Theme Park* centered on a particular theme. Past ones included The Smell Show, Bad Hair Day, and The Cowbell Show. This week, they'd asked me to help choose music related to The 52/52 Project.

Thanks to their imagination and extensive music collection, we featured a diverse assortment of both popular and obscure songs. Some were tied to specific experiences, such as "Wedding Bell Blues" by the 5th Dimension (a nod to my wedding-crashing episode) and even a snippet from *The Karate Kid*: "Wax on, Wax off." (Let's hear it for my Brazilian wax.)

Other tunes related more generally to The 52/52 Project, including "I Wouldn't Normally Do This Kind of Thing" by the Pet Shop Boys, "Dare to Be Stupid" by Weird Al Yankovic, and "Undignified Ways to Die" by Bob & Tom. I tried not to take Tim and Vicki's selections too personally.

While the music carried me through much of the two-hour gig, I did make my share of radio newbie mistakes. More than once, I began babbling to my studio cohorts when I believed—mistakenly—that our microphones were turned off. *Sigh.*

In addition, I'd forgotten that the station's Internet link, for those streaming the show, was also accompanied by a studio video image.

My mother later reported that she lost count of how many times she saw me adjust my bra strap.

Regardless, I sensed my on-air performance improved as the time passed. The caffeine gradually kicked in, and I settled into a more coherent and relaxed groove. While I delved into relaying some of my best and worst 52/52 experiences, I even managed a handful of witty comments.

As Vicki and I walked to our cars in the parking lot, I cracked open another can of Diet Coke and called the morning a success. I'd tackled my fear of public speaking, albeit in front of a mostly invisible audience. I only hoped they tuned in at my more articulate moments.

A few listeners contacted me later and told me I did A-OK. Gracious of them. I popped their checks in the mail.

But, to anyone who happened to view the live video stream and saw me staring blankly, dribbling Diet Coke down my chin, or obsessively readjusting my bra strap—keep in mind the camera adds ten pounds of humiliation.

Chapter 34:

IT'S ALL HAPPENING AT THE ZOO

Next to a good Bloody Mary, I love animals most of all. (And next to my family, *of course*. Ahem.)

I'd always had a terrific rapport with animals. At my very first high school job, working concessions at the Toledo Zoo, I spent my lunch hours tossing Hostess pies through a steel-barred cage to my favorite chimpanzee, Cocoa. In return, sweet Cocoa always threw a pile of shit at me.

Nearly thirty years later, I realized I had much to learn about reciprocal friendships, as well as about feeding and caring for zoo animals. Serving as zookeeper for a day would teach me that while small cages were thankfully a thing of the past and Hostess pies were now off-limits entirely, piles of poop remained a perennial zoo fixture.

I had toilet-trained two boys and cleaned up after my own pet menagerie for years. Dealing with zoo-doo, which I indeed mastered that day, wasn't the most challenging aspect of this new experience.

No, the moment that prompted me to question my ability to love and care for all animals on God's Good Earth was when I peered over the open enclosure of a hissing Chinese alligator.

I had no idea what kind of creatures I'd meet or what tasks I'd be handling when Tana—my contact at the Toledo Zoo—spoke to her boss, who spoke to his boss, who finally agreed to my request for an up-close encounter with zoo animals. All I knew was that an alligator encounter wasn't what I anticipated. Couldn't I just cuddle a koala?

Steve, the knowledgeable zoo guide assigned to accompany me, attempted reassurance. He told me that at just under four feet long, Mu Shu the Chinese alligator was considered a runt. Whatever. The gator's size mattered little when he hissed and bared his teeth at me.

I leaped back. "Heh-heh-heh. Cute little guy. Um, any chance he could jump out of this open tank?"

"Probably," Steve said. "But only if he really wanted to."

Steve was a fabulous tour guide, but he'd be wise to steer clear of a career as a motivational speaker.

My job was to feed this menacing reptile. I was counting on breakfast being a bowlful of kibble. My heart sunk when, instead of pointing to a bag of Purina Alligator Chow, Steve gestured toward two dead mice on the counter.

Sure, they were tiny rodents that many people considered vermin. But I was the kind of weak-hearted sucker who, when discovering dozens of mice nesting in my garage, couldn't bring myself to poison or trap-snap the necks of a single one. I live-trapped and released them all in a farm field a few miles from my subdivision. Mea culpa, Waterville farmers.

I braced myself for the task at hand. As Elton John sang so profoundly in *The Lion King*, this was the circle of life. I told myself I was only playing my necessary part. Fortunately, I wasn't forced to hold the mice by their limp, pink tails. Steve handed me a pair of jumbo tweezers. I clutched a mouse in the forceps and dangled it into the exhibit.

It took some prodding by Steve before Mu Shu spied the mouse. Once he did, he stretched, snapped his long jaws shut, and swallowed it whole. I jumped back. His squinty eyes met my wide ones. Apparently the mouse had only whetted Mu Shu's appetite. He stared back at me, still hungry.

Far better a dead mouse clenched within his jaw than my hand ending up there. I loaded up his second helping. I had no sooner begun to lower the mouse into the pool before Mu Shu lunged and grabbed it, nearly taking the forceps with it. He gulped it down and eyed me again. I hoped it would only take a couple minutes for him to realize his stomach was full and I wasn't dessert.

Steve told me only about a hundred Chinese alligators still existed in the wild, mainly due to the pollution in the Yangtze River. These animals could likely become extinct, and zoos like this one were doing their best to maintain a population. I gazed down at Mu Shu with sudden sympathy for his extended family's sad fate.

Even as I was filled with an unexpected affection for this creature, I was happy to move on. Until I saw our next stop was in front of the snake enclosures.

I'd never had a serious fear of snakes. Running across them in the wild didn't frighten me, although my encounters in northwest Ohio had always been with the small and harmless garter snake variety.

Holding a huge ball python, while it curled around my arm, proved to be a slightly different story.

Steve told me to relax and let the snake rest against my arm, wrapping around it like a tree branch. I cradled the python for a few minutes, stroked his silky skin, and admired his beautiful markings. Then, the snake craned his head and hissed at me. As our eyes met, his forked tongue flickered. I thrust him back at Steve.

"OK, we're good to go now," I said. "We can check snakes off our list."

"Oh, he wouldn't hurt you," Steve said, putting the python back in his exhibit. "He's really a good boy."

I eyed the snake. No reason to push my luck. I believe snakes deserve their place in our world: in zoos, in the wild, perhaps even in my own backyard. But just inches from my face? A definitive nope.

As we left the reptile area, I overheard two employees in the zoo's educational center say they were leaving "to take the dingoes for a walk." I could barely contain my excitement.

"Wait, you actually walk dingoes—on a leash?" I asked. They explained the dingoes were young, fairly tame, and being trained for educational shows. We followed them over to the theater for a training session.

The Toledo Zoo obtained the year-and-a-half-old animals when they were five months old. Dingoes, native to Australia, look somewhat like small German shepherds or cattle dogs. Their claim to fame was a viral news headline many years back: "The Dingo Ate My Baby." (Final verdict: It really did.) I felt *pretty* sure neither of these creatures was that exact same dingo. And I was fairly confident I was way too big for one of them to carry me away as dinner.

Steve said the male, Indigo, was skittish, but the female, Tawny, was friendlier. Sure enough, the trainer allowed Tawny to walk right up to me. She sniffed me a couple times and promptly began licking my hand. I whispered to her that I was very sweet but I was certain I wouldn't taste good.

As the lick-fest continued, I realized Tawny apparently just liked me. *Aww!* I instinctively leaned my head in close and began murmuring in baby talk to her, as I do with my dog, Ringo the Wonder Retriever.

Steve yanked me back and shook his head.

"Not so close to your face," he warned.

Oops. Right. Tawny appeared tame and well-trained,

but she was still a naturally wild animal. I'd have hated for the title of this story to read, "The Dingo Ate My Face."

I worked that day with several other animals, including wallabies and a gorgeous kookaburra that I actually heard laugh. (I neglected to ask if he was sitting in an old gum tree.) I spent the bulk of my zookeeper stint, however, with two white rhinos.

As I tiptoed into their pen, I mentally cued the charging rhinoceros scene from the movie *Jumanji*.

Probably no such worries with laid-back Sam and Lulu, who at forty-one and forty-six were considered geriatric. Even so, Robin, their caretaker, noted, "That doesn't mean they couldn't crush you." A fair statement, with each of them weighing in at close to four thousand pounds.

I helped Robin prepare their breakfast. Thankfully, this menu included no dead mice. Their meal was a combination of what did indeed resemble Rhino Chow, along with hay, fresh fruit, and various vitamins and nutrients. Because rhinos have a heightened sense of smell and enjoy a variety of scents, Robin said she also sprinkled their enclosures with an assortment of odiferous items, including fresh basil leaves and Aqua Velva aftershave.

My duties included shoveling rhino poo. It was, literally, some heavy shit. And it did not smell a bit like Aqua Velva.

I squirted, soaped, and scrubbed the floors and walls of Lulu's enclosure while she ate breakfast. Meanwhile, Sam grew restless. He rattled the bars with his huge horn. Robin reprimanded him, and he momentarily paused. But when she walked away to gather additional supplies, he started back up.

"No, Sam," I shouted. "Stop it! Be a good boy!" He stared at me and stood still. I blinked. Huh. Why had this kind of verbal discipline never worked with my cats—or my two sons?

Next, it was bath time. I squirted down Sam, who backed his butt up against the bars, enjoying this daily routine.

Robin looked on and nodded. "Good job. You handle a hose better than most people."

Haha! I laughed, and Robin looked at me blankly. Oh, she probably meant the rubber garden variety of hose.

We continued the rhinos' spa day with an exfoliating treatment. While I had always envisioned rhinos as scaly creatures, their skin is naturally smooth except for tufts of protruding hair. A rhino's scales are simply dead skin cells that need to be sloughed off. I rubbed Sam's back with a rubber mitt brush, and bits of dead, scabby skin flew off.

I moved on from rubbing his side to his left lower hip. Sam collapsed against the bars, in seeming ecstasy with his massage. Suddenly, he lifted his left back leg. I stepped back.

"Oh! I think he's going to pee!"

"Um, no," Robin said. "See his *equipment* down there? This is similar to how we manually ejaculate him."

I squinted at Sam's "equipment." Perhaps I was *too* good at this particular job. Or maybe the Aqua Velva was making him feel a bit sexy. Clearly, Sam the rhinoceros was one horny old dude.

I switched positions and began exfoliating his back instead. Sam might have become my new best friend, but we wouldn't be friends with benefits.

After we finished Sam's spa treatment, Robin suggested we reward him with some treats. I hesitated before reaching out with a handful of rhino kibble.

"Don't worry, he doesn't have front incisors," Robin told me. I cringed as he sucked my entire fist into his mouth—a gigantic wet vacuum. I laughed a bit nervously, but at least I knew Sam's slobber was worse than his bite.

"But his back molars," Robin continued, "could still do some damage." I yanked my hand from his lips.

Sam proved to be a gentle giant indeed. I patted his horn and told him he was a good boy, never minding his one minor indiscretion that day.

I left the zoo with fond memories of my new animal friends, a wealth of knowledge, and an appreciation for all the work done behind the scenes each day at the Toledo Zoo.

And, I added "I gave a rhinoceros an erection" to the list of things I never, *ever* thought I'd hear myself say.

Chapter 35:

LET IT ROLL

*A*s I premeditated and executed my list of new endeavors, life—as it does—carried on. Occasionally, a planned experience dropped off the list and something unintended found its way on. One such unexpected venture resulted from a late night phone call from Son #2.

It wasn't the mad dash out of town for my twenty-two-year-old's emergency surgery that was so noteworthy. Nor my unforeseen overnight stay in a renovated Milwaukee brewery. Not even my cleaning the apartment bathroom of two young bachelors. All three were indeed new life experiences, only one which I ever care to repeat.

What made the weekend trip list-worthy is that I rode for six hours, alone in the car, with my former husband.

George and I had remained friendlier than most divorced couples I knew. Spending Christmas mornings together with our sons while they opened gifts had remained a fairly comfortable annual tradition, since our attention was focused on our children. But our relationship was nowhere near the take-a-roadtrip-together level. This car ride was by far the longest amount of time we'd spent together without our children in almost fifteen years. A drive across four states—with no children or holiday festivities to provide buffers—could only prove to be awkward, at best.

No surprise we spent the bulk of our drive time talking about our two sons. While George and I still lived in the same town and remained in frequent contact mostly due to our children, our lives had branched off in two different directions. What we still shared in common were points of pride and concerns about our young adult sons.

We discussed their jobs, interests, personality differences and similarities, and dating lives. (The last item was all conjecture, since they seldom provided *any* details about that). As we passed snow-covered farm fields in Ohio, Indiana, Illinois, and Wisconsin, our conversation turned toward other topics.

We shared news about our careers, our extended families, and the new houses we'd each recently purchased. It struck me as sadly surreal to talk about our new and separate homes, only months after I sold the house we'd built together and once assumed we'd grow old in, together.

We fell quiet for a few stretches along the road. Was he, like I was, silently reflecting on our once happy past and on our failed future as a couple?

I felt obliged to ask him about his girlfriend of seven years, Julie, a nice-enough woman I'd met a few times. He asked me about my writing and about The 52/52 Project. I relayed a few of my experiences, and he grinned and nodded.

"You're a good writer," he said.

I shrugged and said thank you. I asked him about his business, the company he started after we separated. I told him he should be proud of taking it to such phenomenal success. It was his turn to shrug and say thank you.

Through our somewhat disconnected relationship, we had still managed to appreciate the other's talents and accomplishments. What we were less proud of and never discussed, of course, were each of our weaknesses and failings: the kind of things that break up a marriage and split apart a family.

Those had been discussed too many times, too many years ago. The passing years had clarified some of my own mistakes, and possibly had done the same for him. But enlightenment cannot change our past. It serves us best by guiding our future.

As we veered into a discussion about our children's finances, we clearly disagreed—with no compromise in sight. We both fell quiet. I stared out the window. I wondered if he was thinking, as I was, "Yes, *this*. This inability to see the other's point of view. This is why we didn't work."

We moved on. Why was it less difficult now to detour around a singular dispute and manage to let it go, than it had been fifteen years ago?

After arriving in Milwaukee, we saw Son #2 through his appendix surgery and first couple days of recovery. George and I ate dinner together at a nearby restaurant. We both stayed at a hotel right across from our son's apartment, in separate rooms, of course. The desk clerk appeared confused when we checked in at the same time, under the same name.

"Oh, honey," I wanted to tell him. "Trust me, this whole thing is even weirder for us."

But the drive to Milwaukee and the two days that followed were nothing compared to what I found myself facing on the trip home, when I inadvertently upped the ante of the challenge.

George, whose position as owner and president of a company allowed him more flexibility than my job did, stayed behind a few extra days to take care of our son. I returned to Toledo via Amtrak.

And, I spent most of that return trip sitting on a train seat next to my former husband's current girlfriend.

While my ex and I had been attending to our appen-
dix-afflicted son in Wisconsin, George's girlfriend, Julie, had
been attending her daughter's bachelorette party just an hour
south in Chicago. What were the odds she'd be departing
Chicago the same evening I was leaving Milwaukee, and she
would be taking my own connecting train back to Toledo?

George realized we'd be on the same train and mentioned this to Son #2, who was still recuperating from surgery. Whether influenced by narcotics or youthful optimism,
Son of Mine thought we might like to connect. He texted
that Julie was looking for me in Chicago's Union Station.

My encounters with Julie had always been within a group,
and we'd never exchanged more than a few bits of dialogue.
She had seemed nice enough. But we definitely weren't *friends*.

I sipped my Bloody Mary in Union Station as I contemplated this. Would I have made this same effort to connect
with *her*? I wasn't so sure. I had to give Julie credit for reaching out, even if she felt swayed by obligation. I told my son
to forward her my cell phone number.

Five minutes later, I found myself sitting next to her
on a bench. We waited out our train's delay and eventually
boarded, together.

Julie's daughters had provided her with a couple bottles
of wine, which were stuffed into her overnight bag. I wondered if this was her family's normal protocol, or if the gesture was provided *after* they learned her boyfriend's ex-wife
might be along for the ride.

No matter. She popped open a bottle, and we began
chatting as we rode the rails through the Midwest.

We talked nonstop for more than four hours. We
mostly discussed current events, our children, and our jobs.
We didn't talk much about the man who was our common
denominator. Even over wine, I think we both sensed that
could be a slippery slope.

Julie proved to be intelligent, funny, and delightful. Who'd have guessed? Not me. I'd had no idea, since I'd always kept her at arm's length, like the code of behavior generally dictated for these kinds of relationships.

But why wouldn't she be terrific? Clearly, my ex always had great taste in women.

Somewhere in Indiana, Julie uncorked the second bottle of wine. Not because we still needed it for liquid courage, but just because we were, well, thirsty.

By the time we pulled into Toledo, a huge snowstorm had brewed. Julie and I each called for a cab, but the weather had resulted in major taxi delays. A friendly couple I had met in the Chicago station, who happened to live in a small town near my Toledo suburb, offered me a ride home.

Could they give my friend, Julie, a ride, too?

When we dropped her off at her downtown Toledo condo, Julie and I hugged each other goodbye. Damned if we hadn't become, well, friends. Not the kind to call each other for a girls' night out, surely to George's relief. But the kind with whom I'd find myself comfortably conversing and laughing, the next time I saw her.

Some experiences and some relationships are only as awkward and uncomfortable as we allow them to be. When we open ourselves up to it, life is full of strange surprises.

Sometimes, we just need to roll with it, right down the highway.

Chapter 36:

TIPTOE THROUGH THE
TULIPS WITH ME

*A*s a child of the sixties and seventies, I was weaned on scary movies. Just like our parents allowed us to chase after mosquito control trucks—shrieking and giggling through the toxic fog—they also didn't monitor the movies or TV shows we watched. We were free, at a young age, to poison our lungs *and* our brains. Maybe it was due to our parents' innocence or ignorance. Or maybe they were just too busy bowling or playing cards to pay us any heed.

I endured all the horror classics of my youth. These included *The Omen*, *The Exorcist*, and *The Other*. But through the years, what continued to haunt me most were any films featuring an aged and categorically creepy Bette Davis.

I never recovered from *Whatever Happened to Baby Jane?* I still can't listen to the song "Bette Davis Eyes" without seeing Bette turn to Joan Crawford, who was mid-bite through her sister's thoughtfully prepared meal of what appeared to be chicken. "Oh, Blanche," Bette said oh-so-nonchalantly, "You know we've got rats in the cellar?"

Sometime around my twenties, I grew weary of shielding my eyes from horrific images and trying to erase disturbing dialogue from my mind as I lay awake in bed. The blood and gore didn't trouble me; it was the psychological terror I couldn't handle. The last horror flick I watched was the 1990 TV mini-series of Stephen King's *It*. Thanks to Pennywise, I never watched another scary movie. And clowns haven't been able to find work since.

So, at the age of fifty-two, I decided to test my heightened wimpy level by spending a night watching horror films. My challenge was to stay up the entire night—until sunrise—watching scary movies nonstop. And, I had to do so while totally alone in the house.

If that weren't enough, my mother suggested that I raise the stakes by keeping all my blinds open and my doors unlocked. Thanks for that, oh sweet, nurturing mother of mine. (Note to self: Be sure to finagle an excuse when Mom invites me over for a "chicken" dinner.)

I armed myself with a twelve-pack of Diet Coke to keep me awake and alert, as well as every form of junk food known to gradually kill a human being. If I died of fright, I'd do so while binging on Oreos and chips and dip.

I also advised Ringo the Wonder Retriever that he was on watch duty. After years of his explosive barking at such dire threats as tricycle-riding toddlers or the UPS guy making a delivery across the street, now was his chance to put his skills to good use.

With suggestions by Son #1 and several readers, my horror fest lineup included *The Ring*, *The Blair Witch Project*, *Paranormal Activity*, and *Insidious*. WARNING: The rest of this story contains plot spoilers. If you haven't yet watched but were still planning to see these movies, I apologize. If you have already seen them all and are some type of wacked-out horror film aficionado, I suggest you seek professional help.

Shortly into *The Ring*, I watched as the main character popped the clearly murderous tape into her VCR.

"No, don't watch the video!" I shouted.

Her phone rang, and she eyed it in hesitation.

"NO! Do not answer the phone!" I screamed.

Just as she picked up the phone anyway (*Why?* WHY, I asked her, did you watch that damn tape, and WHY are you answering your phone when you know better?), my own phone rang.

I gawked, frozen-faced, across the coffee table at my phone. It was after 11 p.m. No one ever called me this late. Was it possible that just viewing that deadly tape, *within the movie displayed on my TV screen*, was enough to curse me? Was I, too, now doomed to die in seven days?

No, it was just my mother calling.

Of *course* it was her. And, also, *thank God*, it was her.

"Hi, honey. I just wondered how your movies were going," she said. "Anything really scary so far?"

I sighed. "Mostly this phone call."

After we hung up, I set my ringer on silent. If some evil being *did* call to announce I'd be dead in a week, I'd let the frigging phone go straight to voice mail.

A few minutes later, Ringo began pacing the house, barking frantically. I had let him out to do his business just before the movie started. I paused the video and chewed my bottom lip. I turned on the front porch light and peeked outside: No tricycles or UPS guys in sight. I perused the back yard through the sliding glass patio door: Nothing lurking out back, at least not within the light from my deck.

I let Ringo out, slammed the door shut, and stalled a few minutes before I peered around the curtain again.

Did I mention my yard backs up to a cemetery?

I squinted through the glass, scoping out the blackness beyond my patch of lawn. The graveyard was secluded, bordered by woods and cornfields. A perfect venue for zombies, ghosts, and Children of the Corn.

Ringo patrolled the yard and finally stopped to pee. Once I ascertained no straggly-haired demon had jumped out from behind a tombstone and was waiting nearby, I quickly ushered the dog inside. Then, I locked the door and closed the curtains. Screw my mother's added challenge to the night.

The Ring proved to be way freaky. Maybe not quite as bad as I envisioned—but only because I envisioned really, *really* bad. SPOILER: The evil, immortal little girl in the film had me rocking and hugging myself several times. Still, I figured if the main characters endured a series of awful events yet didn't die some horrible death, it was practically a Hallmark movie.

Next up was *The Blair Witch Project.* Only twenty minutes into this film, I was so annoyed by the three main characters' constant whining and bickering and bad decision-making— especially the girl with the over-the-top sobbing, who was to blame for half the shit that befell them—that I *prayed* someone would kill them.

SPOILER: I found little intriguing or frightening about this movie, except for the last few seconds. Jesus, Mary, and Joseph! What just happened? The final cellar scene provided ingenious and enduring shock value. And, any parents out there looking for a sure-fire punishment for your wayward young children? Make them watch this movie and then send them to the corner for a time-out. They will never misbehave again.

Paranormal Activity was another pseudo-documentary format film. I didn't totally hate the two main characters, but I couldn't conjure up any love for them either. Especially the husband, who lost me at his first moment of stupid.

SPOILER: They both die. And I didn't much care. But I did make a note to permanently seal the ceiling hatch to my attic.

By the time I got to *Insidious*, at nearly 4:30 in the morning, I'd learned a bit about what really engaged and frightened me in horror movies. Perhaps it was the writer in me, but I needed likeable characters who eventually got screwed over, a tight plot without pointless and irritating dialogue, and lots of shocking "*Oh shit*" moments.

Insidious had this all, as well as a childlike demon-creature dancing to "Tiptoe through the Tulips." As if the song's original singer, Tiny Tim, wasn't creepy enough. *Shudder*. The movie was so intense that I actually screamed a couple times, most notably when my Internet faltered and the movie began buffering in the most nail-biting scene.

I panic-popped potato chips all during *Insidious*. If I hadn't sworn off alcohol for the night, vodka shots definitely would have been in order. SPOILER: Just when you think it's a happy ending, it is *so* not.

I finished up my night of film fright around 6:30 a.m. Staying awake until dawn didn't prove to be much of an added challenge. Even in my middle age, I apparently was still a night owl. Who says all-night college parties don't help prepare you for real life?

Although my horror fest elicited a number of heart palpitations, I never once hid beneath a blanket nor seriously toyed with the idea of turning off the TV. I was proud how I powered through this scary chapter of my life. Maybe I could finally put this particular fear behind me.

Before I headed off to bed, just after sunrise, I watched two episodes of *Parks and Recreation*. I might have felt braver than I had ten hours earlier, but I figured a good laugh would lull me to sleep better than any death screams lingering in my head.

As I lay in bed though, I tossed for hours. I wanted to blame it on the Diet Coke and onion dip. But truth be told, I remained plagued by the refrain of "Tiptoe through the Tulips." Weeks later, I still couldn't get that disturbing song—nor the image of the demon child dancing to it—out of my brain.

I might never sleep again.

Because somewhere in an alternate horror universe, I know that Tiny Tim, Pennywise the clown, and Bette Davis are holding hands, singing, and dancing in a circle. You can bet those evil fuckers are laughing at my expense.

Chapter 37:

STRANGER THINGS HAVE HAPPENED

Once upon a time in a youth far, far ago, I enjoyed a reputation as a fabulous party host. In fact, much to my mother's bewilderment, my high school senior class voted me Best Party Giver.

"I don't get it," she said upon reading this news in the school paper. "When did you have parties?"

I was nearly eighteen and would be starting college that fall; I figured I had little to lose by fessing up. I shrugged, allowing a little smirk. "Um, every time you and Dad weren't home."

Other than her raised eyebrows, my mom appeared unruffled by the news. But apparently, she tucked away this bit of knowledge and chose to get her revenge twenty-five years later by dropping this bomb on my fourteen-year-old son. Over the next four years, Son #1 used it as justification for every unsanctioned party he threw. Thanks for that, maternal traitor of mine.

Eventually though, my *own* party skills nose-dived. Most of the parties I held after my twenties entailed juice boxes, pin the tail on the donkey, and little boys peeing their pants while waiting in line for the piñata.

My plans to throw a terrific shindig at the age of fifty-two presented a number of new challenges—the biggest one being that this was a "Stranger Party," and I wouldn't know a single person.

I formed my guest list by asking several friends and coworkers to invite someone. The rules were these: We could never have met (not even online); they couldn't know each other; and they had to attend alone, not even accompanied by the mutual friend who invited them. My own trepidation surely paled in comparison to theirs. They would need to be brave souls, indeed.

My next challenge was to plan a party while knowing virtually nothing about the guests. Unlike my high school and college years, supplying a couple bags of Doritos and asking everyone to pitch in for a keg no longer seemed a safe bet. I bought an assortment of alcoholic beverages and soft drinks, and prepared a huge feast catering to every taste and diet. After all, this was the new millennium. Someone was sure to require vegan, low-carb, or gluten-free.

My mom forgave my youthful misdeeds and helped me tackle my woeful windows and mopboards. I planned games, including the ever-popular "Two Truths and a Lie," to break the ice and break up the inevitable long lulls in conversation.

As prepared as possible, I awaited my new stranger friends. But that night, the Hellacious Winter That Would Never End tossed another storm our way. The phone calls began pouring in as guests battled the blowing snow into the boonies of Waterville, Ohio. A few were having trouble fighting the elements, and one took a wrong turn and got lost for hours. Surely, at least a couple would conclude an uncomfortable evening with strangers at the home of a woman—who, as far as they knew, could be clinically insane—was not worth the effort.

Yet, all seven persevered. That alone proved this would be a remarkable group of women.

Yes, we were all women. Although I'd encouraged my friends and coworkers to invite men as well as women, all the takers were female.

Besides our gender, we shared few similarities. We ranged in age from twenty-two to seventy-four. Our occupations ran the gamut from teacher to realtor to church office manager. We were divorced, married, and single. One had young twins, others had grandchildren, and the youngest was a recent college graduate still living with her parents.

These details came out early, during small talk over wine, stuffed mushrooms, and smoked salmon. "Two Truths and a Lie" did indeed break the ice. (We all *so* wanted to believe that Susan had truly slept with Frank Sinatra.) But our small talk segued, *amazingly* fast, into much more.

We waded into deeper topics, including the socially taboo trifecta of social, political, and religious issues. We each shared our thoughts, with a twinge of outward unease only in the most passionate discussions, particularly about abortion and the last presidential election.

What none of us expected was that we'd so openly share our most embarrassing personal experiences, like one woman's horrific "burning crotch" anecdote and another's tale about the huge spit bubble she produced while engaging with a prospective date.

We roared in laughter and nodded in empathy. We begged each other for other personal confessions, and our new friends didn't disappoint.

What was *happening*? I'd never been at a party like this, never met people quite like these. We conversed and grinned and hugged all evening, as if we'd been lifelong friends. We all agreed it was the most immediate and closest connection we'd ever felt with a group of new people.

Perhaps the pool of guests was already narrowed to our advantage. After all, who else but a fairly outgoing or courageous individual attends an intimate dinner party, alone, with total strangers? We discussed how the course of the evening might have changed if a man had joined our group. Did the fact that we were all women make a difference in our ability to be so open and fully engaged?

Or, did we feel we had nothing to lose by sharing so much of our private selves with people we figured we'd never see again?

We held back little, and no one seemed self-conscious or embarrassed by much. Well, no one except the hostess, who was so busy accommodating guests and drinking wine (and wine-drinking was *not* her forte) that she forgot to eat.

Somewhere in between asking my new friends to challenge themselves that night with their own experiences of dining in the dark and eating insects and my next plan for them to try their hand at belly dancing in my living room, the evening grew blurry. While my fortitude for new experiences had been growing in leaps and bounds, my wine tolerance remained pitiful.

The next morning, as I tried to recollect the foggy conclusion of our evening, I sent off an email to them all. I thanked them, apologized for being "over-served," and said I hoped we still shared the love. A heartwarming thread of emails flew for days.

"I had more fun with you 'strange' ladies than I have had at any party I have ever attended."

"I can honestly say I've not enjoyed myself like that in quite some time."

"We did agree that 'What happens at the Stranger Party, stays at the Stranger Party,' right?" All of us, particularly me, breathed a sigh of relief at that.

And, finally, this email: "Each one of you is so unique and has so much to contribute to this group, which I suggest we call 'The 52 Club,'" she wrote. She suggested this single experience was worthy of a book in itself for me to write: "Our story of eight ladies of diverse backgrounds and ages, and the developing friendships that ensued."

Perhaps she hit upon something there, because our story didn't end that night.

We began to meet monthly, catching up on news of each other's jobs, families, and dating experiences. Each get-together recaptured the warmth and fellowship of that first night. Our evenings together gradually grew more sporadic, as happens with even the best of friends. One member in our group moved out of state. Two of us were diagnosed with cancer—and beat the hell out of it. And both our twenty-two-year-old friend and our rock star *seventy-four-year-old* friend found new romances.

Even so, as time passed and circumstances changed, we remained closely connected. I have a feeling we always will. And even if six months go by before The 52 Club gathers again, that just means we will have more to talk about.

Is it possible for a group of strangers, brought together for a single night as part of one woman's odd personal journey, to become lifelong friends?

Stranger things have happened.

Chapter 38:

WE ALL FLOAT DOWN HERE

y last several adventures had gone swimmingly. Sure,
I experienced some residual hiccups, but on a bravery
scale of one to ten, I was feeling about an eight. And that sort
of cockiness, as anyone knows, is precisely when the Gods of
Fear and Humility show up to knock you on your ass.

As I faced my newest exploit, I felt only a tad uneasy
about testing the waters: even though that water would be
pooled below me, in a dark and soundproof tank.

I was uncertain how I'd react to spending an hour inside a
flotation tank—commonly known as an isolation tank or a sen-
sory deprivation tank. I'd been under more stress than usual,
so I hoped the session would live up to its purported mission
of inducing relaxation, meditation, and increased creativity.

Even so, the devil on my shoulder whispered that floating in a tiny, closed chest of salt water—while virtually blind
and deaf—*might* feel akin to being buried alive. At the bottom of the ocean.

This experience would either relax me into a nearly coma-
tose state, or it would put me over the edge entirely. I chose to

bet on the optimistic slant, partly because I'd never been claustrophobic and also because I was reality-challenged.

I found the nearest tank at a progressive health center a half hour away. Calling to make an appointment, I was told the schedule was wide open all week. That should have served as a bright red flag. I may not have been claustrophobic, but perhaps I was color blind.

The receptionist suggested I bring soap and shampoo, since I'd be required to shower both before and after my session. In addition, she said the eight hundred pounds of salt in the water, which provided the buoyancy to allow a person to float, could irritate the skin. She advised me not to shave my legs for a couple days before my appointment.

Shave my legs? I snorted. Apparently, she'd forgotten this was February. In northwest Ohio.

The isolation tank, appropriately, was situated in a locked room in a remote area in the back of the building. The assistant showed me how to set the timer before I entered the tank. She assured me that even while lying inside a sound-proof vat and wearing wax earplugs to keep out the salt water, I'd hear the alarm signaling when my time was up.

If I wanted to quit sooner for any reason, she said I could simply open the lid and call it a day. I shrugged. Good information to know, but I was a gamer. I told myself I'd stay the full hour in order to get the maximum experience.

After showering, I set the timer, climbed in, and shut the hatch.

Floating in the silent darkness of the small tank, I attempted to close out the world while opening my mind. A few things became immediately clear.

LESSON #1: Time passes *slowwwwly* when you're lying in a sightless and soundless tank of water.

LESSON #2: If you've been experiencing sinus or upper respiratory issues, the humidity inside a closed tank of warm water will rise enough to induce an acute asthma attack.

LESSON #3: Time stands still entirely when you cannot breathe.

Roughly ten minutes had passed when my lungs began to give in to defeat. I reasoned only a few moments remained before certain asphyxiation.

I blinked my eyes open and twisted my head to look around, as if this could help in the pitch black. I began splashing and crawling my way to the opposite end of the tank. It suddenly seemed way bigger than it looked from the outside. I groped around for the exit hatch, seemed to locate it, and pushed.

The lid didn't budge. I pushed again. And again. Nothing.

And then, my asthma morphed into a full-blown panic attack. Or at least what I imagined a panic attack to feel like, since I had never experienced one. Manic heart rate? Check. Inability to breathe? Check. Inability to find a way out of a life-threatening situation? Check.

I thrashed around the dark vat of water. Even within this small space, I became increasingly disoriented. I contemplated screaming, but I knew no one in the front office would hear me from inside a soundproof box in a locked, remote room out back. I had the last scheduled appointment in the tank that day. How much time would pass after the evening's last massage or yoga session before someone might casually ask a coworker, "Hey, whatever happened to that weird lady in the flotation tank? Did you see her leave?"

Worse yet, I suddenly envisioned Pennywise the clown, from Stephen King's *It*, grinning at me with a mouthful of razor-sharp teeth and growling, "We all float down here!"

I was pretty certain no one would find my mangled, salt-encrusted body until the next morning, after it had mysteriously drifted from the shallow waters of the tank to land, floating inside a street sewer.

Just as I began to give in to the futility of my fate, my hands clawed one last time at the walls of the tank. And then, I finally found the hatch—the *actual* escape hatch! I pushed it open.

Bright light and a rush of fresh air greeted me. I jumped out, dripping and hyperventilating.

Once I was able to breathe again, I calmed and recollected myself. I had escaped. I was breathing. And, Pennywise was nowhere in sight.

I glanced at the timer. I still had about forty-five minutes left in my session. I couldn't quit now, especially since I knew what to expect and I had discovered the *real* way out. I sucked in a few more deep breaths and then sucked up my courage, too. I closed the lid again, this time committing its location to memory.

Five minutes later, I found myself scrambling once again for air. Holy hell! There was no chance of a successful end to this experience if I suffocated partway through it.

I cracked the hatch and gulped in fresh air. I lay inside the partially opened vat as I contemplated my next move. With my earplugs and closed eyes, the room remained dark and quiet. Was that sufficient to count toward completing the challenge? Or was it cheating? Surely this modified experience, along with the time I already spent inside the fully closed tank, still counted. And, now that I could breathe, I might finally achieve that carefree meditative state.

I tried to leave my mind blank. I sang soothing songs in my head. I tried to find my "happy place." While I attempted to relax, I instead found myself pondering everything on my extensive to-do list. I contemplated all the work, writing, and

SHERRY STANFA-STANLEY ○ 215

personal tasks that had plagued me into a state of stress for the past couple of weeks. With so much on my agenda, what the hell was I doing, wasting my afternoon lying inside a vat of warm salt water?

Whether I was just too tightly wound that day or whether my asthma attack had thwarted my ability to relax, I finally allowed myself to climb out, halfway through my allotted time.

I was forced to admit that floating in a tank simply didn't float my boat.

Apparently, I wasn't alone in my disenchantment. As I left the center, I noticed a sign posted on the front desk: "Flotation Tank for Sale: $8,000. Comes with all equipment and 100 pounds of salt." I'd save my money for a Jacuzzi.

A year later, with this experience long behind me and nearly forgotten, I found myself scheduled for an MRI. When I checked in, the hospital desk clerk asked if I was claustrophobic.

"Not at all," I reassured her. "I had an MRI a few years ago and had no problem."

I closed my eyes, in relaxation mode, as my body glided into the device.

"Just keep in mind that it's a little tight in there," the technician said.

I felt my arms squeezed between my torso and the inside of the machine. I was unable to move my body even an inch on either side. Either I was bigger than I'd been during my first MRI, or this machine was smaller, or something *else* was different. I opened my eyes but could glimpse nothing except the top of the tunnel enclosing me, inches from my face.

No high humidity or asthma attack could be blamed for what followed.

"Stop!" I shouted. "I can't do this. You need to get me out of here."

The stretcher exited the machine. I sat up and blinked twice.

"I don't understand," I told the technician. "I had one of these before and didn't feel claustrophobic at all. But I totally panicked in there just now. I can't go through with this."

The annoyed tech crossed her arms and suggested I either reschedule for an "open" MRI machine or take a Valium next time. Both might help. Or maybe neither.

It wasn't until I was in the car, halfway home, that I recalled my isolation tank experience. I managed to connect the not-so-distant dots.

A few of our fears are instinctive. Others are clearly acquired.

Some are just too close for comfort.

Chapter 39:

PAJAMA PARTY OF ONE

The bookstore clerk eyed me suspiciously. He trailed a few yards behind me, his head popping around the corner each time I turned down another aisle.

Maybe it was my oversized purse, which potentially could be stuffed with five-finger-discounted books. Perhaps I was just paranoid. Or, maybe it was my outfit: pink pajamas, slippers, and a headful of curlers.

As crazy as I felt, it was probably only *half* as crazy as I looked. But "crazy" had become a relative term—a concept to which I was becoming more immune.

When I first conceived this very public experience, I imagined climbing out of bed that Sunday morning, brushing my teeth (murder by halitosis wasn't among my goals), and then simply heading out for the day in my pajamas. However, I hadn't given this enough consideration the night before. I'd slept in a pair of plaid flannel pants and a T-shirt. It was sleep garb that loads of people now managed to pass off as public attire.

I perused my dresser drawer until I found a pink, lace-trimmed pajama set that would be undeniably recognized as the nightwear it was. I peered in the mirror. Perfect. Except for the minor detail that the sheer fabric clearly displayed my boobage. *That* particular ship had already sailed during my exhibitionist experience at the nude beach. I didn't care to repeat it in any way. I strapped on a bra beneath my pajama top.

Next, I slipped into a pair of fluffy pink slippers. If I must look ridiculous in public, I would at least come off as fashionably color-coordinated.

The coup de grâce was the package of pink and yellow foam curlers I'd procured the day before at Dollar General.

I hadn't worn curlers like these since junior high, before my discovery of Farrah Fawcett and curling irons forever altered my morning routine and my school photos. Since I still remembered the agony of sleeping with foam curlers, I had waited until that morning to deal with them. I failed to recall, however, the time and precision required to put them in place.

I spent twenty minutes attempting to roll my dampened hair. Most dangled limply, and the rest fell into my bathroom sink. Nearly late for my breakfast date, I finally managed to get a dozen curlers entwined in my hair. I shook my curler-covered head at the irony. I'd chosen this experience mostly for the silliness and the public reaction. But I'd gone to a lot of effort to look like I'd made no effort at all.

Breakfast was scheduled for a popular place called Chowders 'N Moor, a fitting nautically named restaurant for someone feeling like a fish out of water. As I crossed the parking lot, I passed a middle-aged couple leaving the restaurant. The woman glanced at me and faux-muttered, "Okaaay. Looking good, honey."

Smiling, I continued walking as I pondered her comment. Nope, probably *not* a compliment.

I gathered many more strange looks and smirks inside the restaurant. Yet our young server barely blinked an eye, even as a curler dropped off my head and landed next to her while she took my order. My breakfast date, Julie M., simply laughed. Over the past several months, my friends had also grown a bit immune to these outings. Unless they were active participants, they were only guilty—and insane—by association.

Next up was grocery shopping. As I roamed my local Kroger's frozen food section, I noted many of the customers were dressed in their best Sunday-Go-to-Meeting clothes. Given their expressions, they believed I was not. Who'd have thought good church-goers would be such a tough crowd.

At first, I evaded the stares and eyerolls, but curiosity prompted me to push the experiment further. I started looking people squarely in the eye and smiling at them. Those who appeared thirtyish or younger proved far more likely to smile back. Middle-aged or older shoppers either averted my glance or gave me a disapproving look. And then, they peeked into my cart to check out my purchases.

I didn't know what they expected my cart to contain, but I hoped a head of lettuce and package of boneless chicken breasts might offset my six-pack of beer, Little Debbie Nutty Bars, and bottle of coal-tar shampoo. (Hey, *lots* of normal and upright citizens suffered from eczema, seborrhea, or psoriasis.)

My final public appearance took place at the bookstore in an upscale suburban shopping center. The same pattern followed: Younger customers barely noticed me, while the older shoppers stared as if I had an enormous green head with two protruding antennas. The sentinel clerk followed me, aisle to aisle, his mind not eased until I made my book purchases and headed to the store's café. Then, I guess, he figured I became the barista's problem.

I sat in the café for another half hour, paging through a new book and drinking my venti mocha. I engaged tentatively in a few stare-downs with the older crowd while the amateur psychologist in me tried to analyze this attitudal discrepancy. This was not only a new experience for me, I assumed it was new for most of the more seasoned bookstore shoppers, too.

Why the difference in reactions I encountered that day? Was it due to younger folks being more open-minded and not yet as judgmental? Or did the younger generation simply have far more lax standards for a public dress code?

After all, does what a person happens to wear define that individual's character? And, where—if anywhere—is the publicly respectable or acceptable line drawn? At pajamas? At jeans sagged to the knees? At a thong? Who am I to say? (If pressed, I'll go with *thong*. No one needs to see that shit. Unless you are somewhere like Haulover Beach, where apparently anything—or nothing at all—is OK.)

I consequently found myself less judgmental about how others were dressed when I passed them in a store or on the street. Hey, you, in the leopard-skin shorts and knee socks! And you, wearing the tiara and tutu! Do your thing, people!

Even so, how others reacted to *my* appearance still bothered me more than I cared to admit. In most situations over the past months, I'd learned to handle humiliation and to brush off others' opinions. Yet when it came to my appearance in more everyday circumstances like these, it seemed I still wanted to appear physically attractive or at least normal. Whether it was due to an engrained sense of vanity or a bit of insecurity, it made me wonder: As I grew older, would I grow more—or less—self-conscious about my appearance?

I probably could make a conclusion from this particular experiment only if I continued my research through additional public pajama parties. Maybe this premiere warmed me up for an encore—especially if I ever got a craving for Nutty Bars at 2 a.m.

The next time I went out in public resembling a viral Internet photo, I'd head straight to Walmart.

I'm guessing I'd find my tribe there.

SPRING

Chapter 40:

A SITTING DUCK

With my recent stranger party being such a hit, I set my sights on befriending a group of very, *very* young strangers—specifically, six-month-old quadruplets.

I'd raised two boys, two years apart, with minimal long-term damage to any of us. Perhaps those earliest maternal memories were fuzzy, or maybe I was a sentimentalist, but I recalled lots of cuddling and cooing. Babysitting quadruplets would provide all that—times four.

Sure, I anticipated that babysitting quads would entail a good amount of work, yet nothing could truly prepare me for the energy and organization required for an afternoon of caring for the Baldwin Quad Squad.

Mama Laura originally agreed to my babysitting offer under the condition that she wouldn't actually leave the house. She'd stay home, catching up on laundry and other chores, while giving me full responsibility for the babies.

Apparently, parents are kind of funny about leaving their babies with a total stranger. Huh.

When I arrived that day, however, Laura said she'd recon-sidered that plan. A couple mutual friends had reassured her I wasn't totally reckless or psychotic. Besides, little Ryan had cried and fretted the entire morning. I could hear him wailing from his crib upstairs, where the rest of the quads were finish-ing their morning nap.

Laura gazed at me, with wild and weary eyes.

"I really, *really* need to get out of the house," she said.

Laura provided on-the-spot instructions for quad care, a crash course entailing extensive written and verbal guide-lines for a mere three-hour gig. Much had changed since my two grown boys were babies twenty-something years ago. My infants slept on their stomachs, a practice now forbidden. I had never heard of swaddle suits, bottle proppers, or Boppy pil-lows. And each step she listed needed to be multiplied by four.

I wrung my hands as she rattled off directions. I started to wonder if this particular new experience might be filled with far more anxiety and far less fun than I imagined. While Laura got herself and her four-year-old daughter, Leah, ready to go to lunch and run errands, I had no choice but to dive in.

I headed upstairs to the nursery. By now, Ryan was howling and the other three babies—Logan, Madalyn, and Reghan—were all awake from their morning naps. I peered into their cribs and was greeted by a montage of tiny bewil-dered faces. Each of them eyed me with furrowed brows, as if thinking, "Wait, you're not my mommy! Who the heck are *you?*" Yet all it took was a bit of sweet talking before each of their frowns turned to smiles.

All the babies appeared hungry and eager to be freed from their barred crib prisons. Laura told me she and her husband, Billy, seasoned pros after six months, generally took two babies downstairs at a time. Hmm. So, I could either carry a single baby, leaving three crying ones behind, or I could attempt to appease two at a time.

Given my questionable coordination, I shuddered at the possible outcome of that latter choice. I opted for four separate trips, tightly cradling each baby with my right arm and grasping the railing with my left, as I maneuvered the stairway.

Once I had them all settled safely downstairs, I commenced The Changing of the Diapers.

A famous scene from I Love Lucy featured Lucy and Ethel attempting to wrap chocolates on a conveyor belt in a candy factory. They started off confident but grew increasingly panicky, because as soon as they managed to wrap one, they were met head-on by one more. And then another.

So it goes with an assembly line of diapering four six-month-old babies. The only difference was I never resorted to frantically stuffing a messy diaper down my blouse. I did, however, find a dirty wipe that night in my pocket.

To my pleasant surprise, these ended up being the only four diapers I changed that entire afternoon. We experienced several false alarms over the next few hours. But after some sniffing and undressing sessions to ascertain the issue, I eventually discovered just a whole lot of tooting going on.

Two of the babies grew quiet and content as soon as they were out of their cribs and in clean bottoms. The other two made it clear they wanted to be fed, pronto. Pronto wasn't an option—not with having to prepare food for four.

I studied Laura's written instructions for the babies' lunch: six ounces of warm water, three scoops of powdered formula, and three scoops of cereal—all shaken well in each bottle. I vaguely recalled that this same routine, with each of my own sons, required about two minutes of preparation. With four bottles, I figured it should take ten minutes, tops.

Making lunch for quads proved to be a far lengthier ordeal, partly due to my trips at roughly two-minute intervals into the adjoining living room to check on the babies.

Sure, I could see them from the kitchen sink. That ten-yard line of vision might have seemed sufficient with my own children—especially with Baby #2, when parental supervision became *way* more lackadaisical.

But this afternoon, I was responsible for *four* infants, and none were mine. Besides, I had read that children were far more advanced now. This could be the day one of them learned to crawl! And, at any moment, she could stumble upon a throat-obstructing-sized object to pop into her mouth! No, none of these babies would choke on my watch! I could not look away for a single minute.

During one such anxious trip into the living room, I made the mistake of carrying the second bottle in mid-preparation, shaking it as I scrutinized each of my young charges. Little Ryan, still crying, spied his lunch-in-process. He fixed his eyes on the bottle and quieted for a moment. But as I walked away to make the next bottle, without making good on my unspoken promise, he began to wail. Obvious lesson learned too late: Never tease a hungry baby.

"Just one more minute, Ryan," I shouted from the kitchen. "I'm almost done, sweetie!"

Sure, I'd lied to my own children as often as necessary. All reasonable parents do. But I felt guiltier lying to this tiny and trusting babe I just met.

Once all the bottles were ready, I arranged each of the quads in their Boppy pillows in a semi-circle on the floor. As Laura had demonstrated earlier, I carefully folded two receiving blankets on top of each pillow. Next, I put the bottles in their stuffed-animal bottle proppers. I braced the bottles on top of the pillows. And finally, I stuck a bottle nipple in each baby's mouth.

This process would have proven trying for a trained engineer.

All four babies began eating, with gusto. I collapsed on

the floor, in the middle of them, congratulating myself on a job well done. Except the job was far from over.

Over the next half hour, I readjusted bottles a dozen times and wiped spit-up twice as often. Laura had suggested I burp them each after every two ounces. Yet there was no way of knowing how much they'd eaten unless I took the bottle out of each baby's mouth and then also removed the bottle-cover propper—which I did obsessively every five minutes.

To my relief, the quads were patient with me. They also proved to be professional burpers. They managed to rid every bit of indigestion from their systems, as was evident by my formula-drenched clothes. I arrived in a black sweater. I left with it colored milky gray.

Logan and Mady fell back to sleep, mid-lunch. Reghan drank half her bottle and then seemed happy just looking around and occasionally cuddling with me. But our cuddles were always short-lived because little Ryan apparently wasn't just hungry; the poor guy wasn't feeling too good either. At six months (and being born two months prematurely), Laura and I agreed it was possible he was cutting his first tooth.

Ryan wanted to be held. Oh, I was all about the holding of babies! Every time I picked him up, his cries turned to smiles. I swooned. There may be no sweeter experience in the world than making a baby's cry turn to a toothless smile. The only problem was that three other babies also needed attention. Every time I snuggled with Ryan, one of the other three needed to be burped, or moved, or held. And each time I put a momentarily smiling Ryan down so I could attend to one of the others, he cried again. Ryan's cries were relentless.

I whimpered once or twice, myself.

My afternoon went like this: Lay down one baby, pick up another. Set down that one, pick up the next. Burp, change a barfy bib, check for pooping or just tooting. Repeat. Sweet

Baby Jesus! This routine wasn't humanly possible! But, I knew Mama Laura did this, day in and day out, with a four-year-old daughter who also needed attention and care.

Laura was my new hero. No, she was clearly a *superhero*.

She laughed when I told her this later. She said she didn't enter confidently into the role of mother to quadruplets. "I cried when we got the news," she admitted.

While parenting four infants and an older sibling had proven to be a heartwarming and rewarding experience, she said patience and priorities were hard-learned lessons. The family adapted to a routine she did her best to enforce. "It helps that they are all incredibly good babies and none of them has been sick," she added. Well, until Ryan seemed to feel out-of-sorts that day.

Babysitting the quads demanded every second of my attention and energy. I never once glanced at the TV, which Laura had left on for my entertainment. *As if.* I crossed my legs and denied myself more than three sips of Diet Coke, afraid to leave the babies unattended if I needed to run for a bathroom break.

What surprised me most wasn't the work involved. It was how quickly I became attached to these babies. In three hours, I fell in love with each of them. I got to know them not just as a collective set, but as four little individuals. I discovered and appreciated their physical differences as well as their already distinct personalities.

By the time Laura and Leah returned, the Quad Squad had grown restless and ready for their afternoon nap. Following Laura's directions, I swaddled three (Reghan, who recently learned to roll over, was no longer wrapped), and I took them upstairs—one at a time, of course. Logan and Mady immediately fell asleep. Reghan simply lay there smiling up at her crib mobile. Meanwhile, Ryan broke free from my clumsy swaddling, whimpered, and needed to be rewrapped.

I softly rubbed his forehead until he calmed. His eyes fluttered shut, and he finally drowsed off. I could have stayed in the nursery for hours, stroking that sleepy baby's head. It resurrected a memory I only vaguely recalled—and didn't fully appreciate at the time.

Four babies had proven to be *forty* times the joy. And forty times the work.

I left that day exhausted but captivated by the thought of grandchildren. Bring 'em on! It would take some time and convincing, I knew, for my two single, twenty-something sons to get on board.

I hoped, someday, they'd be up to the challenge—preferably one baby at a time.

Chapter 41:

ON THE ROPES

C ompared to many of the experiences on my list, I didn't give a high ropes course much forethought. I spoke to a couple folks who'd tackled a similar challenge, and I glanced at the venue's website. The guidelines specified only that participants be at least fourteen years old and four-feet-ten-inches tall. I figured that made me safe by thirty-eight years and two inches.

I made my arrangements and left it at that. It wasn't that I presumed I would totally breeze through such an endeavor. But I was preoccupied at the time with a double scoop of life crap, as life tends to throw us, while I was busy getting my remaining experiences scheduled on my calendar. I figured I'd deal with this particular challenge when I must.

The morning of my excursion, I pulled up the website for further investigation. The high ropes course at The University of Toledo's Student Recreation Center was situated forty feet above the center's basketball courts. It included a series of swaying ropes and wooden swings strung from the three-story-high ceiling. The goal was to climb, crawl, stretch, and step one's way across this mid-air obstacle course. Presumably, a harness and single cable prevented one from crashing to the ground.

From this lengthier perusal of the course description and photos, it appeared far more menacing. Maybe kind of fun. *Nope.* This was possibly my biggest nightmare.

I didn't possess an actual fear of heights, yet I was terrified of the sensation of *falling* from high places. I could stand on the top observation deck of a seemingly stable skyscraper and I could drive across a high bridge, with minimal quivering. But any high structure that moved, or any experience that resulted in *my* moving and potentially facing a downward plunge, was a deal-breaker.

Before committing to this activity, perhaps I should have allowed it a full two minutes of consideration. Still, what could possibly go wrong? No. What could possibly go right?

My friend, Laura W. (not to be confused with Laura the Quad Squad Mama, who was enduring her own daily obstacle course), and her fourteen-year-old cousin, Haley, came in town to join me. This wasn't Laura's first rodeo. She had attempted a similar high ropes course at a summer camp when she was fifteen. Partway along that course, she fully panicked. She finally convinced the powers-that-be to allow her to escape by climbing down a rappel rope.

She admitted the whole experience had been traumatic. At the age of thirty-three, she was now willing—with great reservation—to give it another shot.

I didn't know the extent of this story until the morning of our outing. Hearing these details was a bit disconcerting. But I welcomed Laura as a courage-seeking comrade. We'd make a good match as two chicken shits supporting each other through an agonizing escapade. And young Haley, who appeared fearless, would provide the necessary naïve bravado to encourage us upward and onward.

Our litany of excuses for backing out commenced as soon as we climbed into the car. Laura and I considered calling it off because poor Haley had a stomachache. Plus, the parking lot was pretty full; we weren't certain we could find a spot. And, it was possible the rec center office misplaced our guest passes. By the time we climbed the three levels of stairs to the course, we devised a half-dozen excuses before we ran out of any viable ones.

Once we filled out our waivers (liability waivers—*never* a good sign for safety or survival), we took our place in the long line. We surveyed the crowd. All the other participants appeared to be college students: lean, muscular, and in their physical prime.

And then we stood at the railing and took a good look out at the course.

"Holy shit," I said. "This is even worse than I imagined."

The online photos didn't give any justice to the terror. The height wasn't the only challenge. It was obvious this task relied on both intricate coordination and great upper-body strength in order to grab each consecutive rope, balance upon the swing, and step onto the next. How had we been roped into this? As fit and agile as these college students looked, to say they appeared struggling on the course was an understatement.

I peered down at my stubby arms and chubby legs. This would be one small step for man, one giant leap for my kind.

We watched a young man maneuvering his way across the course. He painstakingly studied his steps, trying to catch hold of the next rocking wooden plank, all the while pulling his security cable along the way. His odds for success seemed as shaky as his footing.

He paused and shouted to someone on the catwalk. "OK, *this* is why they make you sign a freaking waiver!"

I unfolded the waiver in my hand and read it. It noted

the dangers could result in "physical or emotional injury, paralysis, death or damage to myself, to property or to third parties." Specific risks included "falls and falling... or even more severe life-threatening hazards."

I wasn't certain what could be *more* life-threatening than falling three stories onto the inflexible surface of a basketball court. The fate of the hoops players below wasn't looking so good either.

I cringed and looked back toward the course. My attention was drawn to a young woman in a tie-dyed shirt, attempting to step from one swing to another. The swings were situated a couple of feet apart, but as she stretched her leg from one swing to the next, the beam kept rocking further away. Over and over, she stepped and missed. She finally grabbed the rope in front of her and managed to secure one foot on the next swing. Stretching her second foot over, she succeeded in balancing her body on the wildly rocking plank.

Just as she appeared to get her footing, the swaying board flipped backward. We watched as she slipped off. She dropped, seemingly in a freefall, before the security cable clipped onto her harness finally jolted her to a stop.

She dangled and swiveled, mid-air.

Laura, Haley, and I collectively muttered, "Oh, shit." We couldn't watch another minute.

I turned to one of the college-aged attendants. "Um, so how often have you seen people slip off and dangle like this?"

She peered out at the still spinning woman and paused from chewing her gum long enough to answer. "Pretty often." She shrugged.

I glanced at Laura and Haley. Our panicked eyes met. We observed the course participants for another ten minutes. Finally, without another word, we subtly stepped out of line to consider our options. The time had come to take flight or to flee.

"This is way worse than the one I did when I was fifteen," Laura admitted. "And I was in far better shape then. I'm not sure I have the physical strength to do this. And, I think I might puke a bit in my mouth."

My head bobbed in up-and-down spasms. "Right? Right! And what freaks me out more is the coordination this requires. I mean, coordination? I have a whole lot of *none*."

I could feasibly handle, albeit with a queasy stomach, airplane flights and other height-intensive excursions that relied on the skills of trained pilots or technicians. But my safety here, on these recreational gallows, was fully at the mercy of my lifelong faulty coordination. One misstep would leave me hanging in a harness, from a thin wire cable, three stories above the ground. And, still spinning from that cable was a best-case scenario.

My misstep wasn't merely a possibility; I knew, with all my heart and soul and chronic clumsiness, that it was inevitable. No one could help me across those ropes and swings. Left up to my own inadequate devices, I was certain I'd be SOL.

I eyeballed the waiver again. It noted that the student instructors "seek safety, but are not infallible. They might be unaware of a participant's fitness or abilities."

The instructors might be oblivious of my inabilities, but I was *fully* aware. And that, for the first time during all my new adventures, proved to be a deal-breaker.

"I hate to admit it," I told my friends, unable to look them in the eye. "But I'm pretty sure I can't go through with this."

"Oh my God. Me, either," Laura said. "I'm certain I'd have a panic attack midway through. What then? I don't see any escape ropes like they had when I was fifteen. When you're halfway across and can't take another step, how else do you get down?"

I recalled the swimming lessons I took when I was eight. One of the final test requirements was jumping off the ten-foot diving board. I stood on that shaking board for fifteen minutes until the instructor realized no amount of encouraging, bribing, or ridiculing me would make me jump. She finally let me climb back down the ladder. I failed the class, but even now I remained convinced that last-minute escape saved my life.

There were no rescue ropes or ladders stationed along this course. No easy way to chicken out while standing on a swaying swing, three stories above ground.

I turned to Haley, who'd remained mostly silent during this debate. "How about you?" I asked her. "What do you want to do?"

Haley stepped back and threw her arms up in the air. "Not *this*! *This* should be illegal!"

It was a consensus. We agreed this was a disaster simply waiting to happen. Those ropes might just as well have been wrapped around our necks.

Over the past several months, I'd succeeded through every new challenge I faced. This was the first I'd failed to see through fruition. As we crumpled our waivers and headed downstairs, my failure troubled me.

I hung my head. "I can't believe I couldn't go through with it."

"Maybe we could just Photoshop ourselves into a picture and post it online," Haley suggested. We all agreed it was a fabulous idea, until I decided cheating was wrong. Plus, I didn't know how to use Photoshop.

Laura, always the consummate writer, patted my back. "You've only failed at this *one* thing. Look at it like a narrative arc in a story. There always has to be one really low period, one major conflict for the protagonist. And this was yours."

From a writer's view, she had a point. Maybe there was more to it, too.

While the high ropes course proved to be my only fully

failed attempt in The 52/52 Project, the experience wasn't without its own lesson.

Perhaps acknowledging our limitations is an essential part of self-discovery. Maybe we learn just as much about life and about ourselves by discovering our weaknesses as well as our strengths. Maybe we succeed in growing even as we fail. Just maybe we get credit in life for simply showing up.

Besides, the afternoon's entertainment factor wasn't a total loss. While we each observed and envisioned our agony and defeat, my cohorts spewed out some amazing one-liners. An hour of giggling until we ached surely proved to be a more enjoyable experience than if we'd actually gone through with this whole hot hell of a mess.

I'd never simultaneously faced fear and laughed so much at the same time. How can you regret a win-lose situation like that?

I didn't step one foot on one of those treacherous swings.

But damn if it wasn't one of the best experiences I never had.

Chapter 42:

CATCHING A FLIGHT TO NOWHERE

I had never been an obsessive worrier, nor—as was evident by one glance at my mopboards—a compulsive cleaner. Yet my approach to planning and organizing my life practically screamed OCD. I was the kind of planner who wrote a detailed to-do list every morning and every night. I compiled *lists* of lists. Occasionally, I even amended a list to include unscheduled tasks I'd already accomplished, just for the satisfaction of crossing them off.

I plotted out my days, my evenings, and even my vacations. Before I headed out on a trip, I wrote out a detailed itinerary for every minute, including how I would spend my time on the plane.

Clearly, I wasn't the type to ever consider getting up one day and driving an hour to the airport, booking the next available flight out to wherever it was going, and then hopping aboard—with no hotel reservations, no car rental, and no agenda.

Until I did.

Although The 52/52 Project was teaching me much about going with the flow, I panicked at the idea of embarking on a trip with little premeditation. Not only would this new experience take me far outside my comfort zone, it also would take me… well, I had no freaking idea *where* it would take me.

Other than ruling out international travel due to time and expense, I didn't allow myself to make any choices or plan any specifics. Only a few pre-travel details required forethought. I scheduled that Friday off work, hired a pet-sitter, and puzzled out the idea of packing.

How did one begin to pack for a long weekend to a mystery location, especially in March with its lamb-and-lion weather? Considering I could land anywhere from Miami to Seattle to Fargo, I scribbled out a packing list. (Thank God, this *one* list was allowed.) I figured I'd cover all my bases with a bathing suit, cover-up, and a pair of Sperrys—as well as a winter coat, gloves, and boots.

I also had to consider how I would pay for the trip. Minor details. I had no idea how much a last-minute flight, potentially all the way across the country, might set me back. When I blogged about my plans the night before my departure, readers began quoting me very disturbing estimates. In a panic, I threw out a half-joking request for donated air miles.

An hour later, a longtime friend offered me enough airline points for my entire flight. *Score!* I called Delta and was assured I could simultaneously transfer those miles and book a flight when I arrived the next day at Delta's Detroit Metro counter.

The next morning, for the first time ever, I found myself able to take my time driving to the airport. Forget my usual race through the terminal, praying I didn't miss my plane. This time, I knew I'd arrive right on time for my flight; I just was clueless about which flight that would be.

As I sat on the shuttle bus from an off-site parking lot, I

considered the possibilities. I could wind up somewhere like Hopeulikit, Georgia or maybe Hooker Corner, Indiana, both of which I'd recently discovered were totally real towns. I was sure both these places were lovely. Still, I preferred to end up either in a big city I'd never visited or, even though it was a long shot, a warm beach. I'd grown so, *so* weary of the sadistic Ohio winter that had roared in my frostbitten face for the last five months.

My fate would be left up to the timing of my arrival and the ticketing agent. It was exciting. And more than a bit unnerving. Based on several friends' comments, I also grew concerned that my last-minute booking might get me flagged as a terrorist threat. While I doubted many terrorists allowed the airline to choose their flight, I didn't relish the possibility of being pulled aside for an in-depth search and interrogation.

I wandered into the terminal, taking several deep breaths and practicing a vague recollection of Lamaze-style breathing. That had done me little good two decades ago, when both my children's births ended in C-sections.

Approaching the Delta counter, I explained my complex story to the attendant. She gave me a confused smile.

"I'd love to help you," she said. "But I have no way at all of knowing which departing flights have available seats, let alone which ones are eligible for SkyMile points. You'll need to call the SkyMiles toll-free number to arrange that."

Readjusting my dropped chin, I stepped out of line and plopped onto a bench across from the counter. I found my SkyMiles card in my wallet and dialed the toll-free phone number. When I finally reached a real person, I launched into a long explanation of my mission and my dilemma.

My new best friend at Delta loved the idea of The 52/52 Project, but she didn't seem to fully comprehend my objective.

"OK," she said. "Sure, I can make your reservation. Where exactly do you want to go?"

"You don't understand. I don't care where I go. Well, I *care*, of course, but I'm not allowed to choose," I explained again. "Just tell me the next flight out from Detroit, wherever it is going, which hasn't begun boarding and still has an available seat eligible for SkyMiles."

"Oh." She paused. A very long pause. "So, you're asking me to choose a flight *for* you?"

"Exactly," I said. "Hey, I'm really sorry. Am I putting too much pressure on you?"

"Yeah, this is definitely the first time someone has asked me to do this. But, alright, if you truly just want the next available flight from Detroit, it would be... well... it looks like it's Fort Myers, Florida."

Seriously? A warm beach it was! I did a happy dance around the terminal.

But my celebration proved premature. My SkyMiles BFF told me she couldn't book the flight until the donated miles were transferred to my account. And *that* could only be done online.

My hands began shaking. Did these people not understand my planning anxieties? I required a boarding pass *pronto*! I needed to learn exactly where I was going and when I was leaving, so I could then check those rather significant items off my mental list. While I freaked out, I made another mental list of every Delta employee who had lied or had misinformed me about this whole flight fiasco, so I could file a formal complaint.

I plopped back down on the bench. Sure, I had both my iPhone and my laptop with me, but I knew my best bet was to call Son #2, the techno-geek in the family. He was likely sitting in front of a computer and could manage the entire process far faster than I could even Google the Delta website.

Sure enough, he managed in minutes to navigate the site and drill down to the exact online form we needed. But after numerous attempts, he continued to get error messages. I paced in circles. A half hour passed with no progress.

I faced the growing doom that the Fort Myers flight would board before I was booked, and I'd end up on the next—unknown—flight instead. I knew it inevitably would be Fargo. Not that there was anything wrong with that.

And then suddenly, my confirmation for the Fort Myers flight flashed across my phone.

Happy dance resumed! I collected my boarding pass from the still confused desk clerk, texted a quick thank-you to Son #2, and raced through the airport.

As I was whisked along the terminal's endless series of moving sidewalks, I searched on my iPhone for Fort Myers hotel options. Huh. Apparently, Florida was a popular destination in March. Thanks to school spring breaks, most hotels were either full or were charging prime rates and a kidney for any remaining rooms.

Nearing my gate, I discovered a flight delay left me with thirty spare minutes before boarding. I headed to the closest airport bar for a Bloody Mary.

I believe I've mentioned my deep-seated dread of flying? One pre-flight Bloody Mary generally took off the edge just enough to get me through any turbulence and fear of a faulty-engine crash landing. I ordered my drink and glanced up at a TV, where I spied a breaking news report. A Malaysian plane had disappeared, mid-flight. Just *poof*—gone and totally off the freaking radar.

Maybe I'd suck that drink right down and order another.

I distracted myself with my hotel search and called my sister, DC, a travel guru. Within minutes, she texted back with information about one last available room at an ocean-front hotel in Fort Myers Beach. But the rate was way more than I planned or could afford.

I debated with myself. Sensible Sherry said, "Don't do

it! Book a cheap place by the airport instead!" But Senseless Sherry attempted to justify the cost. "Your airfare is already covered. And, if you're going to all this trouble, you clearly *must* stay by the beach. Aren't you worth an overpriced hotel?"

Besides, the hotel couldn't hold me accountable for any credit card charges once my plane crashed en route.

Senseless Sherry made several compelling points. As usual.

Thankfully, the most eventful part of the flight was finding myself seated directly across from a colleague, Barbara. Out of dozens of flights out of Detroit, and with neither of us knowing the other was headed to Fort Myers that day, what were the odds? As I explained the circumstances of my trip, I discovered that the woman seated next to Barbara, whom neither of us knew, followed The 52/52 Project online. Coincidence or fate? I had already begun to believe there was no such thing as a coincidence.

My new friend, Gina, bought me another Bloody Mary. Between our conversation and the vodka, I never once noticed if the plane—or my hands—were shaking.

Once in Fort Myers, I checked in at my hotel and was promised a reduced rate. Could my good fortune get any better? Yes, indeed it could. My balcony overlooked the pool, the tiki bar, and the ocean. The grand slam? Fort Myers was sunny and eighty degrees. As I dug through my suitcase to find my swimsuit, I gleefully tossed aside my coat, mittens, and boots.

As good fate continued, my old high school friends, Marion and Mike, happened to be vacationing in Naples. When they read my Facebook post noting my final destination, they cruised over to Fort Myers. We caught up over a couple celebratory drinks at the resort and then dinner on Captiva Island.

After my friends headed back to Naples that evening, I hung out at the hotel's beachside tiki bar. Disappointed in the crowd, which was not particularly warm and fuzzy, I wandered back toward my room to sit on the balcony.

Long after the bar closed, I overheard a rowdy group of people on the pool deck. They were having serious fun. The introverted, unmotivated, and exhausted voices in my head advised me to sit tight on my balcony.

But through the past months, I'd learned that pushing myself and taking a chance generally paid off. I could either remain a social creeper that night or make the move to reach out. So, I headed downstairs and invited myself to join their group.

Of all the strangers I met that weekend, these six guys and their sole female companion ended up being the most warm and welcoming. All were twenty-something. All were Muslim. And although they were gathered together for a short vacation in Florida, their homes were scattered around the globe. These details each proved interesting in our conversation yet irrelevant to our connection. We talked until the wee hours of the morning.

Much like the Stranger Party I hosted a couple months back, the evening proved that new alliances don't always require having a whole lot in common.

Other than these two social experiences, I spent much of the weekend alone, strolling the beach and eating seafood. Was there any better plan of action for a short Florida vacation? Especially when the objective was not planning a thing?

I originally anticipated spending two nights away on this impromptu trip and then flying home on Sunday. Yet as soon as I learned I'd been blessed with such a sunny setting, I had called my office from the Detroit airport and told them I'd be staying an extra day. Duh. I rescheduled my return flight for Monday.

It never crossed my mind that Monday was St. Patrick's Day until that very morning. As I rolled my suitcase across the parking lot, I heard music. Pushing through a huge crowd gathered along the curb, I spied a parade marching down the street, directly in front of my hotel.

Call me un-American or—in this case—un-Irish, but I had never been a fan of parades. And this one, although apparently entertaining for the rest of the folks on hand, literally stood in my way of heading home.

The driver of the taxi I'd ordered called to say he was waiting for me on a side street about a mile up the blocked-off road. *Terrific.* I didn't have time for these shenanigans. I had a flight to catch and a Bloody Mary to down. I sighed, pulled my wheeled-suitcase behind me, and hurried alongside the parade.

But a funny thing happened on the way to my taxi. As I watched the floats, Irish dancers, and costumed leprechauns, I found myself humming the *Hello Dolly* song, "Before the Parade Passes By."

By now, I recognized fate when it stared me in the face. I didn't care if my waiting taxi meter was already clicking into the double digits. Unlike all the other parades in my life that I had disregarded or avoided, I decided this one would not pass me by. I knew I had to get in step while there was still time left.

I jumped in line and marched along with the floats. I stopped to take some photos with the crowd and mingle with the crazies. For a few short moments, I was Ferris Bueller, waving to my would-be fans while I pondered how to sing "Danke Schoen" in Gaelic.

My trip could only have ended more perfectly if I'd been able to delay my flight that morning to join the crowd on the curb for a green beer or two. No worries. I'd settle for that Bloody Mary on the plane home.

When I made my list of potential 52/52 experiences, this impromptu adventure appeared to be my most half-assed idea ever. For the new me, who was slowly learning to let so much roll off my shoulders, that spontaneity made it the best—by a sky mile.

On the flight back home, I contemplated Life Lesson #42: Sometimes the *best* plan is no plan at all.

Chapter 43:

AN ITALIAN/IRISH/GERMAN/ FRENCH WOMAN WALKS INTO A BAR...

I held a variety of jobs in my lifetime, including stints as a newspaper reporter, park service ditch-digger, and shopping mall Easter Bunny. Side note: The Easter Bunny gig paid the best, yet after getting peed on, I figured I deserved every penny of that five dollars an hour.

Throughout a dozen jobs though, I never once worked as a waitress or bartender.

Waitressing had been ruled out because, let's be honest, I'd have dropped three or four trays of food before my very first—and likely last—paycheck. And the idea of bartending made me wary for another reason: I'd spent enough time in bars during my wayward youth to make it a point to avoid serving drinks to people like the college-aged me.

In the midst of my unbucket list, while watching an old episode of *Cheers*, I noticed that Sam seldom had to deal with obnoxious and droning drunks (other than Cliff Clavin). And if Carla never dropped a tray of food, perhaps I—a similarly short and part-Italian-blooded smart ass—could manage as well. I decided decisions, naturally, are best based upon old sitcoms. So, I set my sights on a place where at least one or two people might know my name.

The good people at Caper's, the venue for my pizza-eating contest, agreed to test my virgin bartending skills. Perhaps on a hunch, they subtly ignored my inquiry about waitressing, too. Good play, Caper's.

I knew a great deal about beer drinking; after all, I received a bachelor's degree in it. Other than operating a wine corkscrew or adding vodka to Bloody Mary mix, I knew little else about being stationed *behind* a bar. I envisioned myself as a quick study though, and reckoned I had other talents to bring to the table—or, more specifically—to the bar.

I pictured myself leaning in and nodding thoughtfully as patrons poured out their troubles to me. My people skills, my above-par memory, and my patience were sure to carry me through my premiere bartending gig.

Patience might prove to be the most important asset, I soon determined, because Caper's informed me they'd be putting me to work on the granddaddy of drunken holidays: St. Patrick's Day.

Next to New Year's Eve, it was a tavern's most lucrative and looney-filled day of business. The thought of bartending on St. Paddy's Day was one part intriguing and two parts intimidating.

Given that morning's spur-of-the-moment parade and curbside crowd, I'd already observed my share of St. Patrick's Day celebrating. I had originally anticipated a day of rest after my trip to places unknown. But since I extended my stay at Fort Myers Beach, I found myself in a rush on my way to Caper's from the Detroit airport. I only had time for a quick stop at my mother's house to borrow a green shirt to wear under my bartending apron—and to be privy to my mom's always good advice: "Have fun, and don't let anyone throw up on you."

The bar and restaurant were busy but not as jam-packed as I expected. Caper's manager, Emily, gave me the lowdown on St. Patrick's Day drinking. She said the majority of bar patrons on this pseudo-Irish holiday *started* early and *ended* early. Most came before dinner, and a number showed up well before lunch. By the time my shift started, many had their fill and had tottered home.

Guessing I was not only inexperienced but also ill-equipped for the job, Emily positioned me, not at the main bar, but at an auxiliary drink station. My charge was pouring glasses of Guinness, shots of whiskey, and Irish Car Bombs.

I was a bit disappointed that I wouldn't possess full bar authority. However, let it be said that Guinness, whiskey, and Irish Car Bombs are apparently the lifeblood of St. Patrick's Day drinkers.

Back in my youth, my personal drink of choice that day had been a standard green beer. I'd never even tasted an Irish Car Bomb, let alone prepared one.

Fortunately, my best customers, Josh and Emily C., lived under the philosophy of "Drink early, drink often, and drink right." As Irish Car Bomb aficionados, they schooled me on how to properly position the glass, pour the liquors, and ensure the perfect proportion of Guinness, Baileys Irish Cream, and Jameson Irish Whiskey.

I dispensed approximately five hundred gallons of Guinness and concocted enough Irish Car Bombs to rock south Toledo. As I poured drinks and made change (thank God this required only subtraction skills and not algebra), I was able to make small talk with dozens of customers.

The most colorful character was a guy who told me he'd hit five bars that day and dyed the water green in every toilet.

He was sort of my new hero. I also spent ten minutes consoling a young woman who'd just gone through a bad breakup. He'd broken up with her over the phone, two weeks before their planned trip to Mexico. I refrained from calling him names (cheating *bastard*), but I bought her a drink and told her she was gorgeous. An hour later, I spotted her dancing with another guy. She grinned and waved at me from across the room. I made a mental note to add "therapist" to that long list of jobs on my résumé.

What I mostly observed all evening was happy conversation, laughter, and an occasional song. Few of the patrons appeared fully inebriated. I was pleased to report to my mom that I didn't see a single person vomit.

However, my performance as a newbie bartender didn't go off without a hitch. My biggest snafu was forgetting the whiskey in an order of Car Bombs. Tipsy as they were, Josh and Emily C. set me straight on that.

And, coming as no surprise after my recent bar-staining fiasco, I knocked over a couple glasses of Guinness. I shouted to a waitress to bring more bar rags: too late, since most of the errant beer flowed into an already inch-deep pool on the floor around my serving station. Next time I bartended, I'd wear rubber boots.

Either way, I called the evening a victory. I also garnered nearly thirty dollars in tips. I planned to donate this to a local charity until I recalled that the weekend's Fort Myers trip had overloaded my credit card. I was currently my own charity.

Before I left, I drank my first Irish Car Bomb—*damn* tasty—and toasted to the patron saint of Ireland. All hail to St. Patrick, the guy who drove the snakes out of the bars of Ireland, so I wouldn't have to deal with them.

Sure and begorra, St. Patrick's Day is one of camaraderie and community, even if you're only one part Irish and three parts sober.

Chapter 44:

GOING IN CIRCLES

$\mathcal{H}$ow to prepare for a stock car driving experience:

First, be sure to never watch a single car race in your life, not even a televised clip. This way, the outrageous speeds and life-endangering risks will prove a pleasant surprise.

Do not read the fine print on the discounted racing voucher you purchased online, months ago. It's more fun to find out at the last minute that you will *not* be driving—an experience that would have allowed you control of your speed as well as the ability to opt out at any moment along the track. Wait until you arrive to discover you will, instead, be riding along in the passenger seat next to a driver insane enough to do this for a living—whose fear level is negligible and who will likely show you no mercy.

In your effort to be acknowledged as a seasoned pro, work into a track-side discussion with the crowd—all of them major racing fans—how you visited the Toledo Speedway for a concert when you were nineteen. Elevate your status by mentioning how you fainted that afternoon from a combination of heat exhaustion and beer drinking.

While you wait, watch the cars tear around the track. Convince yourself it looks less hazardous than a Detroit freeway.

As your stomach rolls, recall that you never ate breakfast or lunch and that it's now two o'clock. Reassure yourself that if you happen to vomit mid-ride, at least you will only dry-heave.

Order a hot dog and popcorn from the concession stand anyway. Potential puking aside, you deserve a last meal.

When you are finally admitted to the pit, strike up a conversation with the only other female there, a grandmother waiting to drive tandem with her fourteen-year-old grandson. The seventy-four-year-old woman's fearlessness will shame you. The teenager's anxiety, as he watches the cars whiz by, will perk you back up.

"All I know," he mumbles, "is I'm glad I went to the bathroom before we came out here."

Chuckle at this, but find this light moment turning dark again when one of the ride-side employees admits he indeed has witnessed a few riders wet themselves. Grow increasingly uneasy about this risk, considering that these days you can pee with a simple sneeze.

Distract yourself from your inevitable incontinence by asking the track assistant about any other strange things he has witnessed. When he grins sheepishly, prod him to continue.

Listen intently as he whispers, confidentially, that the drivers occasionally have female riders who seem to *really* enjoy their experience. "We've had a few women," he tells you, "who, um, 'rub' themselves while they're in the passenger's seat."

Jump back at this news and shout, *"No!?!"*

"Oh, yeah," he replies. "The drivers have to stop and ask them to get out of the car."

Contemplate this bizarre possibility, but conclude that *no* number of good vibrations in a hurtling race car are likely to move you in that way.

As you await your turn, observe two cars being taken out of commission due to mechanical difficulties. Force yourself to believe this puts the odds in your favor that your car will not lose its fuel pump mid-race.

Be sure to request a racing jumpsuit based on the size you last wore in the eighties—when jumpsuits were the height of fashion—and not the size you require now. As the woman issuing uniforms holds it out, she wordlessly eyes you up and down. Reconsider your choice. Ask for the next largest size instead, which is only *one* size smaller than you probably wear.

Once you manage to get it zipped, the skintight black uniform is sure to make you look svelte and ultra-cool. Say a silent prayer that the layer of sweat already emerging around your waist won't prove all it takes to burst the seams. Add another prayer that you won't have to pee while you wait, since it may take hours to peel the suit off.

Your undersized uniform also makes the next step more entertaining for everyone on site.

Be certain dozens of people are watching as you attempt to climb inside the car, which apparently can only be accomplished by crawling through the passenger side window. Do not bother to hide your dismay about this dilemma. Cry, "Seriously? You've got to be kidding me," loud enough that two track-side employees rush over to see if someone's been injured.

If you happen to be height-deprived, wait for someone to bring a spare tire for you to use as a stepstool. If he thinks you appear old enough to be his grandmother, even though you are certain you have *children* younger than him, he will speak to you in a condescending manner. The fact that he has accurately assessed your incompetence and uncoordination will further piss you off.

The tire stepstool allows you to *reach* the window but

does not aid your ability to climb through it. Due to the constraints of your snug jumpsuit, you are unable to bend your legs. The track assistants, who are already behind schedule and likely way underpaid, are sure to get a kick out of how long it takes them to contort and maneuver your rigid body through the car window and squeeze you into the passenger seat.

Although you are certain *nothing* can pry you from the tight seat into which you have been wedged, the pit crew will double-strap you into the car anyway. Do not complain. Four or five straps might be just enough to keep you safe.

Once you're inside, eye your driver, who introduces himself as Andy. You figure Andy seems a nice, normal name for someone with your life in his hands. Better than, say, Lucifer.

Make nervous small talk for a moment with Andy, who assures you he's been driving for seven years and has never had a *fatal* accident. Squint and frown at him. Suggest to Andy that in the future, he might be a bit less specific.

Andy doesn't appear the reckless or irresponsible sort. Conclude that, given your coordination, it may be best that he—and not you—will be racing this high-powered vehicle around a track.

Then, take a glance around and observe all those folks who *did* succeed in signing up for the driving—and not the ride-along—package. Let it sink in that a half-dozen inexperienced people, who have never once been behind the wheel of a race car, will now be whizzing a few feet next to you at speeds over a hundred miles per hour.

Realize there is no easy way out of this now obligatory situation. Prepare to rip the bandage off quickly. Turn to Andy and say, "OK, let's do this."

As your car jumps to a start, close your eyes and question whether you will die by fainting, throwing up, or crashing. Fainting is your best option, given your last Toledo Speedway experience.

Crashing doesn't seem the best choice. I suggest you vote against that.

Open your eyes momentarily as you feel the car skidding around the first corner. Try to measure how close you came to slamming into the wall. Were you two feet or two *inches* from sure death? Feel grateful that geometry was never your strong subject.

When Andy announces you've made it around the first lap, with just two more to go, gather your courage. Promise yourself you will keep your eyes open the remainder of the ride.

As Andy suddenly swerves, nearly sideswiping the car next to you, close your eyes again.

"Sorry—some kind of object was lying in the middle of the track," he explains.

Probably just the battered corpse of a passenger ejected from another car. Be sure to commend Andy on avoiding it.

Try to count each lap, with closed eyes, but lose track after the next few dizzying turns. When your car suddenly lurches to an abrupt stop, open your eyes and glimpse around, certain you've managed to escape another crash.

Instead, catch your breath as Andy turns to you and says, "Well, that's it. Hope you enjoyed it."

Pause and reply, "Oh, already?" And then blow out a sigh before grinning.

After two hours of agonized apprehension, discover the actual experience is over in a matter of minutes. The trip isn't without an exhilarating thrill or two, and not quite as horrifying as you expected, mostly because the ride is *so freaking fast*.

On your way out, stop at the front counter to pick up your pre-ride photo—the one of you suited up and perched in the car window. Your cocky expression in the photo doesn't convey your panic about your impending ride or your anxiety about your tightly zipped jumpsuit bursting open as you climb out of the car. Who cares if photographs are deceiving when you look so freaking cool?

Climb into your own vehicle, buckle your seatbelt, and proceed to pass several cars on the expressway en route to your suburban subdivision.

Lean back in the driver's seat of your minivan, in full confidence that you are officially a racing badass.

Chapter 45:

COMING FULL CIRCLE

𝓑 eing voted "Best Party Giver" wasn't my only high school legacy. I also got my classmates' nod for "Best Sense of Humor." Oddly, neither of these academic accolades garnered me a single college scholarship.

Thirty-five years later, when I received an unexpected email from my alma mater, I suspected I'd entered a parallel universe—the one where my former high school asked me to return to give the keynote speech at its spring academic awards banquet.

They probably had me confused with *another* Sherry Stanfa from E.L. Bowsher High School in Toledo.

No, it seemed the principal and vice principal both had read about my project in the *Toledo Blade* and thought my story might be inspirational to the students and their parents. I was bewildered and amused, but mostly I was honored.

Until I remembered my fear of public speaking. Then I was mainly freaked.

Sure, I had survived a radio show appearance, but that audience had been invisible. Speaking in person in front of a large crowd was far more intimidating, especially since this audience included some of the city's brightest teenagers. Maybe, and it was a long shot, I might manage to mumble out a few words between my quivering lips. But, let's be honest, how could I ever be an inspiration to these young overachievers when I'd never been more than a cautionary tale?

My own high school academic career saw its highs and lows, as well as lots of ho-hum averages. I excelled in English and art. Not so much in science or math. Should I mention to these scholars that I flunked algebra? The jury was still out on whether that failure was due to my inability to master the curriculum or simply to my inability to show up for class. I topped my class in truancy.

As the certified class clown, I also held the record for demerits in gym class. The dean of students and I were, affably enough, on a first-name basis.

I had been what my mother, with her softening maternal spin, now called a *spirited* teenager. I wasn't malicious and seldom overtly disrespectful; I just wanted to have fun. Apparently, some things in life never change.

Given the awards banquet audience, it was probably best to withhold a bit of my sketchy high school past; yet I couldn't be a poser. I chose to tell the truth, albeit with a few withheld details.

I admitted I was mostly an average student and not always a rule-abiding one. Still, I told them, I felt I did make my mark by my involvement in high school activities, especially as the editor of the school newspaper. The paper, seemingly named in my unruly honor, was called *The Rebellion*.

(Note: Bowsher originally capitalized on its location as the south-end high school within a Midwest city. Our nickname was the Rebels. We played "Dixie" at sporting events, and we waved the Confederate flag. Nothing political, racial, or unpatriotic was intended or even considered back then.

Times have changed, and I learned those school rituals, however innocent, are long gone. Understandable, yet somehow
disappointing to older alumni.)

My heart sank further when I discovered the school
paper, by *any* name, no longer existed. Public education must
clearly take steps to meet the changing times. For budding
writers, I feared this was a big step backward.

The school newspaper wasn't the coolest organization,
I explained, but that hadn't mattered to me. My involvement
with the paper was the highlight of my high school academic
career. Besides writing stories and eventually serving as editor, I also oversaw a section titled "Poetry Corner." While
most of my classmates knew me as an outgoing jokester, I
possessed a quiet, introspective side. *I wrote poetry.*

Unlike being an athlete or a cheerleader, baring one's
young soul as a poet is seldom a road to popularity. I told
these teenagers that even as I realized this back then, I managed to push back the fear of being judged negatively. I not
only wrote poems, in the safe confines of my teenage bedroom, but I even allowed my classmates to read them.

Maybe I was a fairly confident nonconformist, or maybe
I took this risk because I had discovered—by the time I was
only eight—that writing was *my thing.* I realized how much
writing and publishing both my own and other students'
poems and stories meant to me when our school-sanctioned
Senior Skip Day rolled around my senior year.

As my friends planned pool parties or trips to the mall,
I went to school that day anyway; we had a publishing deadline. I'd been truant every other Senior Skip Day since my
freshman year. As editor, getting the paper out on time was
more important to me than enjoying a legal day off.

This personal passion proved to be a major focus of my
talk to these students. Like the cowboy Curly told Billy Crys-
tal's character in *City Slickers* (were any of these kids even old

enough to know this movie?), the secret of life is "Just one thing. ... You stick to that and the rest don't mean sh*t."

I suggested that maybe we were all cowboys and that this *one thing* was what we all needed to figure out and hold on to. Maybe they didn't yet know what that one thing was, but they would eventually find out. Perhaps it was success in a particular profession, raising a family, or something else they hoped would provide a sense of integrity and self-fulfillment. They needed to stick to that and follow their heart, even as they inevitably encountered disruptions, detours, and hurdles along the way.

Had I done so in my own life? Did I have any regrets? I told these students I thought regrets generally served a purpose only if you could do something to change them. Besides, I believed most people had more regrets about what they *hadn't* done than what they *had* done.

With that in mind, I admitted I did have a couple misgivings about my high school and college years. I wished I'd worked harder in school, while still having much of the crazy fun I had enjoyed. I wondered where I'd be now if I'd pushed myself and taken more chances, even if it was hard work and the odds seemed stacked against me. How many books might I have written? How many more different and rewarding experiences might I have enjoyed—even if I failed at a few along the way?

Perhaps, now, I was trying to make up for lost time on all accounts.

You *can* do it all, I assured them. You can work hard, chase your dreams, and still enjoy all other aspects of your life, simultaneously. Just put yourselves out there and don't be afraid to open any door even if you're unsure what you might face when you do.

For now, I advised them to not worry so much about how others may view them. Write poetry if you want, I said.

Try out for a school play or the quiz bowl team, even if none of your friends have the same interests. Say "yes" when it's the difficult but the right answer, and say "no" when you know you should.

It's often impossible to tell when teenagers are listening to you at all, let alone if anything you've said has struck a single chord. I'd had long discussions with my own children when I doubted they ever heard a word. Yet I was occasionally surprised months later when they repeated—and agreed with—exactly what I'd said.

I had zoned out in enough speeches and meetings in my life to know some of these students spent the entirety of my talk memorizing chemical elements for the next day's test or else texting on their phones. But when I finished and allowed fifteen minutes for questions, we actually ran out of time. A few students and parents came up to talk to me later. If my presentation impacted even one of them, I couldn't ask for more.

And, from a personal standpoint, I survived one of the challenges that had terrified me most. Public speaking would probably never be something I embraced. But this single experience led me to accept other speaking invitations, with an increasing level of confidence and a slightly less shaky voice.

I hoped my closing words summed up what I had learned from my experiences so far and what I hoped these young people and their parents might walk away remembering:

"I'll soon be wrapping up The 52/52 Project. The past months have been a whirlwind of anxiety, excitement, and enlightenment. I'm not sure I'd change one minute because I know it's changed me.

"I've learned to never say never; I've learned to let more things slide off my shoulders; and I've learned we discover much more about ourselves and about others when our world is broader and our mind is open.

"As I stand here tonight, I'm clearly not the girl I was

way back at Bowsher High School. I'm not even the woman I was a year ago. At the age of fifty-two, although I've preserved many pieces of whom I was at fifty-one and even at sixteen, I have become someone entirely new. In some ways, I've come full circle.

"I've learned it's never too late to reinvent yourself."

Occasionally, I still think about those young people I met that night, those amazing yet sometimes faltering and unfulfilled teenagers with the promise of their whole lives ahead of them.

I hope their paths are filled with much success and love and laughter.

Oh, the places they will go.

Chapter 46:

MY BIG FAT GREEK PARTY

Having nailed the stranger bash I hosted, I figured I still knew a thing or two about parties. Even so, I might be raising the bar a bit high this time, crashing a fraternity party.

I had happened upon a fraternity party or two in my youth. Attending a frat party at age fifty-two qualified as a wholly new experience. This time around, I'd be drinking legally, unlikely to meet up with any of my college classmates, and not apt to hit on the cutest boy there, since I was nearly old enough to be his grandmother.

Apparently, Son #2—a former member of this chapter—had ensured I wouldn't be a complete party crasher. As we entered the frat house, I was surprised to face a check-in table with a list of invited guests. And my name was on it.

"Wow, frat parties have changed a lot since my college days," I whispered to him as we were approved and directed down the stairs. "Since when did these things become so official and formal?"

He shrugged. "Just since this chapter finally got off a long probation."

Ahh. So, the Marquette chapter of Sigma Chi had been on "double-secret probation." Maybe frat parties hadn't changed much since the *Animal House* days after all. Strange, though, that Son #2 had never mentioned this imposed penalty while he'd been a student and active fraternity member.

As awkward and out-of-place as I felt walking in, I immediately found myself swept into the middle of crazy fun. These Sigma Chi guys knew how to host a party. Want to throw a beach bash in chilly Milwaukee in April? Fill the basement with sand! (The ever-suffering freshman pledges had to shovel it out the basement windows the next day.) Want to make a random old lady feel at home? Ask the DJ to play "Shout!" and dance with that middle-aged stranger without even questioning why she's there.

Disclaimer: One young female guest did tap my shoulder as we were dancing and ask, "Who *are* you and why are you here?" I told her I was pledging the fraternity. She nodded and continued dancing, seeming totally OK with that.

As an older and more seasoned party guest, I also knew a thing or two about the social etiquette of bringing a gift. In this case, instead of bringing a bottle of wine, I deposited a six-pack of beer upon the basement bar.

Before I get charged with contributing to the delinquency of minors, I should note the guys at the entrance checked IDs and secured yellow wristbands on the legal drinkers. Sigma Chi could not afford another double-secret probation. Besides, given the stacks of cardboard cases behind the bar, they had plenty of *better* beer on hand. I doubted the chapter bartender would have to contend with anyone else begging for my Miller 64, once dubbed by my disgusted sister, Lori, as "pisswater."

With a beer in hand and keeping my pledge to not ride on my son's former fraternity coat tails, I suggested the two of us split up. He put up no argument.

Maneuvering through the wall-to-wall crowd was the first challenge. Thankfully, my recent bout of claustrophobia didn't repeat itself. And as far as being more than twice the age of anyone else there? I fantasized this age discrepancy was *hardly* perceptible.

Making conversation, however, proved far more difficult than I expected: since I couldn't hear a word over the ear-piercing music. Perhaps I should have borrowed my mother's hearing aids.

Mid-conversation, I found myself trying to read lips and then simply nodding with a blank stare at my new friends, these college kids with their nearly virgin ears. *Just wait*, I thought, until decades of full-volume earbuds and concerts catch up with you. Who will be laughing then? Me, that's who! Even if I can't *hear* myself laugh.

I desperately wanted to ask the DJ to turn down the volume. But if you want to prove ancient and decrepit in a crowd of college students, try complaining about the tunes.

I sighed inaudibly to myself and headed across the basement for another bottle of pisswater. The bartender-for-a-night handed me a beer and then winked at me, producing an unmarked beige bottle from behind the bar.

I squinted at the bottle of orangeish liquid. "What's this?" I shouted.

"Moonshine," he shouted back.

Moonshine? I winced. Sure, I feared the god-awful taste as well as the heady repercussion from this high-proof alcohol of undetermined origin. But mostly I was suspicious about drinking from a communal bottle. It was still flu season. I was leaving for Italy in a week. I was old and wary. Who knew where all those college-aged lips had been before they'd been puckered around the neck of that mysterious bottle?

The barkeep reassured me only a select few guests had swigged from the bottle. *A select few* at a *frat party*. Was that not an oxymoron?

But The 52/52 Project was about immersing myself in new experiences, even if they entailed a risk or two. I wiped the rim of the bottle, closed my eyes, and chugged. Huh. It wasn't garbage. I took another swig, just to be certain.

I was hardly surprised a few days later when I was hit by a horrendous upper respiratory infection. I left for Italy pumped full of antibiotics.

Even so, I had no real regrets about the moonshine. I did somewhat regret the watered-down beer I drank that night, since it eventually required me to ask directions to the bathroom—*a frat house bathroom.* (I will pause now as you envision this.) And I also momentarily regretted wandering into a back room of the basement, a dark one with strobe lights and couples entwined together in each corner. Even the moonshine I swigged didn't prepare me for those flashing images. An Animal House it might have been, but Dean Wormer's wife I clearly was not.

I figured this was a good time to take my talents to a local college bar, which Son #2 and I managed to close up. I prided myself on hanging with those youthful late-nighters, although I regretted that just a tad the next morning.

Good decisions make great memories; bad decisions make great stories. My Big Fat Greek Party resulted in both.

It was official: I was re-enrolling in college and pledging Sigma Chi. My fraternity pledge was pretty much guaranteed. As long as I agreed to join the freshmen in shoveling the beach party sand out the basement windows—and I borrowed my mother's hearing aids.

I'd bring my own bottle of moonshine.

Chapter 47:

A SEGWAY INTO CATASTROPHE

When a newspaper reporter asked how I came up with
the idea to undertake fifty-two new challenges, it
dawned on me that the idea had been brewing subconsciously
since my first trip to Italy. I spent half of that with my youngest son, who was serving a college assistantship in a small
Italian town. The rest of the trip, I traveled the country alone.

I had never been to Europe. With the exception of several visits to our northern neighbor, I had never been outside
the United States. Besides the required customs stop at the
Ambassador Bridge just an hour from home ("No, Officer, I
am carrying no firearms or fresh fruit"), Canada hardly qualified as international travel.

Solo-tripping through Italy had been both an organi-
zational dream and nightmare for a self-professed obsessive
planner. I plotted an itinerary. I scheduled flights. I booked
rooms in Rome, Florence, Siena, and Venice. I researched
cross-country train and bus transportation. (Here's an interesting tidbit about traveling in Italy: The conductor seldom

asks for your ticket or announces where that particular bus or train, on which you are already seated, is going. So you'd best be damn sure you're on the right one.)

Often without a tour guide or companion to set me on track when I second-guessed myself—which was *always*—I somehow managed to arrive at all my planned destinations and see most major sights. I ordered fabulous food and wine, and mingled with locals and other international tourists, without speaking more than a few words of Italian.

I never did learn how to ask, in Italian, "Where is the bus station?" or "Where is the ladies room?" Those phrases would have proven advantageous. However, the only Italian I managed to master was "Un altro, per favore." *"Another one, please."*

I came away from that trip discovering I was more independent, capable, and courageous than I ever imagined. We all are braver and more competent than we realize, if only we challenge ourselves. That newfound awareness was likely the true impetus for my year of new adventures. I wondered: What other intimidating experiences could I accomplish if I simply attempted them?

I remained so under Italy's spell, that I had promised myself I'd move there as soon as I won the Mega Millions jackpot. (Note to self: Probably best to start playing the lottery if I plan to win.) Two years later, my mother proposed we return there, together. I leaped at her suggestion—as well as her offer to subsidize the trip.

But to justify spending ten days in Italy, I reasoned I should incorporate at least one 52/52 challenge into the trip.

I had scratched "Driving a Motorcycle" from my list of potential exploits months earlier. Apparently, the United States had some silly law requiring a motorcycle license. Additionally, *none* of my cycling friends would relinquish their bike to me. Something about my lack of experience and coordination. Yadda-yadda-yadda…

While I realized I clearly needed new friends, I hadn't fully given up my quest to go motoring.

Enter Italy: Land of *molti* motor bikes, flimsy regulations, and possibly the world's craziest drivers. My plan seemed foolproof.

As I approached the motorbike rental shop in Florence, I envisioned myself as Audrey Hepburn in *Roman Holiday*: I'd dazzle spectators with my royal beauty and grace as I set forth on an adventure through the city, perched upon a classic Vespa.

But my cycling plans switched gears as soon as I spied the shop's sign for Segway rentals. My brain went into overdrive. The new me, the one with a fledgling ability to be spontaneous, took over. While I couldn't quite picture the classy and sophisticated Audrey joyriding on one of these goofy contraptions, I immediately embraced the idea.

"Italian motorbikes are cool," I told my mother, "but Segways are practically *exotic*."

My mom's eyes lit up as she nodded. Yes, in our family, the nut doesn't fall far from the tree.

The shop was new and business was slow, especially since the gray and drizzly day had deterred most customers. The clerk appeared eager to sign a rental. No experience? No problem! She had plenty of time on her hands to provide some instruction.

Following a few false starts, I got a feel for putting the upright vehicle into motion by leaning slightly forward. But *stopping* the Segway was more problematic. After a series of residual spurts whenever I tried to come to a halt, I eventually learned to stand up straight and motionless to ease the scooter to a stop.

Disembarking proved more challenging. Whenever I managed to stop and tried to step off, I tended to bend forward. This jolted the Segway back into gear, and jolted my heart into palpitations. Each time I inadvertently lurched across the lobby with one foot on and one foot off, the ever-patient clerk chased after me. She finally taught me to bring the vehicle to rest against a wall, averting any further movement before I safely climbed off.

After fifteen minutes of observing me cruise a few feet before stopping and then halfway hopping/falling off, the growingly confident—or growingly restless—clerk suggested I give it one last test by circling the entire lobby.

I raced around the perimeter of the store (I presumed the ability to control my speed would come later), before coming to a stop against a wall and agilely climbing off.

I flashed the clerk a grin. "There! I've definitely got it now!"

She nodded. "I think you're OK to go. Let's head back to the front counter to take care of the paperwork."

I leaned forward and attempted to turn the scooter. And that was when *everything* took a bad turn.

Apparently, I tried to make a wide turn when I should have kept it tight. I began whirling in circles in a back corner of the lobby. As I spun around, and around, and around again, I became aware of little except passing flashes of walls, rows of parked Segways, and the distressed shop clerk.

As I tried to make out her incomprehensible orders, the satanic Segway took on a life of its own. The harder I tried to stop, the quicker I spun. I tried jumping off, but the scooter and the room around me were spinning fast. As I twisted around in circles, the Segway began crashing against the walls, bouncing off, and then throwing me into another spin.

Dizzy and disoriented, I slammed into a wall one final time. I flew off backward and landed on the floor, beneath the still sputtering Segway. The clerk ran to my rescue, perhaps a moment too late. As she righted the vehicle, I crawled to my feet.

"I'm fine, I'm fine," I reassured her.

My mom, who'd been in the bathroom directly behind the last wall I'd hit, ran out as quickly as her legs and her cane could carry her.

"What happened?" she shouted. "Are you alright? I heard a huge crash! The whole bathroom shook!"

As my frantic mother and I followed the clerk's silent stare, I knew no explanation was necessary. My accident had left me only bruised, physically and mentally. The Segway, too, appeared unscathed. Yet the brand new shop's now savaged walls told the tale sufficiently. Well, the scraped walls *and* the two baseboards I had smashed and entirely broken off. Several strips of wooden trim lay shattered across the floor. The store was in shambles.

"I'm so, *so* sorry," I told the clerk. I bit my thumbnail and searched her face for my next cue, uncertain whether to laugh or cry or just get the hell out of there, pronto.

She looked around at the destruction and cleared her throat.

"It's OK," she said. "I'm sure this can all be easily fixed." I waited for her to add, "Besides, this happens *all* the time."

No, it was a safe assumption that this particular catastrophe was a first. And that my brief Segway experience would be my last.

Maybe the clerk took pity on me, or maybe she was paid by commission. She hesitated only a few moments before signing off on my rental. How could I argue with the assurance of a professional? Besides, I had a new venture to complete this week, and small details like my chronic uncoordination and resulting collateral damage shouldn't stop me. So, I signed the liability waiver, and headed out to explore Florence, Segway-style.

Perhaps the clerk's judgment, and mine, were a bit shortsighted. In my defense, I figured I already set the Segway-riding bar exceedingly low, so what did I have to lose? Following my new mantra, borrowed from a group of Kent State University students I'd befriended the previous night in an Italian café, I told myself, "Perche' non?"

Why not, indeed?

My mom seemed less convinced.

"You're sure? Really? You're going? OK. Good luck. Be careful," she shouted as I took off. "I love you!"

She likely imagined they were the last words she would ever say to me.

I flashed her a thumbs-up, inadvertently leaning forward and jolting the Segway into motion. No worries, I thought as I hurdled over the curb. I *had* this.

Within a couple blocks, I found myself gliding blissfully, with my hair flying in the breeze and the formerly possessed Segway now safely exorcised. I stayed clear of the busiest streets. The less-traveled, cobblestone roads made for a bumpier ride but allowed me the advantage of seeing old Florence's hidden treasures.

These days, I normally relied on my cell phone to keep track of time. But my first visit to Italy had taught me— the expensive way—about international calls and data, so I hadn't even brought my phone on this trip. After a lengthy Segway spin around Florence, I glanced at the watch my mom loaned me when I left the shop. Probably time to head back.

Congratulating myself on another safe and wide turn around an intersection, I veered back in the direction of the shop. I'd been careful to drive in strategic circles around the city so I wouldn't get lost. Oh, I was adventurous, yet I was also quite clever.

A few blocks later, however, I still didn't stumble upon the street I was searching for. As I squinted at the "via" names etched in the corners of intersection buildings, I grew confused—and very, *very* leery of my devil-may-care exploration. After I passed several blocks that definitely did not look familiar, it dawned on me: Many of Florence's streets inexplicably changed names along their course.

I had no idea where I was or which of these streets might morph into the one on which the Segway rental shop was located. I was lost in the middle of BFE, or more precisely, BFI.

I took a deep breath while I contemplated the Italian word for "*Fuuuck!*"

I had no map. I had no cell phone. I didn't know the phone number, address, or even the name of the Segway shop. I spoke virtually no Italian, other than being able to ask for another drink. I would have welcomed a drink. Unfortunately, I'd left my purse, containing all my money and credit cards, with my mom at the shop.

Even a hundred Euros wouldn't buy my way back to the shop though. Since I also had no driver's license or passport, no one would be able to identify my body if I crashed or finally died from dehydration.

In the heat of panic, I knew I needed to pull over and collect my thoughts. I slowed and tried to stop at the side of the road. But without a convenient wall to rely upon, as I had been trained, I bounced off the curb and began spinning into the street. A car swerved around me, and the driver leaned out the window and shouted at me.

I wasn't certain what this Italian man was screaming, yet I suspected it included the four-letter word I'd just been searching for.

I circled the city for another fifteen minutes, until the street emptied into a piazza. The iconic Florence Duomo loomed before me.

Spying this familiar sight, I zoomed forward and then jerked to a stop against a storefront. Fearful at the outcome of trying to step off the Segway, I instead leaned sideways toward the man next to me and nodded to the map in his hand.

Communication was no issue, since I quickly learned

he was a Norwegian tourist who spoke four languages. He also knew exactly where he was and where he was going. He shrugged and handed me the map.

"I haven't really needed it anyway," he said.

Some people are blessed with an amazing sense of direction. Other spin in circles in store lobbies.

I finally located the obscure street on which the shop was located and, with my index finger, traced my route back. I pocketed the map, just to be safe. I might not be multilingual, but I'd grown way smarter in the last hour.

Five minutes later, I pulled up in front of the shop.

My mother and the clerk were waiting at the doorway. As they spotted me, a look of relief washed over their faces. *They* were relieved?

I couldn't let on what had transpired over the past hour though. While lacking coordination and common sense, I still had my pride.

Sure, I was more Kevin James in *Mall Cop* than Audrey Hepburn in *Roman Holiday*. But damned if I couldn't pretend, at least for thirty seconds, that I was an Italian princess and this was my kingdom.

I smiled at them and coolly cruised on for another block. As I passed by, before executing one final and perfect turn, I gave them both a royal wave.

Chapter 48:

RUNNING FOR MY LIFE

had rushed into several of my new ventures with pitiful preparation. But I knew one item remaining on my list, if I were to pull it off, would require months of baby steps.

Running a 5K was *miles* outside my comfort zone—just over three miles, to be exact.

Being over-the-hill, overweight, out-of-shape, and out-of-breath, I tended to evade working out at all costs. Did I avoid exercise because I was in this condition? Or was I in this condition because I avoided exercise? Clearly, it was pause for the chicken-and-egg question.

All I knew was that I was totally chicken about making this particular commitment. After all, I was the type who piled items at the bottom of the stairs all day to prevent any unnecessary trips up the steps. (Because I was time-efficient!) The type who promised Ringo the Wonder Retriever a long walk, yet turned back after two blocks. (Because it was too cold, too hot, or too dark—for poor Ringo, of course!) The type who, when I moved to my new condo, insisted on dragging along the treadmill I hadn't used in years. (Because I might use it!) (Disclaimer: After moving, I never again stepped within two feet of it.)

I always began a new exercise routine with good intentions, but I managed to justify never seeing it through. I promised myself to work out tomorrow, or the next day, but never *ever* today. That made participating in a 5K one of the first challenges I added to my 52/52 list, but one of the last I would finally attempt. Why put off until tomorrow what you can put off for an entire year?

Although I was slothful, I had learned a lot about my strengths and weaknesses. I knew I could never get through that race if I didn't begin training months ahead. So, early that fall—eight months before my scheduled 5K event in the spring—I laced up my new shoes for my first training run.

I tried to recall the last time I ran. It was probably twenty years ago, and it was likely to the bar for last-call.

Before heading out the door, I glanced at my cell phone to check my starting time—and to make sure I had 911 programmed on speed-dial. As an extra precaution, I called my mom.

"If you don't hear from me within an hour," I told her, "send an EMT squad. I can't be sure exactly where they'll find my body, but less than fifty feet from my house is a good guess."

"You're going to try to run? Oh, bless your heart," she said, sounding more condescending than concerned.

I managed half a block before my arthritic knees buckled and my lungs began spasming. I stopped and stooped over. Who was I kidding? I got winded just rolling over in bed. If I couldn't run a hundred yards, how would I ever manage a three-mile race?

But I had made a 5K commitment—a publicly announced one, at that. So, I began a sporadic routine of what my friend, Toni, called *wogging*: a combination of walking and jogging. I wogged nearly a dozen times over the next couple of weeks, forcing myself to hit the trail even when it was the last thing I wanted to do. And it was *always* the last thing I wanted to do.

I kept waiting for those infamous endorphins to kick in and take me to some biochemical high. The endorphins eluded me, and I never found myself delighting in a run. I did, however, begin to see traces of some headway in both my distance and my stamina. *That* was a reward, of sorts.

As I carried on, my confidence spiked. I figured by my race the following spring, I'd not only breeze through the five kilometers but would find myself bored and tapping my toes at the finish line while all the wannabe runners finally shuffled through.

No good deed, however, goes unpunished. I soon started wincing from pain in my back thigh, right below my butt. After it persisted for a couple of weeks, I made a doctor's appointment.

"So," my doctor asked me, "where does it hurt?" Apparently, this is an *actual* medical question, not just the setup for an old joke.

"Right here," I said, pointing to the general area.

She poked and prodded. "Hmm. Guessing it's your hamstring. You probably pulled it."

When I explained I had started running a few weeks ago, she nodded.

"No more running until it heals. Could take a few weeks."

A few weeks? A month before, I'd have been eager for any excuse at all to stop running. Now, just as I'd begun to feel committed and to see progress, I was incredibly disappointed. Maybe I was evolving after all.

"Meanwhile, I can either prescribe some steroid pills to help with the inflammation, or we can give you a shot today," she said. "Your choice."

I chose the shot in my ass. This year of new experiences was either making me very brave or very stupid.

Weeks later, just as my hamstring seemed to heal, the

early and vengeful winter—as mentioned in prior chapters— blew in.

My hometown, Toledo, made Internet headlines that year by being given the dubious distinction of the worst winter in the nation. As the temperatures plummeted into negative numbers and local schools seemed to be closed more often than they were open, I told myself that running outdoors would be risky and irresponsible.

I enjoyed a couple comfortable months of sitting on my gluteus maximus, until a runner friend guilted me into giving it another go. The temperature had hit twenty degrees that day. Practically balmy.

I dressed myself in four layers and trudged out the door. The temperature may have stretched to twenty-two degrees, but I failed to consider the wind chill factor. I managed a ten-minute, blustery wog before my face became freezer-burned, my nostrils froze shut, and—in a final but not surprising assault—my feet hit an ice patch. Fortunately, my fall was softened by a three-foot high snowbank, six inches of clothing, and a naturally padded posterior.

I limped back home, nostalgic for the happier days of camping next to serial killers.

With no respite over the rest of the risky and wicked winter, I never ventured back out. Both my sons suggested I join a gym with a running track; I assured them I couldn't afford such a luxury. Somehow, I managed to conveniently forget about the treadmill rusting in a corner of my basement.

I once again grew content and comfortable with my safe and sedentary lifestyle. My race wasn't until mid-May. I reasoned I could wait until early spring to simply pick up where I had left off.

By April, the sidewalks and streets began to clear. I began plodding once again through my neighborhood. I quickly realized my five-month hiatus had left me starting from scratch. WTH? *Inconceivable.*

I wogged religiously for three consecutive evenings. Just as I began to develop a routine, I was hit by a massive upper respiratory infection. (Thank you, Sigma Chi communal moonshine bottle!) It sidelined me for days. And, as soon as I could once again breathe without hacking, I left for my ten-day vacation in Italy. How could I continue my training there with everything this trip entailed? Busy bus tours! Hazardous cobblestone streets! Wine with every meal!

The evening I returned home from Italy, I checked my calendar. I realized I was supposed to be checking "Run a 5K" off my list in just nine days. It appeared my newest running routine consisted mainly of running out of excuses.

After months of little training, and with just over a week before D-Day, I headed out the next afternoon.

Following our horrific winter, Toledo skipped spring entirely. May slipped straight into the hot hells of summer. After taking roughly nine steps, in ninety-degree temps, I feared the humidity might suffocate me. I recalled all those months of my bitching and moaning about the cold and snow. I had probably exceeded my quota of weather complaints. So I sucked it up and pushed on.

I succeeded to cover three miles that day, but in reality I ran less than one. I managed the other two at a pace no faster than the mud-covered turtle I encountered that day along the park trail. Gosh, this little guy was cute! I paused for ten minutes to take photos of my new reptilian friend, telling myself the break was due to an irresistible Kodak moment.

Who was I kidding? I needed those ten minutes to catch my breath. The turtle knew this, too. By the way he seemed to sneer at me, I was pretty sure he was a *mock* turtle.

When race day rolled around, I woke up after a sleepless night, panicked. I had a two-fer 52/52 Project day planned. Not only was I running in the 5K that morning, I was also slated to take part in a ghost hunt that night. I found myself worried about being unable to run *far* enough at the first event and *fast* enough—to escape from spooks—at the second.

The race starting line was on a blocked-off street bordering the Toledo Zoo. As I took my place toward the back of a sea of hundreds of other participants, I surveyed my competition. It wasn't difficult to discern most of the hardcore racers from the more recreational runners and casual walkers. I was relieved to observe several people older than me and some in equally questionable physical shape. A number of families with young children were also on hand. I assumed most of them had selected the non-timed walking option. I, however, had elected to be a true race contender.

I might not be the first to pass the finish line, nor even the 200th. But given the number of seniors and small children, I wouldn't be the last! Assuming, of course, that I actually finished.

I never heard the proverbial shotgun start, but I knew the race had begun as soon as the mob in front of me began to push forward. I moved ahead with the crowd.

Son #2, who recently completed his first full marathon, had advised me that pacing was imperative. I started off at a slow jog and figured I'd pick up speed at a quarter mile. Unfortunately, quarter-mile points along the course weren't marked. I tried to gauge the distance, and after a few blocks, I guessed it was time to kick it up.

I ran for five minutes before being forced to put on the brakes. Holy hell! Mama needs a new pair of lungs!

But I had promised myself I'd run, at least at a Sherry-style pace, for the first mile. No walking allowed until I passed that one-mile marker. Then, I'd alternate between running and power walking.

I became obsessed with spying that first mile marker sign. It should be just ahead. Or only a few feet more. Or right around that next corner.

"Hey," I shouted to the runner next to me. "Shouldn't we have hit the one-mile mark by now?"

"No, I've run this course before," he yelled back as he passed me. "We're only around the half-mile point."

I sighed and forced a sprint: of sorts. The sooner I reached that target, the sooner I could give my lungs, and my legs, a reprieve.

Spotting the one-mile mark sign didn't prove necessary, since I heard the curbside crowd cheering as we approached. I was surprised how much that encouragement from strangers at each mile-marker boosted my spirit and my adrenalin.

Wheezing, I slowed to a near stop and walked the next block. After I caught my breath, I fell back into my usual routine—power-walking a couple blocks and then running a few more.

While not timing myself, I felt pleased with my progress and my pace. Until a woman with a stroller approached from behind me. I smiled down at the baby and then glanced up at the woman: She was at least ten years older than me, presumably out for a brisk walk with her grandchild.

She grinned at me and shouted, "Beautiful day, isn't it?"

"Uh-huh, *gorgeous*," I yelled back, panting between syllables.

"Enjoy yourself," she chirped, not sounding breathless in the least. She raced past me. I mumbled something about "freaks of nature," but she didn't catch that. She and the stroller were already three yards ahead.

After the two-mile mark, everything began to blur. I huffed and I puffed, and my right knee taunted me. "Whatcha think," it seemed to hiss, "shall I drop us right here?"

Just as I began to wonder if I'd need to walk the rest, the course wound into the zoo grounds. The final leg! As I passed by the monkey exhibit, I spied a banner ahead of me. This was it! The end was in sight!

I picked up speed, running far faster than I ever anticipated my lungs and legs were capable. As I reached the banner, I collapsed and nearly wept with relief and joy.

Someone shouted my name, and I turned to see my neighbor, Lynn, who happened to be manning this race station. In between my hyperventilating, I smiled up at her, anticipating her words of congratulations. I was mistaken.

"No, don't stop now, Sherry! Keep going," she yelled. "This isn't the finish line!"

Apparently, the banner I'd just passed under was merely some late-race advertisement by a sponsor. The end was not in sight after all. Race planners are sadistic creatures.

I have no idea how much farther I ran before I reached the real finish line. Fifty yards? A half mile? That final leg seemed to last days.

All I know is I managed to make it to the end. And when I did, when I sprinted underneath that last course banner, an amazing feeling overcame me. Maybe those elusive endorphins somehow kicked in, or maybe I was just relieved the trauma had ended.

As I bent over, managing to remain semi-upright and breathing, I felt my greatest sense of self-accomplishment ever. Yes, I did have to walk portions of the course, but I had run nearly two miles of it. That was two miles more than I ran, cumulatively, in the entire two decades preceding The 52/52 Project.

When results were posted online that afternoon, I discovered I finished in forty-seven minutes, forty-nine seconds. In my category (women aged fifty to fifty-four), I placed thirty-seventh out of thirty-nine. Sure, I received no accolades for this. But if they had awarded a medal for the participant most out-of-shape and most ill-prepared, that gold would be mine.

Finishing the race was really all I had hoped for. As pleased as I was with that accomplishment, it was more of a shocker to those who knew me so well.

"You actually *ran?*" questioned Son #1. "Honestly, I can only picture you kind of hobbling."

Nice vote of confidence, beloved fruit of my loins.

I hobbled the next two days.

Chapter 49:

I DO BELIEVE IN SPOOKS

A half-dozen celebrity ghost hunters, more than a hundred amateur aficionados, and one paranormal virgin enter a haunted prison.

Oh, you're waiting for the punch line? Nope, no joke here, just one weird and eerie experience.

Lots of folks love a good ghost story. Me? Not so much. Having an aversion to even the fictional forms (see my previous horror movie marathon chapter), I harbored an even bigger fear of ghosts that might actually exist.

As with most mysterious phenomena—aliens, Bigfoot, the Tooth Fairy—I wasn't certain if ghosts were real. If they were, would a ghostly encounter prove to be like a *Casper* cartoon or more like *The Conjuring?* With no way to know, I found it best to avoid ghosts rather than to seek them out.

This, of course, obligated me to add ghost hunting to my year of fear.

I wouldn't be attempting this expedition solo. Since my goal was not only to seek out ghostly apparitions but also to learn about them, a structured event appeared the way to lose my paranormal virginity. My friend, Marion, joined me on a ghost hunting tour at the former Ohio State Reformatory in Mansfield, Ohio. This old prison, which had been closed for about two decades, was the creepy filming location for *The Shawshank Redemption*. It was notorious worldwide for its spooks.

As we entered the city of Mansfield, our GPS led us into the expansive reformatory grounds. We rounded a corner and passed a "restricted" sign.

Marion frowned. "Wait, the sign says this area is restricted. I don't think we're allowed to be here."

"Nah, we're good," I told her. "We bought tickets, remember?"

She squinted at me, unconvinced, but kept driving.

We circled the prison cemetery, and both of us broke out in visible goose bumps. I assured Marion this was due to "self-induced fear" and nothing more. Not that I believed my own words.

As we passed a large, newish-looking building for the second time, a patrolling security guard flagged us down.

"Excuse me, ladies. Hold it right there," he said. He peeked in our car and sized us up. "What are you doing here? This area is restricted."

"Oh, it's OK," I informed him. "We paid for a tour." I pulled the event tickets from my purse and waved them in front of him.

The guard grimaced. "No. Those things are held at the old, closed reformatory," he told me in short, halting words, as if talking to a four year old. "This here is the current *working* prison. You can't be here."

Marion glared at me. She mouthed, "I told you so."

Apparently though, two clueless middle-aged women didn't pose a major security threat. He waved us off, pointing us in the right direction.

As we rounded another corner, the old penitentiary loomed before us: a magnificent and imposing piece of architecture. As we entered, however, we discovered the inside was something entirely else. The structure contained not just the standard frightening fare of ubiquitous cobwebs but also rotted wood, rusty fixtures, and broken concrete. Ghosts seemed fitting fare.

Marion and I were accompanied at this event by experts from several paranormal TV shows, including *Ghost Hunters* and *Haunted Collector*—plus a hundred and fifty of their fanatic followers. One paranormal group drove in several hours from Indiana in a hearse. These folks were hardcore. I was way out of their supernatural league.

As someone who watched little TV, I had no idea of the huge following these celebrities had. The visiting pros included Steve Gonsalves, Amy Bruni, Adam Berry, John Zaffis, Josh Gates, and Chip Coffey. They proved to be a knowledgeable and entertaining bunch.

If there were any ghosts lurking in a dark hallway that night, these guys would find them. And once they did, I planned to fast-track it to the farthest corner, where I would curl up and cry. Sluggish after participating in my first 5K that morning, I doubted I could even outrun the Stay Puft Marshmallow Man.

Originally a boys' reformatory before becoming a men's state prison in the late eighteen hundreds, the building had a long history of hauntings. These tales, relayed throughout our tour by the TV ghost hunters and seasoned reformatory volunteers, kept us captivated—and paranoid.

Marion and I learned certain locations within the prison were particularly fraught with paranormal activity. Ghosts were seen frequently in the area where a prisoner had murdered a guard. A vision of a strange woman was often witnessed wandering through the warden's living quarters; a former warden's wife had died there when a loaded pistol fell from a closet shelf. Apparitions also appeared regularly in a cell block where an inmate committed suicide by setting himself on fire.

Marion and I huddled closer together, our eyes darting in all directions, as we listened.

She nudged me and whispered. "What?"

"What do you mean, 'what?'"

"Didn't you just touch my head?"

"No. Why?"

"I could have sworn someone was just playing with my hair."

"You're just imagining it," I whispered back.

"No, I *definitely* felt a hand brushing my head," Marion said. She clutched my arm. "This is freaking me out. This was a bad idea. Why are we doing this?"

"Wait, you're the one who watches this stuff on TV," I reminded her. "Besides, these are just *stories*. Who's to say any of this is real? I'm a writer, remember? I make up stories all the time."

She nodded. Our eyes met. We continued after our guide, resuming our nervous glances around.

The stories we heard were only one piece of the paranormal pie. And with so many people roaming through the prison, it was difficult to validate all the strange lights, shadows, or sounds. We managed to disregard many, and we learned that true ghost hunters relied on the results of paranormal tests from equipment such as flashlights, lasers, and "voice boxes."

As we stood in the old shower room, an area well known for spirit activity, the guide's flashlight inexplicably flickered. I shrugged this off. After all, flashlights were temperamental tools. Could be a loose bulb or a dying battery. The fact that the light shut on and off upon command—exactly when the guide asked the spirit to do so—I couldn't explain that so easily.

Marion and I wandered a while on our own and then returned to the shower room. Eight people were now gathered around a voice box. Given my limited know-how, I was unfamiliar with these devices, which supposedly transmitted supernatural sounds through radio waves. The group was listening intently and carrying on a conversation through the box with a presumed spirit named Mark.

Over the next ten minutes, Mark answered endless questions. We talked about his background, the murders he committed, and his experiences while incarcerated here. Some of his responses were muffled and others indecipherable through radio static. But many of his words were coherent. Every time he spoke, those of us assembled would immediately repeat what we thought we heard— and we generally agreed.

Yet, still, a radio providing unequivocal paranormal evidence? I was fascinated and a bit unsettled by the strange conversation, but the skeptic in me determined it could be staged by either the event's PR team or a local radio geek getting his kicks.

When Marion and I later headed up to the sixth-floor attic, we had our second voice box encounter. The attic's celebrity tour guide, John Zaffis, said he and his last group had been carrying on a long discussion with an inmate spirit. His name was Mark. His age, his crimes, and the other details he provided all matched those of the earlier conversation Marion and I witnessed in the shower room.

During our meet and greet earlier that evening, John had appeared the most conservative and practical celebrity in the bunch. As we relayed our similar experience with the first voice box, he seemed stunned. He questioned us extensively, as if he didn't believe this repeat encounter was likely. But "Mark" remained on the air in the attic, talking to us through this second voice box. Although this device was more static-filled than the one in the shower room, Marion and I agreed it was the same voice.

If it was a scam, it was a well-executed one. I left the attic, in no way convinced but with my mind opened one more notch.

The secluded attic and basement were the areas where the worst prison atrocities had once taken place. No surprise that these sites of horrific abuse and torture of inmates had the most reported paranormal activity.

Steve Gonsalves, our guide for this next leg of the tour, warned that due to the basement's physical condition, including broken steps and a crumbling concrete floor, he couldn't advise going down there.

And so, we headed downstairs.

It didn't seem a drastic or dangerous decision. After hearing a number of tales and warnings that evening, Marion and I—and a woman named Maria, who had befriended us—figured the basement couldn't pose any worse threat. We never anticipated the night's most frightening and compelling supernatural evidence would strike, just around midnight, while the three of us were standing alone in the very dark and very disturbing basement. Without a professional in sight to save our sorry souls.

"Dark" didn't begin to describe the basement. With no windows to allow a glimpse of outside illumination and no other passing guests to provide flickers of light, we relied on the narrow beams of our own flashlights while we explored. The basement was a huge, open area. Unlike the rest of the building, it didn't contain any twists or turns or mazes of hallways. And, it was undoubtedly devoid of anyone but us.

After we searched the room's full circumference, Marion suggested we turn off our flashlights. The basement fell back to black.

Marion's voice punctuated the silence. "If there's anyone out there, we'd like to talk to you," she said. "We're just here to talk. We don't mean you any harm. If you are here, let us know."

Suddenly, I felt like a ten year old at a slumber party séance. I giggled. Marion elbowed me, and I covered my mouth, swallowing my last snorts of laughter.

"We're not here to hurt you," Marion continued. "We just want to know if someone is with us. Signal us in some way that you are here. Give us a sign. Knock three times on the pipes."

Haha! Knock three times, just like the classic seventies song! I smirked and nudged Marion, to offer my latest commentary and maybe a strain of the song's refrain.

But just as my elbow met her ribs, we heard a knock. And a second. And then a third.

The unquestionable clink of metal.

I snapped my flashlight on and swung the beam across the room. I swiveled the light across every inch and every corner. No one but the three of us in the basement. I turned and trained my light on the wall behind us, thinking maybe one of us had inadvertently—or purposely—hit some pipes behind us. After all, we didn't really know if our new acquaintance, Maria, could be trusted.

Nothing behind us but a concrete wall.

With my free arm, I clenched Marion's hand. She clenched mine back. But unlike me, she quickly recouped her courage.

"Turn off your flashlight," she whispered to me. "You might be scaring him."

Wait. I was scaring *him*? I cringed, reluctantly switched off my light, and huddled against the wall.

While Marion continued her efforts to initiate a conversation, we heard nothing more. And then suddenly, she elbowed me. "Stanfa, look to your right. See that light? Holy cow, is that an *orb*?"

I turned my head. A few yards away, a blurry roundish light hovered mid-air. I had never seen an "orb" before and didn't know what one was. But after researching online photographs the next day, this image appeared spot-on.

Whether or not what we saw was an orb, all I knew was we had just witnessed two inexplicable incidents in a dark, windowless, and empty cellar.

And that was when I suggested we high-tail it back upstairs. No one argued.

On the drive back to our hotel, Marion and I pondered our night. Were the things we witnessed only imagined? Or possibly staged? Some phenomena can be logically accounted for. Others can't be explained so easily. As someone who entered this "haunted" prison out of curiosity, open-minded but also skeptical, I left there believing anything was possible.

What remained behind for Marion and me were several haunting photos, a weird audio recording she later discovered on her phone, and a couple bruises we inflicted on each others' arms. Proof enough that it was one crazy and creepy night, yet one which Marion and I—as professional ghostbusters—had survived.

Ghosts? Pfft. I ain't afraid of no ghosts.

Except the ones who announce themselves as I'm cowering in a dark and empty basement in an abandoned prison. Oh, I'm scared as *hell* of those.

SUMMER

Chapter 50:

CATCHING THE BUZZ

*A*s I pried open a wooden crate of bees, I glanced over at the professional beekeeper who had agreed to let me lend him a hand.

Me (nonchalantly): "So, how many bees are in this little kit?"

Beekeeper: "About ten thousand."

Me (inaudibly): "Holy *shit*."

To bee or not to bee? It was way too late in the game for that question or to make a beeline out of there.

I tried to remember the last time I was stung. Maybe thirty years ago? I didn't recall the episode clearly. Unpleasant, for sure, yet nowhere near the agony of something going awry now, as ten thousand bees swarmed around me.

Maybe it bears repeating: *Ten thousand bees.*

This beekeeper gig had drifted on and off my 52/52 list several times, mostly due to my poor planning. Even given my extensive bee expertise—which consisted of knowing bees made honey, were somehow responsible for pollinating plants, and hurt like a bitch when they stung—I was a bit off in my knowledge of the honeybee cycle. When I finally got around to making contact with local beekeepers, most had already started their hives, and it was too early to gather honey.

Thankfully, a local beekeeper, Christian, caught wind of my dilemma and emailed that he was still awaiting a late order of bees. He promised I could assist when the crate arrived. New bees for the newbee: perfect. I waited, on stand-by, for their arrival.

However, there was one small caveat. Christian owned only one protective bee suit which, by the description, would likely be a size too small. I made plans—as I do—to lose twenty pounds in the next week.

If that plan failed, I would be entering into this affair protected only by jeans, a long-sleeved shirt, gloves, and something Christian had called a "veil." I trusted he didn't mean a *bridal* veil. I'd sworn off those for the rest of my life.

At the last minute, I got a message from a local reader, John, who happened to have an extra bee uniform in my size. I left work early that day with the most implausible of excuses. One more thing I never thought I'd hear myself say: "I have to see a man about a bee suit."

Thanks to John, I arrived for my bee play date covered by a slightly snug beekeeper suit and a special helmet with face netting. Ahh—so, *that* was the veil in question.

It was a fabulous look. Outfitted in this white uniform and mask, I was damn certain I resembled a *Star Wars* Stormtrooper.

"You look awesome," yelled my ghost-hunting friend, Marion, standing twenty yards away as she snapped photos. "Wave at the camera!"

While I did look like a sci-fi soldier, a reader had warned me a bee suit wasn't made of armor. Those little bee bastards could still sting their way through it. So, while I went about my work, I made a point of carrying an EpiPen in my pocket.

I had only been stung a few times in my life, and I never experienced an allergic reaction. However, those incidents were *years* ago, and over the past decade I'd developed allergies to almost half of the elements on earth. As far as I knew, the long list of offenders didn't include bee venom. But I wasn't sure this was the best time to test that theory.

I cracked open the last few thin boards of the bee kit, and the bees began to escape into the evening air. I stood stoically in my Stormtrooper uniform. I whispered, "These aren't the drones you're looking for."

I might have laughed at my own geeky joke if only I wasn't so terrified.

While the cloud of bees swirled around me, I attempted to reassure myself that stinging me was *possibly* the last thing on their tiny bee brains. They were simply desperate to find their way into their new hive. Poor little guys. They were probably more afraid than I was.

Still, as they poured out of the kit and into the air, I flinched and blinked twice. Maybe ten thousand times.

Christian stunned the bees into a mellow state by releasing a bit of smoke into the surrounding air. Smoking a little something different might have mellowed me, too, but that didn't seem the most prudent option.

Between the smoke and Christian's expert coaching, nearly all the seemingly amicable creatures made their way into the hive. I escaped with just one sting on my ankle, so painless I didn't even notice until after I left. A pair of socks would have been a wise wardrobe addition.

Thankfully, my EpiPen proved unnecessary. I vowed that the next time I herded bees, I would attempt it as bravely as Christian, who wore no protective gear at all.

My friend, Marion, who trembled and swore multiple

times that afternoon as she took photos, made no such promise of returning. Considering she was once stung by an entire swarm of bees and still showed up to support me, I concluded she was the *true* badass that day.

My only disappointments? As I attempted to free the bees from the kit, I accidentally smashed one. I peered down, nudged his limp little body, and sighed. Even worse, Christian informed me that all ten thousand of these creatures—every one of my winged itty-bitty friends—would die in about five weeks. *Oh, the humanity.*

For all the work they did and the environmental benefits they provided in their brief lives, it seemed a cruel twist of fate. But such is the sorry cycle of life for a busy little bee.

After pulling off my Stormtrooper suit and mask, I peered one last time at the bees making themselves at home in their new hive. Considering the bad rap they got, they served an incredibly important environmental purpose. I gained a whole new appreciation for bees.

As I climbed into my car, my body abuzz with both victory and relief, I hoped the Force was strong with them.

Chapter 51:

SPEED-DATING: SOLO-STYLE

*A*fter I struck out earlier that year in my online dating game, several folks told me I forfeited too soon. I hemmed and hawed but agreed to explore some other method of meeting men. The obvious alternative? Speed-dating.

I would rather face another year of online rejection than face a roomful of strange men, in person, during a single night of one-on-one interviews across a bar table. Queasy as the idea made me, I registered for an upcoming event.

The night before the affair, however, I received a message from the speed-dating company that the event had been cancelled. If I thought my online dating experience had been a bust, it was nothing compared to this. The cause for cancellation? A dozen women had signed up, yet only one man had registered.

One.

If I was a tad disappointed ("disappointed" being a huge overstatement), I figured the individual most frustrated by the cancellation was that one registered guy. With a twelve-to-one ratio, he could have been Bill Cosby or Ted Bundy and his chances at scoring a date would still have surpassed all of the women's odds.

I was nearing the conclusion of my project. Due to a couple timing issues and unexpected cancellations, I was already a few weeks past my planned completion. Rather than waiting around for a rescheduled date and risk that also being cancelled, I decided to take this item into my own incapable hands. And to up the ante.

Enter Sherry's Solo Speed-Dating Adventure.

Over the next week, I pledged to visit seven eating and drinking establishments to personally interview men. And no, "interview" was *not* a euphemism.

Here were my rules:

- I must sit by myself at the bar.
- I must strike up a conversation with at least two guys at each venue.
- I must stay at each place for a minimum of one hour.
- I must work a few planned questions into the conversation. I figured, "Have you ever been convicted of an ax murder?" was a given. Also, "Out of mere curiosity, how many cats do you think a woman may own before you would label her as a crazy cat lady?"
- And, the clincher: If a (presumably) single man piqued my interest and didn't run away, I must ask for his phone number.

If I were twenty-two instead of fifty-two, this venture would have barely budged my boundaries. But I had passed my prime for meeting men in bars. Now, my fingers were a bit shaky just *typing* about it.

When I publicly announced my plans, my Facebook and blog readers offered advice and encouragement.

"Good for you!" one of them wrote. "You've got nothing to lose!"

"Except your dignity," added another.

While many were amused at my solo speed-dating idea, some expressed concern for my safety. Throughout the week, I reassured them with brief online updates.

My first evening went as such:

I headed out right after work for happy hour, which I recalled from the eighties as being high time for the single-mingle. To ease myself into this, I chose a venue in an adjacent suburb, a bar and grill I'd been to a half-dozen times. I had a vague recollection of a cute guy hitting on me there once. I glanced around. Strangely, he wasn't there tonight, thirty years later. I scouted out the small crowd up at the bar and sat two barstools down from the only man sitting alone.

He was a fairly attractive guy, roughly my age. He sat quietly, sipping a beer and watching a soccer match on a nearby TV screen.

I gulped my Bloody Mary as I tried to come up with a clever conversation opener. I knew nothing about soccer. And even less about clever flirtation.

I leaned in. "Big game tonight," I said. "Who's your team?"

He glanced at me. "I don't really care. I'm just waiting here for my wife." He turned back to the TV.

OK then. I hung my head and sucked down a couple sips of my drink. Finally, I pulled out my iPhone to appear busy. Maybe I'd just spend the next hour Facebooking.

With no other viable opportunities over the remaining fifty-five minutes, I moved on to a new establishment. This one had TV screens turned to soccer *and* to Judge Judy. Along with Facebook, that would give me three options to fill the next hour.

Fifteen minutes later, a guy sat down next to me at the bar. I glanced around, waiting for his wife to appear, but I soon concluded he was alone. And he was interested.

He initiated some small talk, which was fortunate considering my own proven ineptitude at that. We talked about music and movies and motorcycles. I feigned a bit of interest in this last topic.

He seemed nice enough, albeit possibly overserved. Regardless, it became clear within fifteen minutes that I felt not one bit of chemistry. He wasn't my type, at all. Although, apart from George Clooney—who'd never shown any real interest in me—I no longer recalled what my type was.

I invested a half hour longer in the experience than I normally would have, just to satisfy my own rules. The conversation wasn't a total loss: I had managed, for the first time in a while, to engage in a long dialogue with a single guy. I had to give myself—and him, too—some credit for that.

When I finally excused myself and was on my way home, I got a text from a blogger friend, Tony, who was in town from Maryland and wanted to meet up. Tony was smart, nice-looking, and a great guy all around, but he lived nearly five-hundred miles away. Besides, we were just friends.

Just friends? And what, exactly, was wrong with that? Not a thing, I told myself.

And so, I ended the night by chatting for hours with a terrific male friend. It only went to prove that fabulous guys were out there, even if they were purely on the buddy level.

The night's score? Romance: Zero. Rewarding friendships: Ten Plus. A damn good outcome of the evening's match, if you asked me.

I recapped these events, online.

"Are any of you still awake? I'm home safe, so no worries," I posted. "I didn't meet a single ax murderer tonight! But, there's always tomorrow."

My second night proved fully uneventful. No ax murderers. No future husbands.

On Night #3 of Solo Speed-Dating, I learned the most awkward of lessons: Even with a thousand dining and drinking establishments in the metropolitan area, you are not likely to meet an attractive and available stranger. You will, however, run into your new boss, the same supervisor with whom you sat down, just two hours earlier, for your first performance review.

While a few folks in my office were aware of that week's endeavor, my new boss—by my strategic exclusion—was not among them. As innocent and nonchalant as I hoped I appeared at the bar, I felt like a kindergartner caught with her hand in the cookie jar.

Unlike me, he wasn't there trolling. He was with his wife and a couple of our organization's leaders, including *his* boss. Although Brenda *did* follow my exploits, she was too professional and too good of a friend to out me to the rest of her party. Probably.

To be safe, I pretended to be with my sister, Lori.

Yes, I had headed there alone and had told no one where I was going. But, in still another small world scenario, Lori and her friend Cay happened to show up and plop down next to me at the bar—at a restaurant I recalled Lori once telling me she didn't even like.

Even in a city with a metropolitan population of more than 650,000, you can run but you cannot hide.

For my fourth night, I chose a sports bar I'd never been and figured I'd be unlikely to run into anyone I knew. I also reasoned this bar and grill, which advertised specialties of cold beer and chicken wings, was a fitting place to finally allow myself a wingman.

An old colleague, Laura A., whom I hadn't seen in twenty years, had messaged me earlier that week and offered to accompany me on an evening out. I considered the possibility that by sitting alone at the bar on my previous outings, I might have appeared too desperate. Having an attractive female friend along might make me more appealing. And, I'd have someone to talk to, no matter what.

While Laura and I perused the menu, I decided against the wings. Instead, I chose a submarine sandwich with a compelling name. Even if I never spoke to a nice-looking guy that night, I could truthfully say I enjoyed a Hot Italian Grinder.

That sandwich was as hot as that evening, or either of the next two evenings, ever got.

By the last day of my solo speed-dating extravaganza, I'd grown weary of spending my evenings at suburban bars. I figured it was time to mix it up. Since I desperately wanted to spend my Sunday evening relaxing at home, I pounced on a reader's idea to instead head out for brunch at a trendy place downtown. I figured I'd broaden my horizons while also attempting to be hip and cool, which was clearly not my norm.

I spied a guy around my age, sitting at the bar, drinking iced tea and writing in a notebook. No wedding ring, either. Single, sober, and a potential writer? It was too good to be true. I parked myself next to him.

He wasn't movie-star handsome yet not unattractive, with a great smile and striking blue eyes. Admittedly, I would have been intrigued by any guy I observed writing in public, even if I discovered he was scribbling a list of needed parts for a car repair. For me, a man with a pen and pad of paper was one hell of an aphrodisiac.

Such an easy intro to a conversation, too. And, as fortune would have it, he was indeed a fledgling writer.

"It's my first book," he said, shrugging apologetically. "I'm a couple thousand words into it. Probably not great writing, but it's a start."

We spent the next hour talking about reading, writing, and

movies. While he was writing science fiction, not my favorite genre, I had explored sci-fi and fantasy enough to respectably discuss them. I could hold my own with *Star Wars* or *Doctor Who* fans. And, as a fifty-two-year-old man (yes, my same age!) who admired J.K. Rowling and read the first few *Harry Potter* books, he deserved bonus points and a minor swoon.

We drew two younger guys, sitting alone at the bar, into our conversation. They were sweet and nerdy, and I soon wanted to adopt both of them.

But my new friend, Tom, was special. I knew it immediately. Fifteen minutes into our conversation, I already decided I would give him my card and tell him to call me. That's how brave, safe, and certain I felt.

He wasn't exactly the kind of guy I usually dated. I'd mostly gone out with white-collar types, and I learned his day job was as a tool-and-die worker. He was former military, which made me wonder how we'd fare on some political and societal topics. I thought he also exuded a bit of machismo, although our conversation clearly indicated a softer side.

But dating the same type of guy doesn't always work to one's advantage. If I hoped to find a man I was interested in dating, as this experience was intended, I needed to open my mind and move past my normal M.O. Tom was by far the most attractive, intelligent, and interesting guy I'd met all week.

This was it. I was in.

As we were both paying our bills, I smiled at him and mentioned what a great place this was.

He nodded. "Yeah, I come here a lot. I live just a few blocks away."

I asked him about his favorite restaurants and bars. A couple other places in the neighborhood were decent, but he said he hadn't yet found a favorite.

"Oh?" I replied, still smiling as I reached into my purse for my card.

"Yeah. It's been tough to find a place I'm really comfortable with," he said. "I'm usually disappointed with most gay bars."

And... The microphone dropped.

As I walked to the parking lot, I alternated between shaking my head and laughing at my naïvety and my clearly inadequate gaydar.

I could have given Tom my card anyway. Even if romance was out of the question, I'm certain he would have made a fabulous new friend. Yet, my card included the link to my blog, and I knew I'd be writing that very night about our encounter. That made any new friendship too awkward.

Still, considering my week of engaging with strange—and not so strange—men, talking with Tom had been a delightful way to spend an afternoon.

As I headed back toward the 'burbs, I wondered if I'd been remiss by sitting at a bar all week. Maybe a different result required a totally different kind of venue. I headed to a nearby bookstore, my own favorite hot spot.

I roamed the aisles for nearly an hour, but the only guy I managed to engage in conversation was a man who was shopping with his wife, buying their daughter the entire *Harry Potter* series. I left there alone but not disappointed, since I did walk away with a plastic bag full of books.

None of my 52/52 dating experiences resulted in one successful date. But as I honestly considered this, I knew I never had been committed to searching for Mr. Right. If he showed up on my doorstep, I might not turn him away. But I didn't *need* Mr. Right, and having a man in my life—at least now—wasn't important enough for me to go looking.

Over the past year, I'd become a more independent woman, fulfilling my life in many ways. If romance happened, on its own, I might welcome it. If it didn't, I'd be good with that, too. I was alone, but not lonely.

Sometimes you find fulfillment through a romantic relationship, and you find pleasure between the bed covers. Yet it's possible to also find happiness in so many areas of your life—maybe even between the covers of a book.

When I got home that evening, I curled up on the couch, cracked open a new paperback, and smiled.

A few pages later, I was already in love.

Chapter 52:

UP, UP, AND AWAIT

Over the past year, I had faced potential injury, anxiety, and humiliation, all with varying degrees of success. I'd grown bolder and braver in many aspects of my life. Yet one particular fear—my greatest nightmare—continued to plague me. While I didn't prove to be allergic to bees, I knew I was still deathly allergic to the thought of crashing to extinction from an ungodly height.

I'd confronted this lifelong fear twice through The 52/52 Project: Zip-lining brought me the thrill of victory, and a high ropes course provided the agony of defeat. But a ride in a hot-air balloon would test this fear by the extreme—specifically, by thousands of feet.

Although the balloon ride was one of the first escapades added to my list, it was the last one checked off. Was this a mere coincidence? Or, through some sadistic irony, had I made it through the entire year only to drop to my death on the very last day?

Scheduling the ride seemed simple enough. Captain Phogg's Balloon Quest in Fenton, Michigan, offered two rides a day, year-round. I had bought a discounted coupon package for four back in February, and the extra tickets were quickly scooped up by my friends, Joan B., Martin, and Roxanne.

For the best weather conditions, the balloon company recommended their sunrise flights. However, a sunset trip scheduled on a weekend worked best for our group. Since none of us was keen about flying in Michigan's toxic winter conditions, we marked our calendars for an evening in April. We also agreed on a couple contingency dates, just in case the first one fell through.

The brochure noted: "Balloons require stable and calm weather conditions. If weather forces cancellation of your flight, simply reschedule and continue to do so until the flight is completed."

Ha. We soon learned this warning was subtle, at best.

When our planned April flight rolled around, I received a midday notice that the trip was cancelled due to high winds. Ditto with the following arranged date. And then, the next.

Kudos to the pilot for erring on the side of safety. But, really? Even though I had major misgivings about this plan, I'd always been a rip-the-bandage-off-quickly type. I wanted to get this final and frightening experience over. How bad could high winds be? I didn't care if our balloon ended up landing in the Emerald City. I just wanted to hoist sail and go.

May arrived, along with disturbing national news: A hot-air balloon had crashed in Virginia, killing all three people aboard. Our next rescheduled launch was set for the very next day. I tried to reassure my friends, and especially myself, that the safest day to go up in a balloon was probably the day after one crashed.

We couldn't confirm this theory though. Wind warnings cancelled that trip, too.

So it went. Again and again. And again. Over that entire spring and into the summer, my fellow passengers and I touched base every afternoon of a scheduled flight, only to learn it was a no-go. Synchronizing a mutually available evening for four people, just to have our plans changed at the last minute, proved to be a logistic nightmare. Each time our trip was cancelled, our reactions fluctuated between disappointment, annoyance, and relief. The sense of relief was mostly mine.

The morning of our eighth rescheduled date—in June—I announced a new scientific discovery: The odds of being struck twice by lightning were far better than the odds of a successful hot-air balloon liftoff. As I awaited the weather verdict, I suggested to my Catholic readers that they offer up a prayer to Saint Jude, the patron saint of lost causes.

Apparently, the weather gods weren't Catholic. I called and gave my cohorts the newest bad news, which all of them said they fully expected.

"Yeah, yeah, yeah. Blah-blah-blah," one of them said. "I actually went ahead and made other plans for tonight. Next time, I'll just assume we're cancelled. Next time, call me only if, by some miracle, we're a go."

At this rate, I figured my year of new adventures at the age of fifty-two might not be completed until I turned *eighty-two*. I considered calling the Sunset House Nursing Home, to see if I could schedule a hot-air balloon launch there in 2043.

We rescheduled, once again, for late July.

The night before our *tenth* rescheduled flight, yet another balloon crashed— after striking a power line in a residential area in Massachusetts. Hordes of readers said I should take this as a sign to cancel. Wise advice, perhaps. But I was *so* close to the end of my 52/52 quest. And, the balloon ride was prepaid, with no refunds. Lose hundreds of dollars or potentially lose my life? Tough call.

Besides, I suspected I wouldn't *need* to chicken out. This damn trip would never come to fruition anyway, through no fault, nor fear, of mine.

Once again, I found myself rationalizing that the odds of two balloon crashes in less than twenty-four hours were miniscule. Surely it was worth the risk.

What, exactly, were the risks? The next morning, as I waited for the pilot's call about the evening's flight, I reviewed the balloon company's brochure again, taking special note of its requirement for a signed waiver. "Balloon flights," the Captain Phogg flyer read, "may involve the possibility of physical risks greater than those encountered in daily life."

Thank you, Captain Obvious.

The brochure also read, "Turn your dreams into reality. Drift free with the wind, suspended from a cloud of color and calling greetings to those unfortunately earthbound."

Being "earthbound," especially after this latest balloon disaster, didn't seem like such a bad option.

The pilot's call came early that afternoon.

"You're calling to cancel, I assume?" His timing was good. I was just deciding what to make for dinner. I was leaning toward microwave popcorn and Diet Coke, for a change.

"No, the forecast looks great," he said. "Tonight's flight is on!"

"But that might change in the next few hours, right? I should expect another call, when we're halfway through our hour-and-a-half drive, to tell us to turn back?"

"Nope. The winds are going to be quite low tonight. This is definitely a go. For sure."

For sure? I'd hold him to that, I vowed, as I called each of my fellow fliers. While I secretly half-hoped our balloon ride would *never* happen, I knew my friends would show him no mercy if he continued to mess with us.

After making the calls, I headed out in my minivan to round up the troops. Son #2, who happened to be in town that weekend, also joined us. It would be comforting, I figured, to have a loved one by my side when I drew my final breath.

Most of the group appeared less concerned about being hoisted a couple thousand feet into the air, however, than they did about the car ride.

Well, sure, we *were* almost late for our long-awaited flight. By the time I picked up all my passengers—and after I took a few wrong turns—the ninety-minute drive took nearly twice as long. And, I took only partial responsibility for our near-death experience when we exited the highway for a bathroom break. After all, it was my first attempt ever at maneuvering a round-about. These were simple mistakes anyone could have made. At least our feet would be on the ground if our car crashed.

We finally arrived, checked in, and signed our waivers. I'd signed my share of these over the past year. But this strangely simplistic one, I had a hunch, could be the last in more ways than one.

Our pilot, Craig, assured us he had forty years of experience and that safety was no concern. In fact, he noted the company's high insurance rate wasn't even related to the flight, but due to the fact that passengers were transported from the landing site by van.

"So, if you were worried about the safety of this flight," he said, "let this reassure you it is far more dangerous to ride in a car."

"See?" Son #2 nudged me. "Nothing to worry about."

"Uh-huh," I whispered back. "You realize he is *paid* to say that. Besides, whether he crashes our balloon or crashes our van, we're as good as dead."

After watching a short video, which tactically omitted accident images of any sort, we headed outside.

The inflated balloon was tethered and sprawled on its side, to provide easier entry into the passenger basket. Accompanied by five other passengers, we crawled inside. It proved less troublesome than, say, entering a race car through a window, yet I still required assistance.

"Always manage to be high-maintenance," remained my motto.

We all leaned inside the basket, nearly stacked horizontally, as the balloon lifted and righted itself. Up, up, and away we went.

I closed my eyes and braced myself.

The balloon seemed to rise effortlessly into the air. I felt none of the turbulence or standard stomach flops experienced on airplane ascents. Opening my eyes, I peeked over the rim of the basket. *Wow.*

As the minutes passed, my fear grew as distant as the disappearing ground below. I gazed down at the colorful patchwork of trees and lakes. Instead of cowering in the middle of the crowd with my eyes closed, as expected, I fought for the best vantage point.

"Wow," I repeated. "This is... amazing!"

Everyone agreed. At least they seemed to agree, given their huge grins. None of us could hear much of what was said, over the roar of the gas fire that pumped the balloon.

Those surges of gas were ear-blasting, and the flames—only inches away—were blistering. We jumped every time the pilot fed the fire. Yet these infernos proved to be the most alarming aspect of our trip. The fact that the ground was now a couple thousand feet below us seemed nearly immaterial.

The entire flight was smooth. My stomach and my nerves remained calm. And the sights? They were *glorious.*

With forests and fifty lakes within a ten-mile radius, this area was a popular balloon route for a reason. As we hovered in the air, we glimpsed two smaller, private balloons and two larger commercial ones like ours. We momentarily dropped lower next to one so we could wave across to its passengers.

A former coworker now living in Michigan posted later on Facebook that she had seen four balloons in the sky that night. Kathy had read of my long rescheduling saga but had no idea where my balloon flight was scheduled or that I'd finally launched. She wondered if, by chance, I was flying that night in the Fenton, Michigan area.

"Yes, that was us!" I wrote back. What was the likelihood that someone I knew would spot me?

Even more, what were the odds I would not only survive the flight but find it exhilarating and enjoyable? Perhaps it was because my fears had been unfounded. As with so many of this year's experiences, I learned the anticipation of something I feared was usually the most agonizing part.

We began our gradual descent and momentarily dropped down further for an up-close view of one of the lakes. As we waved to boaters, we dipped down into the lake. A couple inches of water poured into the basket before we lurched back into the sky.

Was this a planned part of the ride? Captain Craig admitted we'd experienced more of a "down drift" than he expected. "Sorry about that," he said. "Hope none of you got too wet. In a balloon, the wind is both our motor and our steering wheel."

I elbowed my friend, Joan. "Um, maybe we'll be landing in Oz after all."

But Captain Craig told us he had his eyes set on a field just ahead.

We began another slow descent and then accelerated toward the earth. As we landed, the balloon bounced a couple times upon the ground before a few spotters who'd followed along brought us to a gentle landing.

Our flight lasted more than an hour. Unlike several of my escapades, I enjoyed it so much I never found myself counting down the minutes until it would end.

Once the van carried us—safely—back to balloon headquarters, we toasted the success of our trip with champagne. This victory had entailed ten times of rescheduling over five months. We all agreed it was worth every penny, every phone call, and every held breath.

As I had drifted across the sky, in the last of my planned fifty-two new challenges, I swallowed any remaining fear of this final experience. I eyed the huge world around me. I contemplated what other wonders in life might yet await me, if I continued to push past personal barriers and embrace new adventures.

If there had been enough room in that balloon's crowded wicker basket, I would have broken into a celebratory song and dance. Not my planned performance of "Up, Up and Away," but perhaps the "Hokey Pokey."

After all, life was very much like that cheesy song. All you have to do is put your whole self in, shake it all about, and damned if you don't turn yourself around.

Epilogue:

THE END—AND A NEW BEGINNING

This is where my year of new challenges officially ended. And where the rest of my new life began.

Some results and ramifications of the past year were more obvious than others. They included the writing and publishing of this book, which I assume you have nearly finished reading. I owe you a Bloody Mary for that. I hope you enjoyed hearing about my misadventures as much as I enjoyed—well, *mostly* enjoyed—living them.

I learned loads about random subject matter of which I had little prior knowledge: Segways and isolation tanks, rhinos and bees, ghosts and nuns.

I made hundreds of new friends—some through the experiences themselves and others through my blog. I continued to get together with my stranger party guests, and I even babysat the Baldwin Quad Squad a couple more times. Many of my blog readers became Facebook friends, and I went on to meet several in person, too.

The following year, The 52/52 Project motivated me to travel across the country and take on a number of other new exploits. I dubbed this the "National Stranger Party Tour."

Based on the popularity of my original stranger party, I invited readers and other strangers to join me on monthly adventures. These fun and mostly nonthreatening excursions included a scavenger hunt in Boston, a night in a haunted hotel near Denver, a Partridge Family Bus bar crawl in Milwaukee, and drag queen bingo in Orlando. On one trip, after ten years of hesitation, I even took the step to meet up with my father's long-lost brother. After all, I had learned that the experiences I envisioned as the most awkward and uncomfortable ended up being the most rewarding.

A number of folks told me I inspired them to take more risks and to jump-start their own lives. Several readers embarked on similar quests. That continued to inspire me, too.

When I considered all the wonderful people I inadvertently met and the unanticipated outcomes of so many of my experiences, I began to believe there was no such thing as pure chance. Some things are surely meant to be. We don't always hear serendipity knocking, but it's often there to greet us if we just open the door.

My year of new adventures even enriched my relationships with my family. My mother came along on a handful of challenges and told me if she was even ten years younger, she'd have asked to join me on more. And my two grown sons were occasionally horrified but mostly proud.

After watching an interview with one of the hosts of *Jackass*, my oldest son told me the guy's remarks reminded him of The 52/52 Project. "So, that's cool," said Son #1. "I'll bet you never thought your life would mirror Johnny Knoxville's." Indeed.

When I nonchalantly told Son #2 that I couldn't meet for lunch because I was scheduled for a zookeeper gig, he paused. "I have to say, when this is all over, I am really going to miss these strange conversations of ours." What we both eventually realized, however, was that it was likely *never* to be over, not even when I completed everything on my list. This mission changed my life in other more subtle and enduring ways.

I discovered a midlife sense of new energy. Sure, there remained times when the plans on my plate and the chaos in my life seemed so overwhelming that I did the most logical thing: I put on my pajamas at 7 p.m. and said, "Screw it." These moments became more rare though. I learned to take a breather when I needed it, and then to pick up the pieces and pick up the pace and carry on.

I became less hesitant to confront what I found frightening or intimidating. No surprise, considering I had endured a year in which I often said to myself, "Which should I choose to do this week, the terrifying thing that will disgust me or the terrifying thing that will humiliate me?" As I told the students at the high school honors banquet, pushing your limits builds your character through both humility and empowerment. The most rewarding life experiences may be the ones we've been sidestepping all along.

Life is full of hurdles, but the biggest obstacle is our decision to stop at a bump or a crossroad, fearful to move on. What's most important is to take that first step and, if we stumble, to just keep going. We're only losers if we've never tried.

I learned to face change with far more ease. One of many new mantras I adopted was, "Change is good. Change is *good*. Right?" Granted, this philosophy sometimes still took a bit of convincing, especially when life took its most unexpected and terrifying turns, such as my diagnosis of uterine cancer, just six months after my balloon ride.

Cancer wasn't a new experience I ever expected or wished to face. But like most of my other new experiences, it proved less frightening and more successfully conquered than anticipated.

Whether due to that brief glimpse into my mortality or

the lingering effects of The 52/52 Project, I also began tackling items not just on my unbucket list but also on my *true* bucket list. I scheduled more vacations. I attended more concerts, plays, and author readings. These are the kind of experiences that brought me great joy, even if they once seemed a luxury. I also made more concrete plans for retirement. Although that goal remained many years away, I planned to find some way to make it attainable sooner rather than later.

Did this year of new experiences make me a happier person? It's almost impossible to quantify or qualify happiness. With all its individual components and nuances, happiness—like love—is not something easily rated on a scale of one to ten. All I knew was I felt more accomplished, confident, and complete.

I expect I'll still be searching, learning, and evolving thirty years from now.

Above all, The 52/52 Project taught me to live my life. I experienced more fear, exhilaration, and laughter than I had in much of the fifty-one years preceding it. When your world is broader and your mind is open, it's never too late to reinvent yourself.

Facing our fears perhaps prevents one of life's greatest fears of all, of someday asking ourselves, "What if?" Instead, as my young friends in Italy taught me, we might begin asking, "Perche' non?"

Why not, indeed?

ACKNOWLEDGMENTS

Mentioning everyone who played a part in The 52/52 Project would require another 50,000 words, and it would be my most futile challenge of all. Just know I thank all of you from the depths of my humbled, humored, and often humiliated heart.

Thank you to the staff of She Writes Press, especially Brooke Warner and Cait Levin, for taking my collection of words and giving them life, and to the entire SWP editorial and design staff. And thanks to the BookSparks publicity team!

A huge thank you to readers of some early story drafts: Betsy Lerner, Roxane Gay, Holly Miller, and Dennis Hensley. I might have quit before I hardly got started if not for your encouragement.

For their eagle eyes and expert editing advice, I send out huge hugs to Vicki Kroll, Whitney Bryan, Gloria Stanfa, DC Stanfa, Terri Spilman, Patty Gelb, and Laura Maylene Walter. Acknowledgments to Vicki, again, as well as Kendra Wright and Chris Maloney, for book title inspiration.

Thanks to Tony Napoleone, who ensures me he provided the impetus for this whole thing through a blog comment when we each turned fifty.

Many writer friends offered support through social media, promotion, and personal guidance. They include Gina Barreca, Nikki Knepper, Cathryn Michon, DC Stanfa, and Katrina Willis. A special thanks for their input and support, over years of my writing projects, to the circle of friends I met through Betsy Lerner's blog: Deb Aijo, Teri Carter, Averil Dean, Amy Gesenhues, Jessica Lahey, Erika Marks, Catherine McNamara, Downith Monaghan, Lyra Nelson, Sarah Wesson, Lisa Williams, Suzy Vitello Soule', and others I may have missed here. FTF? Indeed!

I need to give a shout-out also to the fabulous folks I met through the Erma Bombeck Writers Workshop and the Midwest Writers Workshop.

Great appreciation to my original Stranger Party friends, who helped set the stage for much that has followed since that wonderful evening: Susan Jane Berson, Dawn Hammer, Tamara Johnson, Cindy McComb, Elizabeth Ulmer Page, Stella Reeber, and Kathleen Sallah.

My escapades would not have been the same without those courageous and crazy individuals who joined me on my 52/52 experiences and on my subsequent National Stranger Party Tour. Too many of you to name, but you know who you are. I hope you, too, have no stranger danger regrets.

Thanks to Lynn Konoff, for being a constant source of support, and to Mary Kasper, whose encouragement of my very earliest writing meant more than she will ever know. (Teachers rock!) I am grateful, also, to my oldest group of friends: Cindy Kozak, Diane Wielinski Stark, Karen Hoehn Miller, Joan Bruning, Mary Bruning Forshey, Molly McHugh Branyan, Linda Murphy Savercool, Peggy Harms Sullivan, and Sharon Suski Blakely, who didn't abandon me when I turned down countless social invitations while I lived out these stories and then stayed home for endless evenings, writing about them. Hey, call me now!

To the readers of my blog and my 52/52 Project Facebook page, who have become new friends: You are my heroes. Your engagement and comments inspired and motivated me. You proved this wasn't just one woman's story, but a journey for all of us.

Most of all, I must thank the usual suspects: my family. Much love to my mother, Gloria Stanfa; sisters, DC Stanfa and Lori Stanfa Schroeder; and my two sons, Jorden and Kyle Stanley. Life with you guys is always an adventure. I look forward to many more.

ABOUT THE AUTHOR

Sherry Stanfa-Stanley is a writer, humorist, and squeamish adventurer. She writes about her midlife escapades and other topics on Facebook (The 52 at 52 Project) and also blogs at www.sherrystanfa-stanley.com. By day, Sherry attempts to respectably represent her alma mater as a communication director at The University of Toledo. An empty nester after raising Son #1 and Son #2, she now indulges a menagerie of badly behaved pets.

Author photo © Mary Pencheff Photography

SELECTED TITLES FROM SHE WRITES PRESS

She Writes Press is an independent publishing
company founded to serve women writers everywhere.
Visit us at www.shewritespress.com.

Daring to Date Again: A Memoir by Ann Anderson Evans. $16.95,
978-1-63152-909-2. A hilarious, no-holds-barred memoir about a
legal secretary turned professor who dives back into the dating pool
headfirst after twelve years of celibacy.

*Peanut Butter and Naan: Stories of an American Mother in The Far
East* by Jennifer Magnuson. $16.95, 978-1-63152-911-5. The hilarious tale of what happened when Jennifer Magnuson moved her
family of seven from Nashville to India in an effort to shake things
up—and got more than she bargained for.

This Trip Will Change Your Life: A Shaman's Story of Spirit Evolution
by Jennifer B. Monahan. $16.95, 978-1-63152-111-9. One woman's
inspirational story of finding her life purpose and the messages and
training she received from the spirit world as she became a shamanic healer.

Renewable: One Woman's Search for Simplicity, Faithfulness, and Hope
by Eileen Flanagan. $16.95, 978-1-63152-968-9. At age forty-nine,
Eileen Flanagan had an aching feeling that she wasn't living up to
her youthful ideals or potential, so she started trying to change the
world—and in doing so, she found the courage to change her life.

Miracle at Midlife: A Transatlantic Romance by Roni Beth Tower.
$16.95, 978-1-63152-123-2. An inspiring memoir chronicling the
sudden, unexpected, and life-changing two-year courtship between a
divorced American lawyer living on a houseboat in the center of Paris
and an empty-nested clinical psychologist living in Connecticut.

Gap Year Girl by Marianne Bohr. $16.95, 978-1-63152-820-0. Thirty-plus years after first backpacking through Europe, Marianne Bohr
and her husband leave their lives behind and take off on a yearlong
quest for adventure.